WHITHER ISRAEL?
The Domestic Challenges

Edited by
Keith Kyle and Joel Peters

The Royal Institute of International Affairs

in association with

I.B. Tauris & Co Ltd
Publishers
London · New York

First published in 1993 by

I.B. Tauris & Co Ltd
45 Bloomsbury Square
London WC1A 2HY

175 Fifth Avenue
New York
NY 10010

in association with

The Royal Institute of International Affairs
Chatham House
10 St James's Square
London SW1Y 4LE

Updated paperback edition published in 1994

In the United States of America
and Canada distributed by
St Martin's Press
175 Fifth Avenue
New York
NY 10010

Library of Congress catalog card number: 94–060884

A full CIP record for this book is available from the British Library

A full CIP record for this book is available from the Library of Congress

ISBN 1–85043–868–4

Typeset by Cambridge Composing (UK) Ltd, Cambridge
Printed and bound in Great Britain by
WBC Ltd, Bridgend, MidGlamorgan

CONTENTS

v

Part III: Issues in Israeli Society

PREFACE TO THE PAPERBACK EDITION

At the end of August 1993, when the first edition of *Whither Israel?* was already at the printer, Israel and the Palestine Liberation Organization between them found a way of astonishing the world. They disclosed that they had been negotiating secretly in Oslo for months, well away from the official peace process in Washington that had grown out of the Madrid conference of 1991, and that they had reached agreement to recognize each other and to make a start on the policy of autonomy in the occupied territories by establishing Palestinian rule first in the Gaza Strip and Jericho. On 13 September, following an exchange of letters between Yitzhak Rabin and Yasser Arafat establishing mutual recognition, there took place in Washington the signature of the Declaration of Principles and the celebrated handshake between the two of them on the White House lawn. It was to take until 4 May 1994 before a detailed agreement on implementation of the Gaza-Jericho deal was signed by the two leaders, and even then some details were not fully worked out.

Clearly in one sense nothing was ever going to be the same again in Israel after this upheaval, which for the first time creates what Foreign Minister Shimon Peres termed 'a piece of Palestinian reality'. Yet in another sense it can just as surely be predicted that the effect of this dramatic stroke will be to enhance the validity and the relevance of the domestic challenges to Israel discussed in this book. The reason is that, once freed of its regional isolation, Israel wants to be an economic 'tiger' after the fashion of some Far Eastern economies and seeks to capitalize on the recent wave of Russian immigrants of high educational and professional standing to help bring that about. But this will only occur if the 'systemic' change discussed in subsequent chapters is much accelerated.

The transformation of Yasser Arafat from a man officially portrayed in Israel as the unspeakable head of a terrorist organization (with whom, until a short time before, it had been a criminal offence for any Israeli to have contact) into Israel's indispensable partner was dramatic and truly remarkable. One of the chief tasks for the Israeli negotiators became that of convincing the Arab leaders – not only Arafat but also President Assad of Syria, who held the key, it was generally conceded, to the acceptance of Israel by the Arab states – that they now had to start playing an active role in drumming up support among the Israeli population for the next stages of the peace process. This is so, despite the evident economic rewards of a peace settlement, because of the overwhelming significance of the security issue since the birth of the State of Israel.

Yitzhak Rabin had won the 1992 election on a peace pledge, but he had only just won it and the pledge was most severely circumscribed. During the campaign he had given the impression that he knew how to conclude swiftly, within a matter of months, the hitherto lagging negotiations with the Palestinians over the first stage of a two-stage approach to a peace settlement; that during this first stage he would not compromise over the security of all Jews, including the status and safety of every single one of the existing Jewish settlements in the occupied territories; and that the negotiations, as before, would be only with the representatives of the occupied territories, not with the PLO as such. Concurrently the bilateral talks with Jordan, Syria and Lebanon would be pressed forward and some territorial concession, of unstipulated extent, might be made to Syria on the Golan Heights in return for 'real peace', by which was understood the establishment of full diplomatic and commercial relations. A year later, it was apparent that something would have to give, and quickly, if the Labour-led coalition was not to lose all credibility. What gave was the sidelining of the Tunis-based PLO. Here the totally unexpected factor was the effective partnership of the Israeli premier and his foreign minister. The story of the rivalry between Rabin and Peres, himself a former Labour Party leader and prime minister, was so notorious and long-standing (see p. 112) that it was never supposed that Peres would be permitted any significant share in the peace negotiations. Yet the secret diplomatic coup was brought off through the agency of Peres and his immediate entourage and with Rabin's complete approval.

Advocates and opponents of the Declaration of Principles might both say that it will lead inevitably to a Palestinian state, but the present government has stuck to the view that the really difficult questions of sovereignty over the West Bank and Gaza, permanent boundaries between Israel and the (sovereign or non-sovereign) Palestinian entity, links between that entity and Jordan, settlement of Palestinian refugees and the destiny of East Jerusalem should not arise until the second stage. The argument is that without the experience of a trial period of Palestinian autonomy there would not be nearly enough Israeli confidence in coexistence to create a critical mass of support for such decisions. As one who keeps his cards close to his chest, Rabin has given little indication of what answers to these questions he himself would favour, though he has repeatedly said that he will insist on a united Jerusalem which shall be the eternal capital of Israel. In the extended negotiations on the implementation of the Oslo agreement, the Palestinians had a clear strategic goal – a sovereign Palestinian state with its capital in (East) Jerusalem – but the Israelis had not, and some of the Israeli negotiators felt that distinction keenly.

But of course it is not only on the Israeli side that opponents of the deal are vocal and numerous. Arafat had not felt able to present a programme based on a two-state solution to the Palestine National Council (the PLO's parliament-in-exile) until October 1988. Even then the endorsement in that forum was far from unanimous. Besides the minority of the National Council, the Muslim fundamentalist organizations in the occupied territories – Hamas and Islamic Jihad and a variety of smaller Palestinian organizations, ten of them operating out of Damascus – vehemently rejected it and have an interest in its being sabotaged.

Two instant reactions to the Oslo accord represent the tone of opposition to be expected on both sides. 'They came in the night and stole away our minds,' said Yitzhak Shamir, the former Likud party leader who had been prime minister until June 1992, reproaching his successor with asset-stripping Israel. Ahmed Jibril, the leader of one of the most extreme Palestinian rejectionist groups, said that Arafat deserved death for allowing himself to be made by the Jews into a Third World sheriff for Gaza and Jericho. Another leading Arab dissident compared Arafat to Marshal Philippe Ptain.

Optimists in Israel, especially those around Shimon Peres and his deputy foreign minister, Yossi Beilin, look forward to an early end to the state's regional isolation and foresee an Israel playing an active role in the Middle East as well as in the United Nations and other international fora. Such a role is seen as developing out of the multilateral talks, involving the US, Canada, Russia, the European Union and Japan alongside both the Arab states and Israel, which have been busy wrestling with such problems as water resources, refugees, arms control and regional security, the environment and regional economic development, which affect the Middle East as a whole, in parallel with the much more publicized bilateral negotiations.[1]

Prominent figures in the Israeli business sector, such as Benjamin Gaon, the president and chief executive of Koor Industries, Israel's largest industrial corporation, express the bullish conclusion that 'the peace process has gathered a momentum that cannot be stopped by any government of any political stripe'. Koor, Gaon says, is positioning itself on the assumption that the new markets which will be vital for Israel if it is to become, as it hopes, another Singapore, are principally to be found in the Middle East and in the former Soviet Union.[2] But this would require a dramatic reversal of Israel's regional isolation – perhaps, as Nabil Sha'ath, the Palestinians' chief negotiator, foresaw 25 years ago in a speech in Cairo to the Conference of the Friends of the Arab States, in partnership with Palestinian businessmen who could introduce them to the Arab world.

As the political chapters in this book will disclose, all this is being done on the Israeli side on the narrowest possible political base (pp. 2–3, 246–50). On the very day that Rabin returned from Washington, his government became technically a minority government, because the resignations of the one cabinet minister and three deputy ministers belonging to Shas (Torah Observing Sephardim) took effect.[3] This small ultra-Orthodox religious party (whose background is explained on pp. 196–201) had supplied the six seats that had given the Labour-led coalition its two-vote majority in the Knesset. Although Shas's Knesset leader, Rabbi Aryeh Deri, made public statements expressing serious doubts about the agreement with Arafat, the reason for his resignation as minister of the interior was quite different. He had been indicted on charges of bribe-taking, aggravated fraud, violation of public trust and falsification of documents, for which he had been under continuous police investigation during the last three-and-a-half of his five years as a minister. One of the Shas deputy ministers was also charged with a criminal offence. Although these two had been required (by the judiciary) to resign as individuals, their extra-parliamentary leader, Rabbi Ovadia Yosef, decided that Shas as a party would leave the coalition.

Thus Rabin, at his moment of triumph, was left with a minority of 56 seats in a Knesset of 120. This was not as bad as it might seem since the Communists' three members (two Arabs and one Jew) and the Arab Democratic Party's two were pledged to support him, but he did not wish to be seen to be dependent on Arab parties. On the crucial matter of approval of the Oslo accord he recorded only 61 votes in favour, though abstentions, including the members of Shas and, most significantly, three members of Likud, increased his majority to a respectable 11.

The immediate impact on Israeli opinion of the Oslo accord was favourable – the opinion polls showed an instant reaction of 53 per cent in support and this rose over the next few days until it reached the high sixties. Under pressure, even the new Likud party leader, 'Bibi' Netanyahu, appeared for a while to qualify his initial ferocious opposition. But the dragging out of talks over implementation gave opportunities for saboteurs in both camps. Israeli politics was dominated in the first quarter of 1994 by a succession of terrorist outrages, most of them in Israel proper within the Green Line, while at Hebron one Israeli doctor killed in cold blood 30 Palestinians at prayer and wounded many others in the Makhpelah Cave (Tomb of the Patriarchs), where Abraham was buried and which is sacred to both Arabs and Jews. The consequent Palestinian demonstrations and riots occurred not only in the occupied territories but also, to the consternation of Israeli Jews, among the Israeli Arabs of Yafo (Jaffa) and elsewhere, setting off some ultra-sensitive alarms (pp. 254–5). Support for the agreement dropped below 50 per cent and the opposition from Likud leaders, not to speak of the radical right (pp. 123–33), again became unmeasured.

This book, concentrating on Israel's domestic challenges, is not concerned directly with details of the developing peace process. But since Rabin was elected to bring peace with security – and since the next election due in 1996 is for the first time to be for a directly elected prime minister as well as for the Knesset – the peace issue will condition much of the future political debate. The next election will also coincide, if the timetables of the peace process are adhered to, with the earliest moment at which it has been agreed that negotiations should begin for a permanent settlement with the Palestinians to come into effect after a further three years. The contestants in 1996 will find it difficult to evade (as Labour, for one, was able to do in 1992) the major commitments that this will involve.

One major challenge provided by the peace process which will have a direct impact on domestic politics must be the future of the settlers. These were encouraged by successive governments, including Rabin's previous one (1974–7), to establish communities, especially on hilltops, throughout the occupied territories, which were biblically renamed as Judaea and Samaria. Aside from East Jerusalem (which is a major problem in itself and which, thanks to Israeli housing policy, now has more Jewish inhabitants – 167,511 – than Arab – 154,182), there are 130,000 settlers in the West Bank and Gaza, of whom 20–30 per cent are considered to be ideologically committed to living in biblical territory (see pp. 28–31). The remainder are people, mostly Tel Aviv or Jerusalem commuters, who have opted for cheaper houses with perhaps superior amenities. So far (May 1994) the government has made a policy of having no policy about settlers on the formal grounds that there need be nothing in the first phase of a peace agreement with the Palestinians to prejudice their position and that Israel will remain responsible for their security. But the settlements, most of them very small, are scattered like confetti across the whole surface of the West Bank and Gaza, including 415 religiously motivated settlers at several locations in the middle of the intensely hostile town of Hebron. The issue also arises in connection with separate but concurrent peace negotiations with Syria, since there are settlers, this time many of them secular Labour supporters, on the Golan Heights. Rabin, says Joseph Alpher, the director of the Jaffee Centre for Strategic Studies, 'is evidently seeking to "dry up" and dispirit the settlers, to isolate them politically and weaken their ranks until the time is ripe to initiate their removal'.[4] But this atmosphere of uncertainty could lead the various classes of settler, religious and secular, to coalesce behind the extremists, with whom some sort of confrontation seems inevitable.

The belief of the border police commander at the Makhpelah Cave, when Dr Baruch Goldstein, a member of the racist party Kach, massacred Palestinian worshippers, that Israeli troops were forbidden under any circumstances to open fire on Jews illustrates some of the difficulties with which the government may be faced. While the Israeli government was quick to voice in unequivocal terms its revulsion at Goldstein's action, as the result of which he himself was killed, the volume of local sympathy among settlers displayed for the murderer at his funeral was a sinister warning of the tense encounters that there may be to come between Israel's security forces and extremist settlers (see p. 257).

This massacre might well force Rabin, against his will, to use the security forces to evacuate settlers from exposed positions. Likud's Ariel Sharon, the former general and defence minister, said immediately that such a move would be proof that the government had lost its Zionist direction, since Zionism came about first and foremost to bring Jews back to Jerusalem, Hebron and other places in the West Bank and would call for 'a passive, non-violent popular resistance'.[5] This stands in bleak contrast to the sentiment expressed by the prime minister, on presenting the Declaration of Principles to the Knesset: 'Above all I want to tell you that this is a victory for Zionism, which is now recognized by its most adamant and bitter enemies.' There could scarcely be a more striking illustration of the fissure described by Mordechai Bar-On (pp. 36–7) between different interpreters of contemporary Zionism.

An IDF (Israeli Defence Forces) document leaked to the newspaper *Ha'aretz* warned of the danger of a direct conflict between the democratic majority and the ideals of Zionism as understood by certain groups or individuals, who might 'exhort and call on soldiers not to implement orders resulting from the agreement with the PLO on the claim that these orders are manifestly illegal'.[6] A secret plan for 'practical opposition' to the Oslo accord, revealed in the *Yediot Aharonot* of 1 December 1993, was said to 'make the government face a . . . situation . . . with which it cannot deal (it is impossible to station a soldier on every hill)'. A vigilante movement, claimed to be 600 strong, boasted to *Ha'aretz* (23 November 1993) that it had already carried out substantial attacks on Arab property in retaliation for the Palestinian *intifada* (uprising). After the Hebron massacre the government banned two radical right organizations, Kach and Kahane Hay; it had been claimed on Kach's behalf that 500 of its members were abroad receiving military training, mainly, it is thought, in the United States.

But while the security aspect of the peace process has been to the fore its impact on the Israeli economy and that economy's ability to respond are also highly significant. Pinchas Landau, author of Chapter 4, writes:

By 1994 the Israeli economy is in its fifth successive year of rapid economic growth. This process has its roots in the restructuring that characterized the late 1980s and was powered by the mass immigration of the early 1990s. To these positive factors of a purely economic or socio-economic nature may be added the expectations of a fundamental geopolitical change, which from 1990–1 became a distinct element driving the economy.

The Oslo Agreement and the formal Israel–PLO mutual recognition of September 1993 brought these expectations to a climax. As 'hot money' poured in from abroad and a lax monetary policy stoked the domestic furnace, the economy overheated, with real GNP growth reaching an annual rate of some 10 per cent in the second half of the year.

The financial markets boiled over early in 1994 after the Central Bank abruptly changed the direction of monetary policy and hiked short-term interest rates. However, underlying these short-term swings are more serious issues. The pace of economic reform has slowed and, in many areas, came to a virtual stop during 1993–4. Many underlying structural problems have been addressed only partially and require considerable further treatment. For the economy, therefore, progress towards peace, or at least a general regional accommodation, remains a necessary, but in itself not a sufficient condition for the achievement of sustainable growth.

The truth is that by May 1994 the Labour government had not yet made a sufficient contribution to the modernizing process to ensure that the economy would be able to take proper advantage of 'real peace' if it came. There had even been (as with the reform of the health service) setbacks which appeared ominous, though the overwhelming success in the Histadrut labour federation elections of Haim Ramon, who had resigned as minister of health when his radical reforms had been derailed thanks to the manoeuvres of old-fashioned trade unionists, might well prove a pointer to change. Nor at this point is 'real peace' yet assured. The tentative tone of many of the assessments that follow still holds. Furthering the cause of peace will absorb much of the Rabin government's time but it can ill afford to ignore the domestic agenda if it is to be ready to reap the tantalizing rewards of peace.

Keith Kyle and Joel Peters
May 1994

Notes

1. See Joel Peters, *Building Bridges: The Arab–Israeli Multilateral Talks* (London, The Royal Institute of International Affairs, Middle East Programme, 1994).

2. Benjamin Gaon, 'Promoting Regional Economic Cooperation: An Israeli Perspective', in Yehuda Mirsky and Daniel Seligson (eds), *Gaza-Jericho and Beyond* (Proceedings of the Eighth Annual Conference, Washington Institute for Near East Policy, 1993), p. 38.

3. In Israel ministerial resignations can be formally submitted only at cabinet meetings and do not take effect for another 48 hours.

4. Joseph Alpher, 'A Way to Avert the Next Atrocity', *Jerusalem Post*, International Edition, 19 March 1994.

5. Ariel Sharon, 'Hebron isn't Yamit', *Jerusalem Post*, International Edition, 15 April 1994.

6. Gid'on Alon in *Ha'aretz*, 28 October 1993, and Eytan Rabin, in *Ha'aretz*, 19 November 1993, pp. A1 and B2. The report, entitled 'The Political Process – Explanatory Emphases', was written by Colonel Eytan Meir and distributed to all education officers in the IDF. See also a *Ha'aretz* report by Nadav Shragay on 23 November 1993, p. B2, on the 600-strong vigilante movement affiliated to Kach.

FOREWORD

This book is the culmination of a research project on Israel at Chatham House spanning more than three years. One of the early initiatives of the project was a four-day international symposium in June 1991 at the Institute which brought together scholars and experts from Israel and Britain. It was followed in December 1991 by a return meeting in Israel. This book grew as a logical conclusion to these two events.

The motivation for the original project was to consider the impact of rapid and profound change on Israeli society. Two central and recurring themes quickly emerged: the massive increase in Jewish immigration, and whether the Israeli economy and political system has the ability to cope with such demographic change and its consequences. It was also evident that the future shape of Israeli foreign policy, and the nature of Israeli involvement in the peace process, would in turn be conditioned, at least in part, by such factors.

Throughout the course of the preparation of both the symposium and the book it has been a pleasure to deal with our colleagues and friends from Israel. Their vigorous debate has helped to illuminate much about Israeli society, culture and politics. I thank them for their stimulating contributions at Chatham House, in Israel, and in this volume. I would also like to mention the considerable efforts of the book's two editors, Keith Kyle and Dr Joel Peters. Keith has been a leading figure at the Institute for over 20 years. I have always valued his sharp eye and shrewd judgment, and admired his boundless enthusiasm and literary style. Joel joined us as an associate fellow to work on this project. His tireless efforts and great dedication were crucial in making the symposium a success, and in the production of such a rigorously well-edited volume. Finally, I would like to thank the sponsors of the project. The National Institute of Research Advancement in Tokyo and the Foreign and Commonwealth Office in London gave fundamental financial support to the project. The Anglo-Israel Association assisted with the travel expenses for the Israeli participants to come to Chatham House, and also in the production of the book. I would also like to thank the association, and in particular its director, Cedric Mercer, for financing a study visit to Israel. This enabled me to increase our academic contacts in Israel, spanning the whole of that country's university system.

The Middle East research programme at the Institute continues to be committed to working at any one time on some aspect of the Arab–Israeli dispute. Before this book we published *Towards a Palestinian Entity* by Paul Lalor. We have now turned our attentions to the multilateral track of the Middle East peace process. We intend to publish a report on the activities of the multilaterals with Joel Peters as author. It is hoped that such analysis can then be followed up by work that puts the multilaterals in historical and theoretical perspective, and which can then address both agenda issues and substance.

Dr Philip Robins
Head, Middle East Programme
Royal Institute of International Affairs
February 1993

GLOSSARY

Agudat Yisrael = Association of Israel, often called 'the *Agudah*'. Ultra-Orthodox, originally anti-Zionist, now non-Zionist political party, with extensive educational network.

Aliyah = ascent. Used to describe migration of Jews (known as **olim** or ascenders) to Israel. The term carries an implication of 'end of exile'.

Arab Democratic Party Founded by Abdul Wahab Darawshe in 1988.

Ashkenazi (pl. **Ashkenazim**) A Jew of Central or Eastern European ancestry.

Basic Laws Elements towards an Israeli Constitution which are being gradually enacted one at a time, viz. Basic Law: the Knesset (1958), Basic Law: The Government (1968). The process is not complete.

Eretz Yisrael = Land of Israel. In contemporary politics, it refers to a 'Greater Israel' (strictly, Eretz Yisrael Hashlema) incorporating the West Bank and Gaza.

Green Line The (provisional) borders of Israel established by the 1949 armistice agreements. Since 1967 the line (not shown on ordinary Israeli road maps) has separated Israel from the occupied territories.

Gush Emunim = Bloc of the Faithful. An extra-parliamentary religious Zionist movement which actively promotes the settlement of Jews throughout the entire area of the West Bank and Gaza.

Hadash (acronym for *Hazit Demokratit LeShalom UlShivyon*) = Democratic Front for Peace and Equality (DFPE). Predominantly Arab and communist party, but with a few Jewish and non-communist members.

Halacha Religious law; those parts of traditional Jewish literature concerned with legal matters.

Hamula Arab term for an extended kinship group.

Haredi (pl. **haredim**) = ultra-Orthodox Jew(s).

Hasidim Members of a Jewish pietist-mystical-revivalist movement that originated in Poland and Lithuania in the eighteenth century.

Histadrut (*Hahistadrut Haklalit shel Ha'ovdim Be'eretz Yisrael*) = The General Federation of Workers in Eretz Yisrael. Israel's main trade union but also Israel's major employer (of 23 per cent of the work force, operating through six conglomerates), its principal supplier of health insurance and hospital services (*Kupat Holim*), and a major cultural impresario.

IDF or **Zahal** (*Zvah Haganah LeIsrael*) = Israel Defence Forces.

Intifada = Uprising, as of the Palestinians in the occupied territories since December, 1987.

Kach = Thus! Extreme right-wing party, advocating expulsion of Arabs from *Eretz Yisrael* and fighting terror with terror. Banned from elections as racist.

Kibbutz (pl. **kibbutzim**) A collective agricultural settlement, based on principles of communal ownership, common provision of needs and equality of incomes.

Knesset = assembly. The name of the unicameral, 120-member Parliament of Israel. Members use MK as a prefix to their names. Particular Knessets are referred to by their number, viz. The thirteenth Knesset, elected on 23 June 1992.

Labour Party (properly *Israel Labour Party*), established as a social democratic party in 1968 when the socialist **Mapai** (the Party of Workers) merged with two others. It subsequently participated in an electoral bloc called *the Alignment* and fought the 1992 Knesset election as 'Labour led by Rabin'.

Land Day Celebrated every 30 March by Israeli Arabs as an annual strike to commemorate the day in 1976 when six demonstrators were killed during a protest against the confiscation of Arab lands.

Law of Return Law passed in 1950 which says, 'Every Jew has the right to immigrate to the country.' A subsequent (1952) law grants automatic citizenship to any Jew who immigrates on the basis of the Law of Return.

Likud = Union. Formed under Menachem Begin in 1973 as a right-wing parliamentary bloc of which the leading force was the **Gahal** (itself a bloc grouping the **Herut** with the Liberal Party). A complete merger was agreed in 1986 but in 1992 there was still no Likud party constitution.

Ma'Hapach = upheaval. Used to refer to the Likud's overthrow of Labour's predominance in the 1977 Knesset election. It has been suggested that the 1992 election also deserves the appellation.

Meretz Alliance formed for the 1992 election between **CRM** (Civil Rights Movement, or **Ratz**), **Mapam** (United Workers' Party – a left-wing socialist party), and **Shinui** (Change), which advocates a free market economy, on the common basis of Palestinian self-determination and separation of religion and state.

Moledet = Homeland. Party founded by General Rahavam Ze'evi to advocate 'transfer' (i.e. expulsion) of the Arab population from Eretz Yisrael.

Moshav (pl. **moshavim**) Co-operative agricultural settlement, run on lines of mutual assistance but less uncompromisingly collective than a kibbutz.

National Religious Party (NRP) or **Mafdal**. The party for religious Zionists.

National Unity Government A 'grand coalition' of Labour and Likud. These existed from 1984–90.

Progressive List for Peace (PLP) A non-Zionist party set up in 1984. Favours complete Israel withdrawal to pre-June 1967 borders and complete equality of Jewish and Arab citizens within the State of Israel.

Sephardi (pl. **Sephardim**) = (strictly) Jews who lived in Spain and were expelled in 1492, many of whom then settled in Muslim countries; also a term generally (though inexactly) used to describe the Oriental Jews (or **Edot Mizrah**) who since the fall of the Second Temple had always lived in the Middle East and North Africa.

Shas (acronym for **Shomrei Torah Sephardim**) = Torah Observing Sephardim. Ultra-Orthodox party founded in 1984 to protest against the under-representation of the Sephardim in the Agudat Yisrael.

State Comptroller Independent agency with powers of inspection and report to Knesset over all branches of central government, local government and all bodies subsidized by the state. Also acts as ombudsman for complaints by the public.

Status quo (religious) The existing balance between the secular and religious parties, affecting public religious observance, the material interests of the various religious establishments and the laws relating to marriage and burial.

Tehiya = Renaissance. Party founded in 1979 in opposition to Camp David Accords between Israel and Egypt, which it regarded as treason to Zionism. Strongly in favour of increased settlement.

Torah = the Pentateuch, the first five books of the Old Testament.

Transfer The idea of removing the Arab population, either voluntarily or by compulsion, from *Eretz Yisrael*. Supported in the Knesset only by the *Moledet* party.

Tzomet = Crossroads. Party formed by General Rafael Eitan in 1983 which stands for clean government, separation of religion and state and *Eretz Yisrael*.

United Torah Jewry (UTJ). Ultra-Orthodox (Haredi) alliance formed for the 1992 Knesset election by the **Agudat Yisrael** and **Degel Hatora**, the party inspired by Rabbi Schach.

Yeshiva (pl. **Yeshivot**) Jewish religious academy.

Yishuv = settlement, community. Used to describe the pre-state Jewish community in Palestine.

1. THE NATURE OF ISRAELI POLITICS AND SOCIETY

Joel Peters

On 23 June 1992, after spending the previous 15 years languishing in opposition or sitting uncomfortably in governments of National Unity with the Likud, the Labour Party, led by Yitzhak Rabin emerged as triumphant in the elections to the thirteenth Knesset. While Labour increased its power to 44 seats, the Likud under Prime Minister Yitzhak Shamir suffered a crushing defeat at the hands of the Israeli electorate, receiving only 32 mandates. Not only did Labour secure the largest number of seats but, more importantly, it was the only party in a position to form a new government. The Israeli electorate had seemingly given Yitzhak Rabin a clear mandate to govern and bring about the changes that he had promised to deliver.

Rabin's victory was heralded as an important turning point in the fortunes of the country. Some went even as far as to describe his triumph as a second *Ma'Hapach* (upheaval), a phrase associated in political terms with the Likud's capture of power in 1977. A wave of optimism swept Israel and the international community alike. Hope was coupled with expectation. Above all, the outcome of the election was portrayed as a vote for peace. The Israeli public had cast its verdict on the peace process, forsaking the intransigence of Yitzhak Shamir and the dream of *Eretz Yisrael Hashlema* (Greater Land of Israel) for the path of peace and compromise.

The Arab–Israeli conflict permeates every aspect of Israeli life and choices over peace and security have played a central role in each of its elections. However, it is misleading to see the 1992 election solely as a referendum on the future of the occupied territories and to regard the result as a final verdict on that issue. Labour rode to power on a wave of socio-economic discontent. Dissatisfaction with the Likud

1

stretched far beyond its handling of the peace process. Labour inherited a domestic agenda packed with items where action has been long overdue. This agenda ranges from the challenge of absorbing the new immigrants from the former Soviet Union to the need for economic growth, the reform of its electoral system, the question of the relationship of religion and state and the treatment of Israel's Arab minority. The roots and causes of many of these issues are independent of Israel's conflict with its Arab neighbours and the need to address them is equally pressing. While the Israeli public will be hoping for progress in the peace talks, the Rabin government must also deliver on the home front as well. It is those domestic challenges which form the central theme of this book.

Within three weeks, in record time and for many with undue haste, Yitzhak Rabin presented his new government to the Knesset for approval. The arithmetical outcome of the election placed Rabin in a position of unrivalled strength, allowing him to approach the task of forming a government without having to face the political intrigue and extortion which had become the hallmark of Israeli politics in the 1980s. From the outset he was assured the active support of Meretz, the newly formed left-wing alliance which had secured 12 seats, and the tacit support, at least, of the Arab Democratic Party and the communist-dominated Democratic Front for Peace and Equality. Combined, this gave him the necessary majority of 61 seats. Rabin needed, however, to broaden the basis for his government. He was acutely aware that the domestic legitimacy for his government would be severely challenged were its survival dependent solely on the support of the Arab parties. Nor did he savour the prospect of his hands being tied by the demands of Meretz. His plan was to form what would have amounted to a National Unity government, extending on the right to the secularist Tzomet, which had risen dramatically from two seats to eight and the religious parties, and on the left to Meretz, with Labour holding the central reins of power, but without the participation of the Likud. Had he been successful, Rabin would have built a 74-member coalition, with left balancing right, secular offsetting religious and created a situation whereby no single party nor any single issue could hold the government to ransom.

At one point it appeared that Rabin might accomplish the formidable task that he had set himself. His grand strategy faltered not over the question of Eretz Yisrael and the future of the occupied territories but on account of his mismanagement of the far less contentious education portfolio. Initially Rabin offered this ministry to Tzomet in order to tempt it into joining his government. The prospect of Rafael Eitan – the hawkish and outspoken former chief of staff who had been roundly condemned by the Kahan Commission for his actions during the Lebanon War – as minister of education and culture, outraged Meretz and caused a certain unease among members of his own party. Rabin was forced to retreat and hand the portfolio to Shulamit Aloni, the leader of Meretz. Aggrieved at the way he was first offered and then refused the education portfolio, Eitan was deaf thereafter to any further overtures to join the government.

Whereas Meretz would not countenance the prospect of Eitan controlling the country's education system, the appointment of Shulamit Aloni was equally unpalatable to the religious parties. Prior to the election the religious parties had lined themselves up on the side of the Likud. The Likud's inability to form a government and their fear of being denied the sources of patronage brought a quick change of heart. Election pronouncements were redefined to meet the new situation. But the thought of Shulamit Aloni, the veteran civil rights campaigner who was renowned for her bitter attacks against the ultra-Orthodox, being responsible for education of the country's youth was too horrible for the religious parties to contemplate. Only Shas, the Sephardi ultra-Orthodox party, assured of retaining the Ministry of Interior, was willing to join the government. In the end, Rabin was forced to settle for a shaky narrowly based coalition of Meretz and Shas, with the tacit support of the Arab parties. Significantly, he did not shut the door and left two ministries (Religion and Social Affairs) open in the hope that, at a later stage, he would be able to broaden the base of his government.

It would be inaccurate to conclude that Rabin would have been successful in forming a broad-based coalition but for the battle over the education portfolio. The idea was over ambitious from the outset and was based on an over-estimation of Labour's new-found strength and an exaggerated view of the weakness of other parties. The divisions that Rabin was trying to bridge were numerous and far too wide. While Eitan ostensibly withdrew from the coalition talks after being denied the Ministry of Education, his opposition to autonomy for the Palestinians together with his fundamental and deep-rooted differences with the Labour Party over the future of the territories made his joining the government difficult to imagine. At the same time, this episode is illustrative of the importance attached to edu-

cation and reflects the inner divisons within Israeli society. It is
noteworthy that Rabin's grand design hit insurmountable difficulties
not over just the peace process but also over who would be responsible
for the country's educational system.

The importance of education can be found at two levels. On the
practical side there is a pressing need to revitalize the school system
and to improve educational standards. Resources have to be allocated
to build more classrooms, extend the teaching day and make teaching
more financially rewarding. The outgoing minister, Zevulun Hammer
of the National Religious Party, presided over a system whose budget
was continually being cut. The ever shrinking school day has forced
parents who possess the financial means to turn to the area of informal
'grey education' as an indispensable supplement to their children's
education. The derisory level of pay has forced teachers in turn to
offer courses outside the formal educational system. Differences exist
over priorities and approaches, but on the overall need to overhaul the
system there is unanimous agreement.[1] It is at the second level, over
the nature and content of the curricula, over what is to be included,
the relative weight to be given to broader universalist concerns and
issues as opposed to an emphasis on Jewish history and values within
the secular school system and how it is to be taught, that critical
differences emerge. It was over the future values and culture of Israeli
society not the management of the system that the battle of the
education portfolio was fought.[2] As Mordechai Bar-On argues per-
suasively, controversies within the Zionist Movement in the past
focused on questions of strategy and tactics. Today the debate rages
around fundamental and over cherished values and goals. While
compromise can be found over interests, it is far harder to reach when
principles are at stake.

The Labour Party won the election on a platform of change. In his
opening remarks to the new Knesset Yitzhak Rabin returned to the
theme that had dominated his election campaign, that his government
would spare no effort in bringing about 'a change in the national order
of priorities'.[3] After focusing on the peace process, Rabin turned his
attention to the 'war of unemployment'. For Pinchas Landau the
challenges facing the Israeli economy are twofold, to create favourable
economic conditions for the successful absorption of the Aliyah from
the Soviet Union and the necessity of integrating Israel into the global
economy. Identifying these challenges is simple; meeting them, however, is more difficult.

The opening of the gates to Jews in the dying years of the Soviet Union created both a challenge and an opportunity for Israel, one that it cannot afford to miss. The pace at which Israel is willing to absorb any number of Jews who wish to migrate from the various republics which formerly made up the Soviet Union defies any economic logic. The reason is rooted firmly in the importance and centrality of the Zionist principle of the 'Ingathering of the Exiles' and the belief that Israel should provide a home for all Jews. Good intentions and open arms are not sufficient by themselves for successful absorption, as the experience of the past couple of years has shown.[4] The Russians (as they all tend to be called) were greeted by housing shortages and unemployment queues. Disillusionment quickly set in and the expected flood failed to materialize. From the heady days of 1990 when nearly 200,000 arrived the numbers have declined steadily. Estimates in 1993 talked of no more than 6,000 a month despite the mounting economic crisis and signs of nascent anti-semitism in the new republics. Most other countries would have welcomed a slow down in the number of immigrants. Yet, as Keith Kyle rightly points out, Israel will be judged, and more importantly will judge itself, by how it responds to this challenge.

Some of the criticisms levelled at the Shamir government were too harsh, reflecting Israel's fervour for quick and neat solutions. The Likud, however, had opened itself up to the charge of sometimes displaying wilful neglect and indifference. The confrontation with the United States over the building of new Jewish settlements in the West Bank and the failure to secure from President Bush the granting of $10 billion of loan guarantees were interpreted by the new immigrants as placing zealous attachment to the idea of *Eretz Yisrael Hashlema* ahead of their immediate needs to find meaningful jobs and adequate housing. This was a theme adopted by the Labour Party and relentlessly pursued throughout the campaign. The Likud paid a heavy price at the polls. When the Soviet Jews first began to arrive in Israel, the Likud was seen as their natural constituency. The increased support would give the party a clear majority and condemn Labour to the opposition benches for the foreseeable future. The opposite proved to be the case. At least half the new immigrants supported Labour, bringing it a crucial four extra seats; the rest dispersed their vote among the other parties. Few in the end voted for Likud. Political loyalty has to be earned, a lesson Labour would do well not to forget.

The arrival of the Soviet Jews sharpened the debate in Israel about the nature and direction of economic policy and the need for economic reform. Pinchas Landau and Yitzhak Klein lay the blame for Israel's economic ills at the door of an outmoded government-dominated system which has led to inefficiency and stagnation. Both argue strongly that if Israel is to meet the challenge of successfully absorbing the new immigrants a number of far-reaching reforms have to be implemented. Landau pulls no punches: more government involvement and control would be a recipe for disaster; measures need to be taken for trade liberalization, capital market liberalization and deregulation, labour market reform, and privatization. He warns that failure to pursue these reforms is likely to result in further economic stagnation which would exacerbate existing social tensions within Israeli society.

Supporters of privatization have more or less won the upper hand in Israel. Rabin has declared that the sale of state-owned firms will be actively promoted. The government will also decrease its involvement in the capital market and open a new market for venture capital. 'A free world,' Rabin informed the Knesset, 'demands a free market.' But simultaneously, Rabin qualified his new-found devotion to the market. The government will allocate funds, he insisted, for investment in transportation, electricity, water and sewerage, high-tech industries, research and development and provide for services in welfare, education, health and housing. That was its job.

Creating the right balance between these two approaches may be beyond the reach of this government. The drive towards a free market economy will inevitably lead to certain economic hardships especially in the short term. Time is something the government does not possess in abundance. Furthermore, as Itzhak Galnoor points out, the Israeli public expects government not only to safeguard its national security but also to serve as a vehicle for fostering social and economic development. Labour gained power promising that it would attend to the pressing social problems facing the country. The constituencies demanding action are numerous, while the resources on hand are not unlimited. Nor is the public liable to be forgiving if action is not forthcoming. When after only a few months of the government taking office, progress or change in the economy failed to materialize, frustrations were vented publicly. Any long-term reform may well have to be put aside for the sake of short-term political survival.

The problems of implementation and the prospects for future

reform are the themes of Yitzhak Klein's chapter. After discussing a number of proposed reforms in both the economic and political sphere, Klein turns his attention to the question of strategy. Meaningful reform has occurred in Israel especially when there has been sufficient public demand. But governments in the past have tended to choose the path of least resistance and have implemented piecemeal changes rather than a comprehensive set of measures. This has allowed, Klein contends, for the battles over reform to be fought on the terms most favourable to its opponents. While pressure from below is important, what is required is leadership from above. The Labour Party has been handed a mandate to effect change. Whether it possesses the calibre, capability and commitment to meet this challenge has yet to be seen.

Israeli society is highly politicized and the level of public participation in the political process is among the highest in democratic societies. But in recent years there has been a marked decline in the public's faith in the political system and in its leaders. This erosion of confidence reached its nadir following the breakdown of the National Unity Government in the spring of 1990 and the scandalous behaviour of the political parties in attempting to form a new government. The paralysis of government and the abuse of power led to the widespread demand for an immediate change to the electoral system.

Many would maintain that the political system is suffering from a crisis of legitimacy and attribute to this the increased activism of extra-parliamentary groups, a growing impatience with the democratic process and a decline in the attachment to democratic values. Yehuda Ben-Meir in his chapter on civil-military relations sounds a cautionary note. While asserting that the Israeli army does not pose any current threat to the democratic institutions of the state, he notes that one of the conditions leading to praetorianism is a weak and ineffective political system. The principle of civilian control is seen as firmly rooted within Israeli values and society. But if the commitment to democracy should ever weaken then the situation might change in the future. Ben-Meir regards the probability of military involvement in the governing of the country as unlikely, but he warns that 'there is still room for doubt and for concern'.

The Israeli public was spared in June 1992 the spectacle of political horse-trading which had become the prime feature of Israeli coalition negotiations. This was by luck rather than by design. Had the results been only slightly different then it might have been forced to endure a repeat performance of the debacle of March 1990. But the public's indignation at that time was ignored. While the pressure from below was great, the resistance from above was sufficient to stem the momentum for reform. Vested interests overruled public concern. Progress was not entirely halted. The electoral threshold for receiving a seat was raised, but only by half a per cent to 1.5 per cent. Though only a bare concession, it did lead to the elimination of one party, Tehiya, which would have received a seat under the old rules and may have contributed to reducing the number of parties in the Knesset from 15 to ten. The bill for the direct election of the prime minister encountered more stubborn resistance in the shape of Yitzhak Shamir who succeeded in ensuring that the bill was not passed in time to be enacted for the election he was about to face. Eventually, the outgoing Knesset in its final hours agreed to the new law which will take effect in 1996.

The prospects for extending and completing the process to include some combination of proportional and constituency based election and a complete written constitution are strong. A clear cross-party majority now exists in the Knesset with the Labour Party, Meretz, Tzomet and most of the Likud in favour of such steps. Opponents, in particular the religious parties, are now powerless to prevent it. Better systems do not necessarily produce better government and there is no guarantee that the direct election of the prime minister will produce the desired effect. It may strengthen the executive but at the same time it could also weaken it considerably should the prime minister find him or herself in opposition to a majority in the Knesset.

While progress in reforming the electoral system has been tortuous, there have been significant changes within the major political parties and the style of Israeli politics. Most important has been the opening up of Labour and Likud, allowing the rank and file members the right to elect their leader and choose their candidates for office. The adoption of the primary system has transformed the image of Israel's political parties. It has opened up the parties, increased membership and moved power away from the smoke-filled central committees and the party bosses.

The Labour Party was the first to adopt the primary system, replacing Shimon Peres with Yitzhak Rabin as its leader and choosing its candidates for the Knesset by this method. While the formula for choosing candidates may have moved rather too far down the path of decentralization, all in all, the primaries did much too boost Labour's image as a more open, representative and democratic party. It is, however, too early, as Emanuel Gutmann points out, to know if this method of choosing candidates will ensure greater responsibility and accountability, two items which to date have been singularly lacking in Israeli politics. Its undisputed success was that it ensured the appointment of a leader who held popular grassroots support and was able to lead the party back to power.

The success of such a measure can be best judged by the speed of the opposition in adopting it. Before even the reality of defeat had sunk in, senior figures in the Likud were demanding that it choose its next leader in the same way. In contrast to Labour, the Likud had entered the elections, as Ehud Sprinzak describes, torn by internal strife and damned by a devastating report by the state comptroller, Miriam Ben-Porat, on corruption and the misuse of public funds in several of the government departments. While there was universal support for following Labour down the path of holding primaries, there was less agreement as to their timing and immediate purpose. Eventually in mid-November the party agreed, by an overwhelming majority to Binyamin ('Bibi') Netanyahu's proposal that the party's chairman, to be elected in March 1993, would also be its candidate for prime minister at the next general election. This would allow the new leader time to rebuild and unify the party without the fear of a challenge to his leadership. Others argued that it was too early to commit the party to a new leader. The system of primaries may not serve the Likud as well as it did Labour. The bitter and heated rivalry between the candidates boiled over with the public accusation made by 'Bibi' Netanyahu on television, that his opponents were trying to blackmail him by threatening to expose his extramarital affair. Though he mentioned no names the finger was clearly pointed at David Levy, the former foreign minister and the most prominent Sephardi politician in the Likud. Whereas the Labour primaries succeeded in muting the personal vendetta between Shimon Peres and Yitzhak Rabin, there is not the equal guarantee that 'Bibi' Netanyahu, in spite of his overwhelming and clear-cut victory, will succeed, after the divisiveness of the primary campaign, in uniting the party behind him. Healing these divides will require considerable political skill on his part and will be the first test of his leadership.

Although the direct election of the prime minister will not start until the next general election, due in 1996, much of the last campaign was conducted as if the new system were already in place. In replacing

Shimon Peres and conducting its campaign under the banner 'Labour led by Rabin', Labour was banking on the broad appeal of Yitzhak Rabin to wide sections of the Israeli electorate, a strategy which proved to be successful. The mould has been set. The 1996 election campaign is likely to be dominated by the issue of personalities where style will be as important as substance. The Likud in choosing the hugely popular Netanyahu, regarded by many as the epitome of the television-age politician, as its new leader has reflected this reality. Sex, glamour and scandal, ever present but hidden quietly in the background of Israeli politics, are emerging on to the front stage. In discussing the future of the Labour Party, Emanuel Gutmann contends that what is important are policies not personalities. Gutmann is correct, but it is a lament from the sidelines. The dawn of television politics has finally arrived in Israel.

It is possible to divide the outcome of the 1992 election into winners and losers. The religious parties as a group fall into the second category. While their percentage of the vote did not fall dramatically the overall distribution of seats means that they no longer hold the balance of power in the Knesset. Relief in many quarters of Israel was clearly visible. The increased political representation of the Haredi ultra-Orthodox parties in the 1980s, the abuse of their political clout, the extortionate demands for the funding of their institutions, their unwillingness to serve in the army and the imposition of religious legislation had led to open hostility among large segments of the Israeli public. This resentment can help explain, in part, the gains made not only by Meretz but also by Tzomet whose views on religion and state and the exemption of Yeshiva students from the army mirror those of the left. The fears in the Haredi world of a secular backlash were only reinforced by the appointment as minister of education and culture of so outspoken a critic of religious coercion as Shulamit Aloni.

Accordingly, there was puzzlement and dismay when Rabin sought to bring the religious parties into the coalition. There was equal surprise, given the vehemence of their attacks on the Labour Party, when the Haredim at first responded positively to these overtures. Menachem Friedman argues that the decline in their electoral power is ominous for the Haredi world and that it poses a serious challenge to the very survival of what he terms 'the society of scholars'. The ultra-Orthodox appear to have no option but to participate even in a Labour-led government in order to guarantee the patronage and funding for their institutions. But the appointment of Shulamit Aloni was a bridge too far for the Haredim. Rabbi Eliezer Schach, the nonagenarian spiritual mentor and erstwhile leader of the ultra-Orthodox community, forbade the Haredi parties to join the coalition. Whereas in March 1990, Shas, the Sephardi ultra-Orthodox party, accepted Schach's *diktat* against joining a Labour-led government, this time they ignored him. Despite severe and sustained pressure, they stood firm and chose to protect their own interests.

Shas and Meretz have found living together in the current coalition to be a difficult experience, but neither can afford to be out of power. While the religious parties as a whole emerged from the election weakened, during the first 12 months of the new government Shas succeeded in manoeuvring itself into a position of strength, underlining the fact that it is a force to be reckoned with. Rabin needs Shas's six seats as much as it needs him. Without them, Labour would lack a parliamentary majority and would be forced to rely on the support of the Arab parties. Shas fortified its position in mid-November following a mini-coalition crisis arising from remarks made by Shulamit Aloni which were seen as offensive to the religious and Haredi public. Emerging victorious from the crisis, Shas obtained additional benefits for the religious public and secured extra ministerial responsibility for itself, including a say in the religious education in state schools. In the negotiations surrounding the 1993 budget, it had little difficulty in successfully preventing the proposed cuts in the funding of *Yeshivot* and other religious institutions. The simmering tension between the two wings of the coalition came to a head at the beginning of May, when the Shas leader, Aryeh Deri, threatened to resign as minister of the interior and leave the government if Shulamit Aloni was not removed from her post. Faced with the potential collapse of the coalition, Meretz had little option but to acquiesce in the public humiliation of its leader at the hands of Shas. After a month of tense negotiations and public mud-slinging between the two leaders, a compromise was eventually reached. Amnon Rubinstein, of Meretz, became the new minister of education and culture; by way of compensation Shulamit Aloni was forced to accept the lesser portfolios of communication, science and technology.

By freeing itself from the control of Rabbi Schach and by being the only religious party prepared to align itself with Labour, Shas has, for the time being, sole access to religious funding. It has also taken a huge step toward its long-term goal of becoming the dominant

religious force within the country, a position previously occupied by
the National Religious Party (NRP).

Having broken the taboo imposed by the religious parties, Labour
has been willing over the past year to countenance Shas's demands in
the hope that it can develop a new entente cordiale, similar to its
partnership with the NRP during the first three decades of the state.
But Rabin has yet to offer it the Ministry of Religious Affairs, the
prize it covets dearly. Instead, he has retained this ministry himself in
an attempt to lure the NRP into joining his coalition.[5] Some regard
this as a forlorn hope. Others argue that the NRP has forfeited its
right to that post by its slide into the arms of the radical right.

Labour needs to tread a careful path. The offering of the religious
portfolio, with its immense control over religious institutions, to a
party whose leaders, while not committed to an anti-Zionist ideology,
nonetheless follow a Haredi way of life would have potentially far-
reaching consequences for the mainstream traditional Zionist religious
public. Furthermore, having spent the past decade watching the
Haredim successively and successfully challenging the religious status
quo, secular Israelis will be looking to this government to restore the
balance. They will find the continued diversion of resources let alone
any further erosion of their liberties difficult to accept.

Whereas the non-Zionist ultra-Orthodox are seen as legitimate
partners for government, the Arabs are not. The Arab Democratic
Party, led by Abdul Wahab Darawshe, with its two seats and the
communist-dominated Democratic Front for Peace and Equality with
three, while regarded as part of the government majority voting bloc,
are not formally part of the coalition. This reflects the marginal
position of Israel's Arab community within Israeli society. Majid Al-
Haj argues that Israel's Arabs find themselves caught between their
allegiance to the Palestinian people of whom they are a part and their
identification with the State of Israel in which they are citizens. As a
consequence they suffer from a 'dual peripheralization' sitting on the
periphery of Israeli and Palestinian society alike. In recent years,
however, Al Haj contends that there has been an increasing tendency
among Israeli Arabs to focus on the citizenship component of their
identity and to seek greater participation within the decision-making
process to address their concerns and advance their own socio-
economic development. This is reflected by the desire of the Arab
Democratic Party to be included within the political consensus, a

theme it emphasized throughout the election campaign and in its willingness to join Rabin's coalition.

Israel's Arabs number around 800,000, approximately one fifth of the country's total population. Yet their numerical strength has not translated itself into a share of national power. The fragmentary nature of Arab politics is one of the reasons for this. The Arabs have been unable to create one party or form an electoral alliance. Votes in the past have even been wasted by an inability to arrive at any surplus-vote agreement. Efforts to overcome these differences before the last election ended in miserable failure. Some political groups, notably the growing Islamic Movement, have also refrained from participating directly in parliamentary politics. Nor have Israel's Arabs bestowed their support exclusively on Arab parties. In 1992, 52 per cent of the Arab vote was given to the Jewish-Zionist parties, primarily to Labour and Meretz. This is not just a reflection of their disillusionment with the Arab political parties but a realization of the inefficacy of a separatist strategy matched with the desire to have a direct impact on the political system.

Israel's Arabs have received meagre rewards from their participation in parliamentary politics. This has led them to channel their efforts in the area of local politics where they are better able to influence the outcomes and where they possess a greater say in the running of their own affairs. They have also mobilized through extra-parliamentary organizations to advance their particular concerns and interests. Al-Haj expects that the minimal returns from national politics and their continued exclusion from government will strengthen activity in these two arenas. But at the same time, he also foresees increased pressure from the Arab public for the formation of a United Arab list in order to participate in the Knesset elections from a position of strength. The Arabs have failed to exploit Israel's system of proportional representation to their benefit. Ironically, the move to the electing of the prime minister directly by the people will afford them a say previously denied and will make them a constituency to be courted.

A society can be judged by how it treats its minorities. In this respect Israel, as Yitzhak Rabin admitted in his opening remarks to the Knesset, has fallen short. He sought to reassure Israel's Arabs that the government would make every effort to close the gap between the Jewish and Arab sectors. Words, however, will not suffice. As Keith Kyle shows, the discrepancies in the infrastructure, welfare, services afforded to Jews and Arabs are vast. Years of discrimination

and neglect has left the Arabs in a state of socio-economic underde-
velopment. Over half of Israel's Arabs live under the poverty line,
unemployment among Arabs is disproportionately high and health and
educational systems require substantial injections of money. There
are no Arabs employed at high levels of government service and few
in public institutions.

Since Rabin took office, some efforts have been made to redress
the balance. Two Arab Knesset members, Nawaf Massalha of Labour
and Walid Tsadik from Meretz, have been appointed as deputy
ministers. The level of child allowance for Arabs is to be brought into
line with the Jewish sector and the 1993 budget almost doubled the
funds earmarked for the Arab sector. These are all important steps in
the right direction. But to echo Keith Kyle, there is much still to be
done.

Inequality extends beyond just Jew and Arab. Israel is also divided
by an ethnic problem between Jews of Oriental or Sephardi origin and
those of an Ashkenazi background. Although the numbers of Oriental
and Ashkenazi Jews are roughly equal, the poor and working classes
are predominantly Oriental while the upper-middle class and the elite
are dominated by Ashkenazim.

Sammy Smooha traces the origins of this ethnic divide and dis-
cusses the factors which account for the persistence of this phenomenon within Israel. There are those who would argue that ethnicity is
receding as an issue in Israeli society. Smooha disagrees. Although
significant headway has been made in the areas of political representation, the incorporation of Sephardi culture in Israeli life and social
assimilation, Smooha argues strongly that the magnitude and persistence of ethnic stratification is a continuous source of deprivation for
Orientals and that it presents a serious problem for Israel. While
ethnic tension has not posed, and is unlikely to pose, any real threat
to political stability, Smooha is struck by the resilience and periodic
resurgence of ethnicity as an issue.

Indeed the arrival of the Soviet Jews has the potential of exacerbating this phenomenon. In the first instance a new Russian ethnic
problem may emerge which will overshadow the Oriental problem.
Secondly the arrival of highly trained and qualified new immigrants
will reduce the Orientals' prospects for social and occupational
mobility. The diverting of resources to the absorption process will also
reduce funds for the provision of welfare services, thereby hitting the
poorer strata of society hardest. The housing crisis of 1990 and

PART ONE
Challenges and Reform

2. ZIONISM INTO ITS SECOND CENTURY: A STOCK-TAKING

Mordechai Bar-On

The term 'Zionism' signifies two different, albeit tightly interwoven, phenomena: on the one hand, an ideology, a school of thought, a set of goals to be achieved, a fabric of dreams expressed in hundreds of books, in thousands of articles and countless lectures and speeches and carried in the minds and hearts of entire generations. On the other hand, a movement, a set of events which have occurred in historical reality, a project accomplished, a process in which actual human behaviour reacted and was reacted upon by certain historical conditions and constraints. While the first meaning of the term is primarily epistemic, the second is factual – the events took place.

Ideologies have often played an important role in the shaping of historical processes.[1] This is particularly true before and during revolutionary upheavals. Yet seldom did ideology play such a central role in determining historical realities as it did in the case of Zionism in its formative stages. Between 1882 and 1924 millions of Jews fled Eastern and Central Europe in a huge wave of migration. The overwhelming majority were moving away from dangers and life-threatening miseries, looking for a safer and better place to live. Opportunistic motivations led them to look for their new haven in the West and especially in the USA, *Die goldene Medineh* (The Golden State).

Only a tiny minority, less than 2 per cent, opted against all personal rationality to settle in Palestine. These pioneers were motivated purely by the force of an ideological impulse. They were utterly convinced that Judaism in its primarily traditional religious forms of existence in the Diaspora had become untenable under conditions of modern nationalism and that, therefore, Jews, too, must recreate their own

20

national homeland in Zion. History has tragically proved them correct inasmuch as Eastern and Central Europe are concerned. However, they did overlook the other possible salvation, which Jews started to experience in the democratic West. These few ideological pioneers laid down the foundation for what would later become the State of Israel.

This unique phenomenon and the overwhelming impact ideology had on its development has led in more recent times to most, if not all, Israelis adopting two dangerous fallacies. On the one hand, they tend to believe that Israel was created by the force of will power alone, against and in spite of all historical odds. On the other hand, many are convinced that ideology, against all political and economic odds, is still the most important factor in determining the fate of Israel in the future.[2]

The scope of this chapter does not permit a detailed examination of our assumption that, important as it may have been in shaping the path along which the Zionist project evolved, ideology was only one of many complex chains of historical causation. What is more important for present purposes is the fact that, over the last five decades, the role of ideological impulse has waned considerably and has been transformed to a large degree from a unifying and mobilizing force into a self-gratifying set of rationalizations at best, and, at worst, a divisive set of political propaganda ploys. This transformation started immediately after the establishment of the Jewish State in 1948. Paradoxically, the very generation of young men and women who fought the Israeli War of Independence sometimes used the word Zionism with disparagement to designate hypocritical and vacuous ideological preaching.[3]

After the Six Day War of 1967, while it looked for a time as if Zionism had won an unexpected renaissance, the schism become complete. The way different factions now used the term Zionism implied diverse and often contradictory meanings. It is true that variants of Zionist ideology and harsh inner ideological strife were abundant in the movement from its outset. Yet even in the 1930s the great schism between the mainstream of the Zionist organization, led by Chaim Weizmann and David Ben-Gurion, and the Revisionist breakaway, led by Ze'ev Jabotinsky, resulted from controversies around issues of strategy and tactics, not around goals and ultimate aims. As we shall see later, the grand national debate in Israel today rages around fundamentals. Stark questions, not only of priorities and

timing but of finite and crucial choices between cherished goals, lie at
the heart of current political and ideological divisions in Israel.

An even more damaging fallacy centres on the question of the
functionality of ideology. Even today, the Zionist ideology continues
to be a strong mobilizing and recruiting force for many people. But at
the same time it is obvious that, on the whole, it affects the
development of the Zionist project only at the margin. The recent
wave of immigration of Soviet Jews may serve as a good example: by
the time of publication, close to 400,000 Jews will have emigrated to
Israel from areas which once constituted the Soviet Union. Most of
these Jews would have clearly opted to migrate elsewhere had the
gates of the USA and other western countries remained open to them.
Certainly, few of them have read, let alone been motivated by, Zionist
ideologues. Yet this huge influx of Jews to Israel is certainly the most
outstanding and influential feature of the Zionist project so far this
decade.

Zionist ideology had a unique mobilizing force at those times when
a real and vital debate was taking place inside the Diaspora itself.
During the first five decades of its existence, in every Jewish *stetl*,[4] in
every Jewish community, in every Jewish household in Eastern and
Central Europe, a vibrant debate raged around the question of
whether to leave and where to go. These were not theoretical
questions. The need to leave the soil which was burning under their
feet and go elsewhere was real and urgent. The question of the
physical and spiritual survival of Judaism had direct personal implications. On the personal level the Zionist option may have looked crazy
to many but it made a lot of sense on the collective level and, as such,
possessed a strong moral force.

An ideological appeal which today comes primarily from Israelis
born in Israel, who have not had to confront the problem of *Aliya*[5] as
a personal dilemma, yet at the same time preach to Jews in the
Diaspora the Zionist precept of 'the Ingathering of Exiles', cannot
have the same moral force as the original idea, which was sparked off
in the stormy almost volcanic Diaspora of the turn of the century. Nor
can it escape the suspicion that it is motivated by concern for self-
preservation and addresses the needs of Israel rather than those of
Jews in the Diaspora.[6]

The weakness of Zionist ideology as a motivating force can also be
seen in the area of land settlement. There can be little doubt that the
followers of Gush Emunim, the extreme right-wing settler movement,

are keenly motivated by their messianic vision. Many small settlements in the West Bank, the Gaza Strip, and the Golan Heights, especially those settled in the first decade of the occupation, against the better judgment of the ruling Labour Party government at the time, were motivated purely by ideology. However, when at the beginning of the 1980s Ariel Sharon, then minister of agriculture in charge of the Land Authority, wanted significantly to expand settlement in the occupied territories, beyond the few thousand who had followed the ideological call, he was obliged to use much more mundane attractions. A spacious villa, in beautiful surroundings for less than half the price of comparable property inside the pre-1967 boundary but 'only thirty minutes away' from the centre of Jerusalem, Netanya or Tel Aviv, presented a much more convincing attraction than the enthusiastic speeches of ideologists like Geula Cohen and her colleagues.[7] Quite understandably, people who opted for a 'villa' tended to justify their choice, ex post facto, with heated ideological argumentation.

Zionist Goals

The Zionist idea advocated five main goals, which originally united all streams of the movement, notwithstanding vocal and often vitriolic controversies around questions of tactics or timing:

1. The Ingathering of the Exiles into the Land of Israel.
2. The carving out of a territorial space for the Jews in that Land.
3. The creation of a modern reality of a Jewish society in the Land.
4. The achievement of political sovereignty.
5. The eventual achievement of peace and international acceptance.

Not all five goals were defined by Zionist thinkers in these exact terms, but all were included, at least implicitly, in the writings of the classical Zionist ideologues and were clearly implied in the platforms of all the Zionist factions. They are amply spelled out in the flood of words that the Zionist movement produced in its first five decades. These were the goals that were to shape new realities.

Paradoxically, but quite understandably, the final goal – achieving peace and international acceptability – appeared only rarely in the early days. In those days it was debated mainly by the extreme wings of the movement: Brit Shalom on the left and the Revisionists on the right.[8] For the former it served as a rationale for Zionist minimalism; for the latter it was a reminder that eventually, even for Zionist maximalists, peace and acceptance must prevail. Most spokesmen of the mainstream, who rarely dealt with this subject at any length or detail, certainly assumed it to be a vital but self-evident goal, without whose eventual achievement the entire project would mean very little.

Today these goals serve as a rationalization for policy choices, more often than as a directive to action. In the following pages I shall analyse what happened to each of them, and what transformations they underwent in the course of time. No goal of any historical movement and revolution can ever be fully achieved. But the goals as outlined above can be used as a means of discussing what has actually happened to the Zionist project and where it may lead us in the future. It is hoped that the parameters of the current Zionist debate, which cuts deep in Israeli society and divides its core right through the middle, will thereby become clearer.

The Ingathering of Exiles

This most basic precept of Zionism has always carried and still carries today a fatalistic assumption about the future of Diaspora Jewry. Zionism assumed from the outset that Jewish life in the Diaspora, under the evolving realities of modern nationalism on the one hand and democratic liberalism on the other, would become increasingly untenable.[9] Most early Zionist thinkers, who came from Eastern Europe, were inclined to express the 'Catastrophic' version of the 'Negation of Exile' (*Shlilat ha Golah* in Hebrew). They believed that Jews would gradually lose the economic and even physical ability to survive in conditions of exile. The Nazi Holocaust was to supply a tragic vindication of this 'Catastrophic' version of Zionism. Under the Weimar Republic in Germany and later on in the United States, Zionist thinkers tended to stress the dangers of Jewish assimilation and intermarriage in the open liberal societies of the democratic West.[10]

Recurrent demographic studies of American Jewry, which indicate a steady erosion of Jewish life in the United States, in terms of both the sheer size of the community and the intensity of its affiliation and identification, serve as a vindication of what might be termed the 'softer' version of the 'Negation of Exile'. Nevertheless, it must be said that, after one hundred years of Cassandra prophesies, Jewish communal and personal life in the Diaspora shows an impressive degree of resilience. The amazing revival of Jewish identification in the Soviet Union, either through immigration to Israel or through the re-establishment of Jewish communal life, is a recent reminder of this resilience.

The fact remains that, after one hundred years, only one out of three identifiable Jews lives in the Jewish State. For the foreseeable future it seems that Israel will remain only the second largest Jewish community in the world. Thus even the more limited goal of the ingathering of the majority of the Jewish people in their ancestral land remains still a far cry. The recent immigration from the ex-Soviet countries and Ethiopia since the beginning of 1990 revived the vigour of the 'Ingathering' process, yet it is now clear that not only are existing Diaspora communities there to stay but also new kinds of Diaspora are simultaneously being formed. Half a million Jews who opted over the years to migrate back from Israel to the Diaspora now form large new communities of Hebrew-speaking Jews in Los Angeles, Queens County (New York) and elsewhere in the United States and Canada. The Soviet Jews who were allowed to build their homes in Brighton Beach, New York, and even in Berlin, make it harder still to predict the future of Jewish exile.

In addition, the growing difficulties in the absorption of the new immigrants in Israel are not only a result of insufficient new housing projects, nor merely a reflection of the greater task of widening the Israeli economy. There is also a poor fit between the vocational and professional structure and placement expectations of the Soviet immigrants and the existing employment structure of the current Israeli economy. There are already indications that the pace of future Soviet immigration may well be dictated by social and economic factors rather than by the ideological zeal which has hitherto determined Israeli immigration policies.

The decision of the Israeli government, backed by an overwhelming majority of Israeli Jews, to keep the gates wide open for all Jews who desire to immigrate and become Israeli citizens, contrary to any rational calculations, either economic or demographic, results from its devotion to the Zionist idea. But in spite of the dramatic increase of the absorptive capacity which the attainment of statehood conferred on the Zionist project, objective constraints and historical conditions still dictate much of the outcome. As in the 1920s and the 1930s, the coincidence of two essential conditions is required in the 1990s also to bring about a large wave of immigration: a strong and urgent desire on the part of Jews in some Diasporas to escape imminent dangers; and far-reaching limitations on their ability to emigrate to countries other than the land of Israel.

Soviet Jews will most probably continue to flow into Israel in great numbers during the next decade, though a gradual reduction in the annual rate and a probable increase in the re-emigration from Israel to other countries may put a ceiling to the scope of net 'ingathering'. As to the other Diaspora communities in the West, the pattern over the last 50 years and a sober analysis of the prevailing conditions in those countries point to the conclusion that, if the size of these communities does continue to decrease, it will most probably be for reasons other than the opting of significant streams of Jews to 'ingather' to their ancestral land.

The 'Negation of Exile' Controversy

Post-Second World War realities in most countries of the Jewish Diaspora and the establishment of the Jewish State obliged Zionist ideologists to amend their concepts about the 'negation of exile' and to reinforce traditional analytic-predictive arguments with normative-moral ones. They had to accept that the Diaspora could well continue to survive in the modern world. Yet exilic existence, they argued now, involved heavy moral flaws. A Jew in the Diaspora, they maintained, could not realize fully his or her Jewishness. Only in a Jewish state, in an integral Jewish environment, could a Jew live fully as a Jew. Also, some argued, to live as an ethnic minority entailed limitations to the fullness of human responsibility and control of one's own fate.[11]

The Israeli state education system does indeed try to merge universal and Jewish elements and perhaps succeeds to some degree in presenting human values in Jewish terminology and Jewish values as part of a universal orientation. Nonetheless, many Diaspora communities do in reality succeed in offering Jews meaningful forms of Jewish life. While Jews who want to give their children a fuller scope of Jewish education find ample ways to do it while still in the Diaspora, those who are already assimilated to such a degree that the Jewish identity of their children is of no concern to them are not likely to be swayed by such arguments.

The very fact that most of the Jews in western Diaspora, even declared Zionists among them, have lost any sense of living 'in exile' and have insisted on replacing that term with the more neutral term 'Diaspora', which implies permanence, is an indication that, whatever theoretical validity the moral argument about negating 'exile' might have, it cannot mean much to most of the Jews who do not live in the Jewish state. Unlike pogroms and persecutions, assimilation can be a comfortable experience. The moral argument around the 'negation of exile' has little real mobilizing force and therefore cannot have a real ideological standing. Indeed a wide gap was created over the last four decades between the common discourse of the Zionist movement and its actual practice. While Zionist congresses, conferences and ideological seminars remained replete with old litanies and lofty sloganeering, the State of Israel and the World Zionist Organization themselves vigorously and consistently led policies which clearly implied a readiness to legitimize Diaspora Jewry and were often directed towards the strengthening of diasporic communities.

Ever since the famous *Gegenwartsarbeit* decision was adopted by the All-Russian Zionist Conference in Helsingfors (Helsinki) in 1906,[12] the Zionist Organization has been committed not only to fight anti-semitism everywhere but also to encourage Jewish cultural and educational work in the Diaspora 'as long as it still existed'. But in 1949 David Ben-Gurion took this logic one dramatic step forward in his exchange of letters with Jacob Blaustein, president of the American Jewish Committee. This exchange, which can be described as a semi-official 'concordat' between the State of Israel and American Jewry, was clearly a trade-off between unequivocal support by US Jewry for the State of Israel and clear legitimization by the Israeli prime minister of Jewish life in western Diasporas. 'Negation' was to be no more mentioned by either side.[13]

The reconstitution of the Jewish Agency in 1970 endorsed a formal partnership between the World Zionist Organization and leaders of the Diaspora communities on an equal footing and, in the 1980s, the joint leadership of this agency moved explicitly to put Jewish education in the Diaspora at the top of its priorities. The huge influx of Soviet and Ethiopian Jews at the beginning of the 1990s has reversed, at least for a while, this trend. In terms of priorities of resource allocation and public attention, the educational efforts to 'save the Diaspora' have been relegated to a secondary role. The hasty escape of close to half a million Jews from their 'lands of bondage' served as a reminder that classic Zionism in its original forms had not yet lost its functionality. Yet it is already clear now that, after immigration from the former Soviet Union has slowed down, the problems of helping the

Diaspora to survive culturally and spiritually, even in Eastern Europe, will come back to haunt Zionist ideology.

Carving a Territorial Base

From the very beginning of Zionism the return of the exiles to their ancestral homeland was named a process of 'redemption'. Harping on biblical metaphors, it was described as the redemption of the Jews from exilic subjugation and powerlessness. This process was, however, inevitably linked with another redemption: the redemption of the Land. The two most used Zionist slogans in the early days were: *Me Avdut le Herut* ('From Slavery to Freedom') and *Geula Titnu la Aretz* ('Bring Redemption to the Land'). The term 'redemption' in this second context implied at one and the same time the liberation of the land from its desolation and its liberation from 'foreign' rule. The land must be reclaimed from the desert and made into a Jewish land. Theodor Herzl was seeking a 'territorial base' for his *Judenstaat* anywhere he could.[14] But after his death the issue was resolved once and for all: the territorial base could be established only in the Holy Land of Israel. Paradoxically, the term 'territorialist' was acquired by those who broke away from the Zionist Organization in search of a haven elsewhere for the persecuted Jews. But the Zionists did not thereby become less 'territory-minded'. It became obvious that the Zionist project would necessitate maximum procurement of land by the Jews in Palestine. The Jewish National Fund, the main Zionist organ for the purchase of land, became also one of the most important tools of Zionism in the first decades of the century. A high premium was attached to the expansion of Jewish agriculture, while defence and security needs dictated the consolidation of Jewish territorial holdings in large stretches of land, covered by self-defending Jewish settlements.

The critical mass of Jewish settlements established on Jewish-owned land in the first five decades of the twentieth century made all the difference in 1948. When the decisive war was ultimately fought, it enabled the Jews not only to defend themselves against the Arab onslaught but also to expand their territorial base, so far acquired by purchase and gradual settlement, by military conquest and then by the rapidly induced settlement of the massive immigration of the 1950s. The fact that the Jewish National Fund had to transform itself from a land-purchasing agency to one dealing primarily with afforestation

demarcation lines and the zealous guarding of its independence from any external interference with its decisions on security and foreign affairs may be becoming a luxury Israel will not be able to afford. A state, the security and economy of which depends on an annual subsidy from the United States of more than 10 per cent of its national budget, can hardly claim total independence.

Any likely resolution of the Israeli–Palestinian conflict, and especially any solutions of the Jerusalem problem, will call for significant limitations on the sovereignty of both sides. More intricate and sophisticated versions of national sovereignty will be necessary in order to diffuse one of the most complex conflicts of our century.

Peace

It was mentioned earlier that the least explicit goal of Zionism, as expressed by its ideologues, was the achievement of peace and acceptance of the Zionist project by its Arab neighbours. This was due to the fact that the early Zionists had taken this goal for granted. Neither Herzl, Pinsker, Borochov nor anyone else among the early Zionist thinkers conceived of the Zionist dream as entailing a hundred years of strife and violence. Even the one thinker who saw the conflict in the most farsighted way, Ze'ev Jabotinsky, who predicted a prolonged zero-sum strife between two contending national movements, felt compelled to end his famous article 'The Iron Wall' with a consoling paragraph about the images of peace and friendly neighbourhood, which would eventually prevail between the two nations. Eventual peace was the only condition, Zionists always believed, which would bring the project to its ultimate fulfilment.

Not before 1967, or perhaps even 1973, could the Israelis take the goal of peace down from the high shelf of pious hopes onto the table where real political contingencies are considered. The peace concluded with Egypt in 1978, the uprooting of the PLO by the Israelis and the Syrians from Lebanon in 1982 and, finally, the initial success of the Intifada in 1988, were necessary preliminaries to the great leap that the Palestinians made from the uncompromising 'Armed Struggle' stance to the table of peace negotiations. By the end of 1991, it seemed at long last that the goal of peace-making had jumped to the top of the Zionist agenda. A consistent majority of more than two-thirds, including supporters of the Likud, had come to the conclusion that the status quo was no longer tenable and that Israel must now strive to achieve some kind of reconciliation with the Palestinians and the Arab world.

The issue of peace could be postponed no more. More and more people were convinced that peace could and must be achieved, if not 'now', at least in the foreseeable future, and that the road which might lead to it had to be mapped out now in real terms of phased agreements. Yitzhak Shamir's 'peace initiative' of May 1989, as murky and equivocal as it was, was a clear indication that even ardent proponents of 'Greater Israel' had come to put peace at the top of Israel's national priorities.

This posture, nonetheless, failed to reach the level of a national consensus, not only because the ways by which peace could be achieved remained a major bone of contention among different schools of thought, but mainly because a sizeable minority of some 20 per cent of the Jewish population of Israel remained unimpressed and intransigent. Much of this debate may be presented in political terms but there can be no doubt that, underneath all these rational and quasi-rational arguments, ideological preferences and value choices lurk. A clear choice between conflicting national goals constitutes the decisive parameter. The Israeli extreme right believes that the Zionist project must proceed as hitherto to achieve the maximum territorial base through land annexation and intensive settling of the land, even if this means more violent strife and wars and the further postponement of peace. According to this view the 'Iron Wall' strategy still holds today and should not be abandoned. This ideological posture is fortified by a strong disbelief in the sincerity of the Arabs and in the feasibility of a credible and secure peace, especially if it is conditional on a retreat from the occupied territories.

The 'Peace Camp', in contrast, implies that, in its march to fulfilment, Zionism gained more territories than it can maintain and must therefore retreat to a more limited living space. This position also implies that the social and economic realities established within the 'Green Line' can provide a base strong enough for further development of the Zionist project, including the absorption of another million or so Soviet immigrants, the maintenance of military security and further economic growth. Moreover, the achievement of peace is deemed by supporters of this camp as a precondition for any further advancement of the Zionist project. The insistence on entrenchment in a larger territorial base is seen as endangering the

Zionist achievement in other areas and perhaps eventually endangering the very existence of the Jewish State.

The way each side of this national divide interprets the significance of the new wave of Soviet immigration is illuminating. The right insists that a larger territorial space is needed to accommodate the dramatically increasing Jewish population of the State.[21] The left, on the other hand, maintains that the continuation of the violent conflict with the Palestinians will eventually endanger the continuation of immigration, while stifling Israel's capacity to absorb the existing mass of immigrants and encouraging growing emigration. A typical banner in a recent demonstration of 'Peace Now', the main Israeli extra-parliamentary peace movement, read, '*Aliyah*, not Territories!'

Jewish Nationhood

The single most important of the assumptions which underlay the Zionist idea was the conviction that the Jews constitute a nation like all other nations and therefore have the right to political self-determination and a state of their own. These early thinkers drew their world view from the multi-ethnic and multi-national East European experience in which Jews possessed all the traits of other nations in that part of the world, except that they had no clear territorial concentration and also constituted an historical religion which was not shared by any other ethnic community.

By the end of the twentieth century, however, in the light of dramatically changing conditions of world Jewish existence, this prime Zionist conviction has become a permanent source of misunderstanding and puzzlement and requires further clarification. Is this conviction, indeed, so simple and self-evident today? Not surprisingly, the Palestine Liberation Organization was keenly interested in this issue. The Palestinian National Charter includes a special paragraph which defines the Jews. It declares that: 'Judaism, being a religion, is not an independent nationality.'[22]

Many neutral observers often have an honest difficulty in understanding this strange phenomenon, which does not fit neatly into any regular categorization. Even Jews in western Diasporas find it sometimes difficult to apply the term 'nation' to define Judaism, since, in their world, the term 'nation' is already employed in defining the state in which they live and of which they feel themselves to be citizens. Moreover, in every secular respect these Jews have become totally socialized and integrated into the societies in which they live. They

identify themselves culturally, politically and in other secular senses as
members of the nation in which they live. Nonetheless, Jewish
worldwide solidarity and the deep sense of concern Jews everywhere
feel *vis-à-vis* the State of Israel are also real facts, alive in the
consciousness of millions of Jews in the Diaspora for whom their
Jewishness is an important, if not the most important, facet of their
complex identity. No purely religious interpretation can fully account
for these facts.[23] To overcome this ideological confusion, Jews often
use terminological palliatives by employing words such as 'people-
hood', 'brotherhood', *Mishpoche* ('family' in Yiddish) or 'we are One'
– the famous slogan of the United Jewish Appeal (UJA).

For the four million Jews who live in the State of Israel, the majority
of whom are secular or at best 'traditional' but in no way 'religious',
the term 'Jewish' serves as the adjective which differentiates them
from other Israeli citizens and tells them 'what kind of Israeli they
are'. The common term 'Israeli' which they more often use to define
their nationality, clearly means for them a short version of 'Israeli who
belongs to the Jewish People'. From the outset Zionism, which was
heavily secular in its make-up, defined the Jewish people in national
rather than in religious terms, though it never denied the prime role
that religion played in the formation of Judaism and its preservation
during the long years of exile. Today this issue has become more
complex and must be expressed in optional and normative rather than
descriptive and analytical terms. Modern Zionists will maintain that
Jews should have the personal right to define their loyalties and sense
of belonging. Political self-determination is recognized universally as
a collective right; so must be the individual right to self-identification.
Zionism therefore insists that, despite all complexities, Jews everywhere should have the right to define themselves as belonging to a
certain nation, and, therefore, if they so opt, should have the right to
emigrate to Israel and live in the 'State of the Jews', namely the state
in which Jews are the majority, in which the prevailing language is
Hebrew and in which all trappings of statehood are their traditional
national trappings. In this respect the Law of Return is an inalienable
right, around which all Zionists unite.

It is, however, our moral obligation to add in this context that no
right is valid if it does not apply universally. Such Zionist conviction
cannot therefore deny the same right of self-definition and political
self-determination to the Palestinian people as well.

Conclusion

Zionism was born amidst a major shake-up of historic Judaism. Millions of Jews migrated to faraway countries, millions perished in the Holocaust, and almost all surviving Jews underwent a deep process of modernization, which brought about far-reaching changes in their daily lives and world views. One hundred years later, significant parts of world Jewry show clear signs of stabilization in new forms of life and new sets of beliefs. Nevertheless, we are still in the middle of great flux. The consequences of the demise of the communist empire, the great social and economic transformation of Eastern Europe, and the unfettering of generations-old shackles, which once more allows millions of Jews to choose their destinies, will certainly continue for quite some time. It is impossible to predict at this stage when and how these millions of Jews will reach a new equilibrium and the modus of a new stability.

Similar problems confront the four million Jews who now live in the land of Israel. The state of Arab–Jewish relations remains unstable, and the impact of the recent waves of immigration on Israeli society has not yet fully unfolded. To predict the course Zionism may take in its second century is a highly risky undertaking. Nonetheless, we should try to draw some conclusions and at least pose some questions which will probably engage Zionist ideology well into its future.

The first comment has to do with its very age. The mere fact that more than a hundred years after its inception, Zionism is still alive and kicking, that people continue to debate it, hold congresses and conventions under its title and try again and again to reformulate and articulate its platforms, is amazing indeed. Yet, despite its recent revival, one cannot escape the impression that it is, after all, on its way out, more through its own success than as a result of its failures. At the tail end of its historic functionality it may become more a set of nostalgic symbols than a guiding and mobilizing force in the lives of the Jewish people.

Secondly, immigration from Eastern Europe will sooner or later level down. Many Jews will probably opt to leave the lands of the former Soviet Union for either Israel (probably the majority) or other western countries (primarily the United States). Some may continue to lose their Jewish identity through assimilation, yet many may succeed in recreating active Jewish communities in the towns and cities of the fallen communist empire. Immigration from the United States and other Western countries into Israel will continue to trickle on, but emigration from Israel into the West may well offset much of the gain.

Peace in the Middle East as well as the coming to political maturity of Israelis of 'Oriental' descent, may well thrust the question of Israel's integration into the Middle East into the centre of the Israeli cultural, economic, and social agenda. For the first time it may indeed become a real issue. Will Israel gradually become another Middle Eastern society and thus remove itself further from other centres of Jewish life, or will it maintain its basic European make-up, and thus remain aloof from its immediate environment? Open borders and unimpeded communication with its Arab neighbours would probably be accompanied by the desire of the Mizrahi (Oriental) Israelis to gain a more central role in society and in politics, thus strongly colouring the evolving identity of the Zionist state. Yet the economic and technological advantages of remaining part of the West are so overwhelming that it is rather unlikely that Israelis in the next century would want to give it up. Also, the democratic structures and prevailing norms seem to be solid enough to sustain deep environmental and internal upheavals; they will most probably continue to prevail and, one may hope, may even improve.

David Ben-Gurion never tired of preaching his conviction that the Jews were and are obliged to remain a 'Light unto the Nations'. He saw in this not a privilege bestowed on the nation but a moral obligation demanded of it. Over the years, as a result of wrong lessons drawn from the Holocaust experience and the prolonged strife with the Arabs, this outlook tended to take on a more chauvinistic meaning. Morality gave in too often to national arrogance. The unique characteristics of Jewish history and what can too easily be perceived as Jewish solitude in the world, fed by a resurgence of anti-semitism, were translated into discourse about power and alienation. Peace in the Middle East and some measure of stabilization in the external relations of Israel may help to weaken negative and ethnocentric interpretations of these legacies of our history. One may hope that, short of being a 'light unto the nations', Israel may at least be 'a light unto itself'. One may indeed hope that the humanistic elements which were always present in the Zionist ideology will prevail and make the Zionist project an enlightened form of Jewish existence in the next century.

3. THE PROBLEM OF SYSTEMIC REFORM

Yitzhak Klein

During most of the 1970s and 1980s Israelis had good reason to be dissatisfied with their political and economic system. Economic growth was painfully slow after 1973, seriously holding back the achievement of such important national goals as increasing the average citizen's welfare, integrating disadvantaged groups into the mainstream of Israeli society, attracting Jewish immigration to Israel and ending dependence on foreign aid. The government amassed a huge public debt, which posed a constant threat to economic stability and consumed resources that might have been put to better purpose.

The problems were chronic and had been recognized for years. This highlights the close connection between social and economic dysfunction in Israel, on the one hand, and political dysfunction on the other. Problems widely acknowledged to exist nevertheless were not effectively addressed, and hence persisted for long periods. Most Israelis would agree that their political system was not, and is not, responsive enough to public concerns. Systemic reform, political as well as economic, has long been on Israel's public agenda. It is actively discussed by social scientists, political elites and ordinary citizens alike, and is endorsed at least nominally by both major political parties.

In any polity effective institutional reform is difficult to accomplish, and the peculiarities of Israel's institutional structure make it especially difficult. Nevertheless during the last few years change has been palpable. The conditions for reform of Israel's political and economic institutions have been created, so that perhaps the next few years could witness an ongoing and accelerating process of reform. Israel's political institutions may become more responsive to public concerns;

the economy may emerge completely from the burdens of the past, growing fast enough to respond effectively to society's growing needs.[1]

Two observations regarding the reform process in Israel are apposite here. First, the 'change to change' is still fragile and could be reversed. Secondly, the impression of a watershed, a sudden shift in the pattern of political behaviour from stagnation to reform, is at least partly illusory. Though Israeli political and economic institutions could in the future change rapidly, the foundations of change have been laid in the context of existing institutions. Extraordinary measures bypassing the normal institutional structure of government are not necessary for reform to take place.

A Systemic Overview
Israel is not the only democratic society where the performance of political and economic institutions is perceived as less than optimal. In the Israeli case, however, institutional dysfunction can be described as systemic in that most of the country's major institutions are implicated; furthermore, problems within different institutions compound one another. Three chief characteristics of Israeli society contribute to the problem:

The Government as Patron
Israel has never had a centralized, state-owned or command economy. However, the state has traditionally played the role of patron of economic and other social actors. This was expressed in a variety of forms, from regulation and trade protection to outright subsidy. Such patronage was once widely thought of as an appropriate way of fulfilling the state's obligation to attend to the welfare of society.[2] This view is now far less widely accepted. Nevertheless, Israel remains unusual among the developed western market-type economies in the scope and the value of government benefits extended to a broad range of interest groups.

The Impoverishment of Public Policy
Demands for government patronage tend to increase over time and become particularly intense during periods of social stress or economic stagnation. This has led since the late 1960s to steady growth in government spending and in cumulative public debt, subjecting public

policy-making in Israel to severe constraints. The state of the public finances is a prime cause of economic instability and government policy in recent years has been preoccupied with the struggle against the twin problems of inflation and recession. Any significant change in public policy, whether to increase, decrease, or reallocate government spending, would involve extensive and painful adjustments by large segments of society and hence large political costs.

The System of Government

Israel's system of government gives marginal groups, whether organized as political parties or not, substantial veto power over policy changes. Political elites hitherto have been chosen indirectly and enjoy considerable security of tenure, regardless of performance. Decision-making power is low.

Israel's socio-economic and political institutions have interacted to produce what has seemed to be a trap, confining society within a vicious circle of economic stagnation and political immobility. The crisis in public finances has exerted a dampening effect on economic growth and social mobility, harming all sectors of society. Yet systemic change has seemed difficult to achieve. For change to happen, someone's interests would have to be hurt, at least in the short term, and the parties affected would resist change. Israel's political system makes such resistance easy.

Change, nevertheless, does occur. Incremental change, much of it of lasting value, happens all the time. Sometimes major reforms are introduced on the basis of a national consensus that change is indispensable and the concomitant costs must be borne. This may happen when most individuals feel that the personal cost to them of eradicating an evil is less than the personal cost of continuing to tolerate it. The economic reform of 1985, instituted to defeat hyper-inflation, is one example. More recently, the Israeli public demonstrated with the passage of the Electoral Reform Bill of 1992 an ability to feel deeply about an issue and force change even when the individual citizen's welfare was not directly and immediately threatened. None of these reforms is adequate in itself but they show that the deadlock of economic and political institutions can be broken when the consensus of public opinion demands it.

Table 1   Public Expenditure and Finance in Israel, 1960–88

(In percentages of annual GNP)

Period	Expenditure	Receipts (Deficit)	Of which: Taxes	Defence	Defence as % of Expenditure
1960–66	37	36 (1)	33	9.7	27
1967–72	56	43 (13)	39	21.1	39
1973–84	76	59 (18)	48	25.7	34
1985–88	66	64 (2)	51	18.6	28

Adapted from Michael Bruno, 'Havra'at Hameshek. Beperspektiva Historit' (The Economic Recovery in Historical Perspective), *Rivon Lekalkala* (Economic Quarterly), No 141, July 1989; table 3, p. 110.

Economic Crisis and Reform

Evidence of Systemic Failure
The process which led to the narrowing of Israel's policy options in the 1970s and 1980s can be summarized by looking at the trends in public expenditure and finance in Israel during 1960–88 (see Table 1). Until 1977 the Labour Party and its allies were in power; yet, during the period 1960–66, public expenditure was on average only 37 per cent of GNP, a figure that was reasonable by the standards of most western market economies at the time. Government's share of the economy then grew steadily until the period 1973–84, when government spending absorbed 76 per cent of GNP and the government deficit averaged an astounding 18 per cent of GNP. By 1985, the total public debt exceeded twice Israel's annual GNP.

The burden of government expenditure progressively came to weigh more heavily upon the Israeli economy. In 1973–84 nearly half the national income was taken in taxes (these rates are average not marginal), an extraordinary percentage by any standard. During 1985–8, in an effort to eliminate the budget deficit, expenditure fell but tax rates rose again. They have continued to rise since.

Perhaps the most telling figures are those that deal with defence

Table 2   Growth of National Product Annual Percentage Increase
Product per worker in parentheses

	1960–73	1974–80	1981–84	1985–87
Israel	4.2 (5.5)	3.3 (2.2)	3.5 (0.1)	5.7 (3.5)
'Semi-industrialized' Nations	6.7 (2.7)	6.0 (3.0)	6.0 (3.9)	6.6 (5.2)
OECD	4.7 (3.6)	2.6 (2.0)	2.2 (1.8)	3.0 (1.4)

Source: Michael Bruno, 'Havra'at Hameshek Be-Perspektiva Historit' (The Economic Recovery in Historical Perspective), *Riv'on LeKalkala* (Economic Quarterly), 141, July 1989; table 3, p 110.

Kippur War (1967–73), when it was absorbing over 20 per cent of GNP and nearly 40 per cent of the budget. Afterwards, defence continued to rise as a percentage of GNP, but total government expenditure rose much faster. Between 1960–66 and 1973–84 non-defence items in the budget expanded from 27 per cent to about 50 per cent of GNP. This increase reflects the rise in special benefits provided to various constituencies, including transfer payments to individuals, price and investment subsidies, and the like. These budget figures do not take account of a large array of off-budget government benefits provided to special constituencies in the form of trade protection, cartelization, and the 'mobilization' of loans from commercial banks on less-than commerical terms, all of which impaired the functioning of the economy.

These figures describe a domestic budget process and a political system out of control. Public expenditure and public debt grew continuously from 1967 onward. The effect upon the welfare of the national economy was not positive; quite the reverse. Until 1965 Israel enjoyed one of the highest growth rates in the world, comparing well with the East Asian 'tigers', but far exceeding them in terms of per capita income. Since 1973 Israel's growth rate has been cut to a little over 3 per cent per year, or about 1 per cent in per capita terms (see Table 2).

By the early 1990s, however, the situation had changed significantly. There is a marked difference between the period 1985–91, especially the early 1990s, and the preceding 18 years. While the figures somewhat overstate the underlying rate of economic growth,[3] the early

Table 3   Annual GDP Growth (%)

	1986	1987	1988	1989	1990	1991	Average*
United States	2.5	2.9	4.4	3.0	0.9	−0.5	2.2
'Major 7'**	NA***	NA***	4.5	3.4	2.2	0.8	2.7
All OECD	2.5	3.1	4.4	3.5	2.3	0.8	2.8
Israel	3.7	5.9	2.7	1.6	5.1	5.9	4.2

* Average of figures in preceding columns; not necessarily equivalent to average growth rates in period under consideration.
** United States, Japan, Germany (Federal Republic), France, Britain, Italy and Canada.
*** Not available in series consulted.

Sources: Lines 1–3: OECD Main Economic Indicators, chart, 'GDP', March issue each year, 1987–91, February 1982; Line 4: ICSO, *Israel Statistical Annual* (Jerusalem 1991), Table 6.1, p 188; ICSO, *Israel Statistical Monthly*, February 1992. p 17.

Table 4   Savings and Investment (percentage of annual GNP)
Productivity (percentage annual increase)

	1981–85	1986–89	1990	1991
Gross Savings	17.7	17.3	17.5	20.0
Gross Investment	19.1	16.1	16.8	21.6
Growth of Labour Productivity		1.2	4.3	2.4
Return on Capital		11.0	12.0	14.7

Note: during the hyper-inflationary early 1980s savings and investment were high but productivity and return on capital were relatively low. The 1985 reform programme depressed savings and investment; these have now begun to recover, even while inflation drops.

Sources: Lines 1–2, Bank Yisrael (Bank of Israel), *Din VeHeshbon Lishnat 1991* (Report for 1991), (Jerusalem, May 1992), Table A–9, p 11; lines 3–4, Ibid., Table A–1, p 1.

1990s nevertheless reflect a sea-change in the Israeli economy: rising investment, falling inflation, and growing business confidence as reflected in the steady rise of the Tel Aviv stock market in 1991 and 1992 (see Tables 3 and 4).

Macroeconomic Reform

It is convenient to think in terms of two distinct agendas of economic reform in Israel: macroeconomic and microeconomic. Macroeconomic reform issues include the promotion of economic stability and growth by balancing the budget and reducing inflation; the reduction of taxes and government spending as a percentage of GNP; and, bordering upon the realm of microeconomic policy, the redirection of government spending from subsidizing private consumption and investment towards investment in public infrastructure (communications, higher education, water management and environmental protection).[4]

The greatest single success in Israel's reform agenda was the macroeconomic stabilization policy implemented in 1985. This policy achieved both of its major goals, namely the ending of hyperinflation (which peaked at a rate of nearly 28 per cent per month in July 1985) and the elimination of the government deficit. It was achieved at the cost of a sharp, if temporary, decline in private consumption and a longer hiatus in investment. Significantly, this painful reform was instituted by a government based on a broad 'national unity' coalition. It therefore rested upon a national consensus, reflecting the individual calculus of most voters, that hyperinflation was intolerable and that considerable sacrifices should be borne in order to eliminate it. The 1985 stabilization programme initiated a lengthy period of macroeconomic discipline. Budget deficits and the exchange rate were carefully managed to keep inflation under control. The gains of the 1985 stabilization could have been forfeited at any time by a breach of macroeconomic discipline; however, this was not done by any government, even during the recession of 1988 and 1989. The experience of hyper-inflation in the early 1980s produced a consensus on macroeconomic stability shared by the public and by policy-makers alike.

Economic stabilization did not address directly the last two issues of macroeconomic reform mentioned above. In particular, taxes and government spending as a percentage of GDP remained too high. Nevertheless, macroeconomic policy after 1985 produced significant changes in the Israeli economy. Israeli companies grew more competitive, business confidence improved as the long-term inflation rate began to decline, investment began to recover after an initial period of slump and the domestic labour market began to respond to the constraints of labour supply and demand. Israel's economy reacquired the potential for long-term, rapid growth. Realization of that potential depends to a great extent upon proceeding to the next stage of macroeconomic reform: cutting taxes and government spending. Such a step would be difficult, however, since specific constituencies would have to bear the pain of budget cuts. They will fight hard to protect their interests.

Microeconomic Reform

Microeconomic reform in Israel, proposed or currently being implemented, covers a large and varied agenda from the liberalization of capital markets and the privatization of business enterprises to reform of the health system. Many of the most important reforms are discussed elsewhere (see Chapter 4 below). We are not concerned in this chapter with the details but, rather with the questions of why reforms do or do not take place and what implications there are for the overall agenda of reform in Israel.

Like most reform, microeconomic reforms of almost any kind are sure to hurt someone's immediate interests. Sometimes this sparks resistance which prevents change; sometimes the resistance is ineffective. Broadly speaking, one can identify three groups whose behaviour can determine the outcome of reform: first, the government, which must initiate reform by changing current patterns of regulation and/ or ownership, secondly, the specific constituency targeted by the reform (banks, importers, exporters, doctors, etc); and thirdly the public at large occasionally figures in the complex set of forces affected.

In order that any particular reform succeed, a necessary though not sufficient condition is for the government of the day to be absolutely determined to carry it through, with a minimum of reservations or inhibitions. Privatization is a case in point. The country's major banks were effectively nationalized in 1983, the consequence of government intervention in a massive share-manipulation fraud. At that time the government viewed its new-found role as owner of the heart of the banking system with distaste, and expressed its resolve to privatize all the banks after five years. Yet this resolve has been tempered by reservations, lest a politically unreliable or otherwise unsuitable foreign investor acquire a bank or lest the government, which has already lost £4 billion in the venture, receive less than its money's worth. Although it is now nearly four years after the official start of privatization only one bank has been sold. Similar reservations have retarded the sale of the national airline (also nationalized after a bankruptcy) and Israel Chemicals Industry, the country's largest minerals producer.

Even where government resolve is not lacking, reform can be derailed by the emergence of a public constituency against it. A 'public constituency' in this context refers to a group of ordinary citizens, perhaps numbering only a few thousand, as opposed to elite groups such as managers of firms. The agricultural sector in Israel employs 3 per cent of the workforce; as in many industrialized countries, agriculture in Israel is heavily regulated and subsidized and subject to recurring financial crises. As in other countries, the agricultural lobby is vocal and wields influence far beyond its size; no reform of the debt-ridden agricultural system is anticipated.

Consider, by contrast, an important reform measure introduced in 1991: the elimination over a five-year period of almost all trade restrictions on manufactured imports. This reform, intended to improve the competitiveness of the Israeli economy, poses serious problems of adjustment for many enterprises. Managers and owners of such enterprises were not able to mobilize an effective public constituency against this reform, and the government succeeded in carrying it through against fragmented and ineffective opposition.

Significantly, the trade reform was instituted by executive decree; the government feared to introduce a tariff bill into the Knesset, where opponents might succeed in lobbying against it or amending it to death. Public constituencies in Israel succeed in defeating reform measures when they succeed in playing on public sympathies or can threaten to cause discomfort to the public at large. Specific reforms can occasionally benefit from the public's unwillingness to identify or sympathize with its 'victims'. An example is the conversion of five government-owned hospitals to private non-profit enterprises. This 'privatization' was opposed by thousands of hospital employees who threatened to respond with a series of work slow-downs and strikes. But the functioning of the public health system in Israel is widely regarded as unsatisfactory; it is afflicted with long queues, poor service and occasional instances of corruption. The Israeli public therefore tends to support radical organizational reform in the health services system and could find it hard to distinguish between the threatened wave of strikes and the ordinary state of affairs obtaining in the hospitals.

Conclusion

Reflection upon the record leads one to the unsurprising conclusion that the success of any particular reform depends chiefly upon the broad mobilization of public opinion in its favour. The significant question is when such mobilization can be expected to occur. Israel's institutional structure leaves decision-makers vulnerable to pressure from small constituencies interested in retarding reform. Political decision-makers feel their position is precarious and hesitate to jeopardize it by doing anything controversial or significant. This attitude, when policy-makers are 'left alone' in the arena with the special interests, means that the achievement of significant reform should not be counted upon.

The Israeli public at large can be motivated to support reform, however, and has done so in the past. When public opinion has proved ripe for it, as with the case of the macroeconomic reform of 1985, the political leadership necessary to prepare such a programme, to justify it to the public, and to implement it was not lacking. If microeconomic or budgetary reform has proceeded in fits and starts, it is because it involves a large number of fragmented issues, the significance of which is not evident to the public at large.

With respect to microeconomic reform, successive governments, out of a lack of nerve or conviction, have been their own worst enemy. Seeking to minimize resistance and controversy, they have tended to pursue incremental reform, presenting their proposed changes as small, moderate, and isolated rather than as part of a comprehensive programme of national significance. This merely ensures that reform battles are fought on terms most favourable to opponents of reform.

Political Reform

The Crisis of Political Legitimacy

The Israeli legislature, the Knesset, is a unicameral body of 120 members to which the government is responsible. The electoral system is proportional within a single constituency which is the whole country. Parties prepare candidate lists, and voters cast ballots for the party of their choice, not for individual representatives. There is an electoral threshold of 1.5 per cent of the votes cast, but this limitation is not very meaningful; a vote significantly smaller would be too small to entitle a party to even one of the 120 seats.[5] In practice, the party composition of the Knesset closely reflects the distribution of votes.

The system gives rise to a number of abuses. In the first place, marginal groups enjoy inordinate power. Proportional representation encourages the formation of special interest parties appealing to small constituencies. Ten parties won representation in the 1992 Knesset elections (15 in 1988). Small parties' successes come at the expense of the major parties which, under a different electoral system, might compete for an outright majority of representation. In practice, no party has ever won an outright majority. Among so many parties, representing so many different points of view, coalition formation is very difficult. Coalition leaders have to 'buy' the support of small parties, sometimes as many as six or eight, any of which may, by withholding their support, make the formation of a government impossible.

Secondly, there is insufficient personal accountability. No individual member of the Knesset receives a vote from the people; only party lists are voted for. No laws determine how parties select the lists of candidates they present to the voter. As a result, until very recently all Knesset members have been dependent primarily upon their party colleagues, rather than upon their constituents, for their tenure. Voters vote for parties because they believe that, in general, the party's programme reflects their preferences. Normally any party represented in one Knesset is likely to win at least a certain proportion of the seats in the next; under the old system, still generally prevalent in 1992 with the exception, as will be explained later, of the Labour Party, so long as a Knesset member can retain the confidence of his party colleagues, he may hope that his name will be placed high enough on the party list to guarantee him a seat, no matter how unpopular he may be among the public at large.

This has in the past sometimes led to a worse abuse. It has not been unknown for Knesset members, once they have been elected, to 'sell' their support to the highest bidder, part of the price being the assurance of a 'safe' seat on the list of one of the major parties. To secure his personal political future, a Knesset member elected on one political programme has been known to change his spots and throw his support behind a programme diametrically opposed to it. Distasteful as this practice was, both buyers and sellers in these transactions evidently calculated that the voter would be unlikely to penalize the party of his choice simply because it had incorporated into its ranks several politicians who were particularly unscrupulous. Moreover, the fragmented nature of the Israeli political system frequently seemed to make such deals necessary. In the long run, though, such practices brought the entire political system of the country into disrepute. In 1990 the Knesset passed a law providing that from now on a Knesset member who leaves his party should lose his seat.

Dilution of Executive Power

The government is responsible to the Knesset, and under the current political system the lion's share of the executive's time and energy must be spent on keeping coalition members placated. Not only marginal parties but also factions within a ruling party must constantly be accommodated, since the defection of even one of them to the opposition can endanger a government's survival. The most destructive consequence of this phenomenon is that the executive seldom retains the energy to pursue a vigorous programme of legislation, and, indeed, usually prefers doing nothing to doing anything even slightly controversial.

Electoral Reform Issues

Any electoral system needs to strike a balance between a number of competing values, such as fairness, responsibility and political efficacy. Fairness refers to the problem of 'wasted' votes, or votes that have no ultimate impact upon the electoral outcome. Responsibility as used here refers to the degree to which elected officials are dependent upon the electorate for their tenure in office. Political efficacy refers to the responsiveness of the political system as a whole to public concerns.

Fairness is sometimes perceived to be compromised by constituency-based electoral systems in which 'the winner takes all'. As many as half the votes cast, and often more, will have been wasted because they were cast for losing candidates. Proportional representation systems counteract this effect. Under the Israeli system, for example, about 95 per cent of the votes cast receive expression, as it were, in the final distribution of Knesset seats. A heavy price is paid, however, in terms of representativeness and political efficacy.

Direct election of individuals can in theory address these two aspects. A legislator or chief executive who is directly elected serves at the pleasure of the people and can be dismissed at election time if he fails to please. Direct election thus may be a method of securing active and effective governors committed to finding and implementing solutions to public problems. Direct election of individuals to the legislature, which necessarily involves a constituency-based system, provides an antidote to the fragmentation of political power typical of proportional systems. Small parties' candidates fall by the wayside. The winner emerges with a parliamentary majority and is able to govern. It should be noted, however, that nations with direct electoral systems have not necessarily found it easy in practice to dismiss incumbents or to secure good government.

Most proposals for electoral reform in Israel involve incorporating elements of constituency-based election for the Knesset and direct election for the head of the government. Taken to its logical conclusion, this would prescribe a system in which all Knesset members were elected from constituencies and the prime minister was elected directly in one nationwide constituency. Two objections have been raised against so radical a change in Israel's current electoral system. In the first place, a change to a pure constituency system would involve too great a sacrifice of the fairness principle. In any case no such proposal, which would demolish the small parties in Israel's current political system, could pass the Knesset. Secondly, Israel has no experience with an executive independent of the Knesset. Some legislative check on the tenure of the executive would be desirable.

In the light of these objections, proponents of electoral reform have formulated a proposal for a governmental system with several novel features.[6] The primary objective of the proposal is to strengthen the executive by loosening, though not severing, its dependence upon the legislature. The main features of the proposal are as follows:

1. The head of the government[7] is to be elected directly and always simultaneously with elections to the Knesset. If any one candidate receives 40 per cent of the votes cast, he/she is elected; otherwise the leading two candidates compete in a second election ten days later.
2. Candidates for head of the government must receive the endorsement of 20 Knesset members or of 200,000 voters (currently about 5.5 per cent of the electorate) for their names to be placed on the ballot. This provision makes it unlikely that anyone other than well-known, mainstream public figures can be nominated.
3. The prime minister appoints and dismisses ministers of the government however; binding decisions of the executive may be made only by the vote of a majority of the government.

4. The Knesset can remove the prime minister and government by a vote of no confidence; however such a motion must pass with a majority of 71 (out of 120 Knesset members). This leads automatically to the dissolution of the Knesset and the calling of new elections for both Knesset and prime minister. Similarly, the resignation of the head of the government dissolves the government and the Knesset simultaneously.

This proposed system preserves the proportional representation system in elections to the Knesset but largely frees the executive of its consequences. The head of the government almost certainly must be a mainstream political figure, but is directly responsible to the people. The Knesset can, as an extraordinary measure, remove the government, but in doing so immediately submits its action to the judgment of the people. Proponents of this mixed, 'parliadential' system[8] maintain that it would increase the effectiveness of the legislature as well as of the executive. The survival of the government would not be put at stake with each piece of major legislation. This would enable the construction of occasional coalitions crossing party lines on the merits of any bill. It would curtail the ability of marginal parties to prevent change or to squeeze concessions out of the government of the day.

Other Reform Proposals
Some thought has been given by proponents of electoral reform to improving the quality of 'responsibility' in the Knesset by combining proportional and constituency election. One proposal is based on the German model, in which half the legislature is directly elected but every party receives representation proportional to its share of the vote. Another attractive feature of the German system is the 5 per cent electoral threshold, which denies representation to marginal parties. Any attempt at reform in this direction is sure to draw the opposition of the small religious parties in Israel, however. Unlike the proposal for 'parliadential' reform, no proposal for reforming the system of elections to the Knesset has got as far as a second reading in that body, except the raising of the electoral threshold before the 1992 election to its present level of 1.5 per cent.

Political parties in Israel choose their own methods for selecting the lists of candidates for the Knesset that they submit to the voters. Such lists are usually drawn up by party elites; party leaders 'reserve' the lead places in the list for themselves, and the rest of the list is nominated by the parties' central committees. Back-room deals and political horse-trading play a prominent role in the selection process. One reform idea is to make these lists more representative by involving the public in their selection. Such a change in the selection rules lies within the provenance of each party and need not depend upon a vote in the Knesset.

Both major parties have considered allowing rank-and-file party members to vote directly for the party's candidates for office. This system, termed the 'primary' system, does permit a relatively large constituency to decide the choice of candidates. The Labour Party at its 1991 convention adopted the primary method of selecting candidates for the office of prime minister and for the party's Knesset list. On 19 February 1992 Yitzhak Rabin was elected head of the Labour Party and its candidate for prime minister in the 1992 elections. Some 70 per cent of the Labour Party's 152,000 rank-and-file members participated in the vote. Elections for the Labour Party's Knesset list involved a complicated formula combining regional as well as nationwide constituencies. This subsequently led to charges of inequity; several relatively unknown candidates made the Knesset list on the basis of a few thousand votes in regional constituencies, while prominent party figures who received many times that number in nationwide elections were nevertheless left out.

Overall, however, the Labour Party's primary system appeared to work well. In the 1992 electoral campaign Labour benefited from its image as a more open, representative, and modern organization than the Likud and, of course, the primary system yielded a highly popular candidate for prime minister. After its defeat in the 1993 election the Likud Party in turn proceeded to choose its new leader by the primary system.

Electoral Reform in Practice

Electoral reform has been an active issue on the Israeli political agenda since the mid-1980s. Since 1984 a group of prominent Israeli scholars, initially under the leadership of the jurist Professor Uriel Reichmann, has studied the issue; many of the reform proposals discussed here originated with members of this group.

Electoral reform is highly popular. Several small parties of the left and right support it as being in the public interest, even though their power would be diluted thereby. With the exception of the pro-Zionist

National Religious Party, however, the small religious parties who hold the balance of power between left and right in Israeli politics do not share this view. Their primary concern is to secure spoils for their constituencies, and electoral reform would weaken their ability to do so.

Both major parties have made statements in the past in support of electoral reform. Under the conditions of stalemate which prevailed in Israeli politics from 1984 to 1992, it was assumed that the cooperation of both parties, against the interests of the religious parties, was necessary for a reform bill to pass. For a number of years, therefore, the issue of reform was held up by a classic example of 'prisoners' dilemma'. Each major party feared to support a reform bill, lest the other defect at the last minute, whereupon the former would find that it had alienated to no good purpose the religious parties without whom it would be impossible to form a government in the foreseeable future. Naturally, the religious parties did nothing to counter the impression that vengeance would be their political guide should any attempt at legislating reform fail.

The breakdown of the National Unity Government in the spring of 1990 and the events which subsequently transpired raised the issue of electoral reform to a new level of salience. The three months that passed until a new, right-wing government was formed witnessed the worst display ever of the evils of the present proportional representation system. The mandate to form a government was given initially to Shimon Peres, then head of the Labour Party. His attempt to present a minority left-of-centre government to the Knesset was balked at the last minute when two members of a small religious party, breaking party discipline, defected on the instructions of a prominent New York rabbi. Subsequently, when the Likud received the mandate to form a government, a small faction of that party threatened to defect to the Labour Party unless its leader, Yitzhak Modai, was made finance minister and its members were guaranteed safe seats in the next elections. At one point this faction demanded that the Likud post a $10 billion bond, to be forfeited if it reneged on the agreement.[9]

Public indignation at these abuses of power was profound and universal; it seemed as if the nation's leadership conducted its affairs without the slightest regard for the ethical standards, not to mention the interests, of their constituents. In a rare statement on a matter of public policy, the president of Israel condemned the manner in which the reputation of the country's political system was suffering and lent his prestige to the cause of electoral reform. A public petition in favour of electoral reform gathered over 600,000 signatures, nearly 20 per cent of the electorate. During 1990 four Knesset members representing a broad spectrum of political opinion submitted roughly similar bills for the direct election of the prime minister. These bills were later fused into a composite text along the lines which have been already described, with the four as co-sponsors.

While the Labour Party made a vote in favour of the bill a matter of party discipline, the ruling Likud Party's central committee rejected it. This was primarily due to the influence of one man, the then prime minister, Yitzhak Shamir, who seemed to feel that the proposed change to direct election of the head of the government was not in his interest. So intense was the pressure exerted upon Likud members by the party leadership that Uriel Lynn, the Likud chairman of the Knesset's Law and Constitution Committee and one of the bill's main sponsors, participated in the attempt to suppress it.

Nonetheless, the bill survived to become law in a form surprisingly close to its original design.[10] Its essential features were preserved. The head of government is to be directly elected and, except in unusual circumstances, the Knesset cannot pass a motion of no confidence in the government without simultaneously dissolving itself. To accommodate Shamir's opposition, the new law was not to take effect until the election following the 1992 election.

Electoral Reform: Popular and Institutional Aspects

The case of electoral reform in Israel is a classic example of successful reform in a democracy. Public sentiment on the issue of electoral reform slowly gathered momentum during the latter half of the 1980s. The spring of 1990 saw that sentiment become broad, deep, well-organized and unequivocally expressed. Public sentiment slowly but inexorably pressed its stamp upon the institutions of government. Several factors contributed to its ultimate success:

Intelligent tactics. Prior to 1990 advocates of electoral reform emphasized the comprehensive application of the principle of direct election of individuals to the Knesset as well as to the executive as leading to greater responsibility and efficacy in government. In practice, direct election to the Knesset would have had much greater impact on small parties than the direct election of the head of government; whereas few of them could ever hope to win the top executive office, constituency elections to the Knesset threatened their political existence.

Advocates of electoral reform made the most of the upsurge of interest in their cause by adopting a tactical compromise. They would blunt the opposition of the small parties by pressing first for direct elections for the head of government. Afterwards, with the executive strengthened, the introduction of further reforms might become easier. The tactic worked; not one of the small religious parties exhibited a solid front against the reform bill.

Broad-spectrum support. Though electoral reform is expected to increase the power of large parties compared to small ones, a number of small non-religious parties supported the bill as a matter of principle. Public sentiment in favour of reform was shared by many Knesset members. Though in 1991 the governing Likud Party officially adopted a position opposing electoral reform, it did not succeed in enforcing party discipline on the issue. This contributed to the Likud leadership's eventual acquiescence to the passage of a compromise bill.

The role of the Labour Party. The success of electoral reform must be identified primarily with the Labour Party. Faced with the standard challenge of an opposition party – how to convince the voter to restore it to power – the Labour Party made electoral reform its own issue. It not only supported direct elections for the head of government on the national level but also adopted electoral reform internally, in the shape of the primary system. Both decisions required courage. Labour chose to risk the religious parties' anger in order to put itself behind a change the public clearly wanted. The classic dynamic of government and opposition in a democracy played itself out; the opposition party succeeded in making an emergent public agenda its own, and rode that agenda to victory at the polls.

Conclusion: Whither Reform?

The macroeconomic stabilization plan of 1985 and the electoral reform of 1992 were both major reforms. They provided important evidence that the Israeli political system is not impervious to significant, systemic change. They are proof that reform proposals can gain the breadth and depth of popular support needed to press them through to a successful conclusion. This is the encouraging side of the record. On the other hand, these two reforms in themselves are incomplete. Only the first steps have been taken towards the reconstruction of Israel's political institutions to make them less beholden to special interests and more responsive to public demands. Most of the changes needed to set the Israeli economy on the path of long-term, rapid growth, the prerequisite for the achievement of most other important social goals, remain to be made. The reforms of the last few years should not in themselves be thought of as comprehensive; they merely have shown that comprehensive reform is achievable in principle.

The key element in reforms that are 'systemic' in nature, that is, that they succeed in overriding entrenched institutional opposition and changing the rules of the game, political or economic, is the mobilization of broad and deep public support. When such mobilization takes place, politicians are forced or tempted to take uncommon risks in order to implement the agenda that the public desires with such intensity. Conversely, the limits to such mobilization set the limits of achievable reform.

Broad and intense public mobilization over an issue is more clearly possible when the issue in question affects most citizens personally, such as the hyper-inflation of the early 1980s. But Israelis have shown themselves willing to be mobilized even when the issue in question does not necessarily affect them directly and personally. The daily life of the average citizen was not directly affected by the manifestations of corruption that accompanied the attempts to form a new government in the spring of 1990. Nevertheless, many hundreds of thousands of citizens were moved to active political participation by the events of that spring. Whatever the Israeli political system lacked at that juncture, it was not the public-spiritedness of its citizens.

By its nature, however, broad public mobilization and concern is a blunt instrument. It is mobilized most easily when the issue at stake is simple and can be simply expressed: 'End hyper-inflation!' or 'Reform a corrupt system!' Both the macroeconomic stabilization programme of 1985 and the electoral reform of 1992 were complex programmes, designed by academic experts and implemented by small groups of political leaders who perhaps understood only partially the implications of what they were doing.[11] The public for its part understood none of the nuances or niceties that, as experts were aware, in both cases made the crucial difference between success and failure.

Reforms that cannot be simply 'packaged' and 'sold' to the public stand far less chance of being implemented. This is a critical problem with Israel's remaining agenda of economic reform, macroeconomic and microeconomic. Microeconomic reform especially presents itself as a series of limited measures, each affecting a small corner of the economy and of no great moment in itself. Professional economists can demonstrate the importance of individual reforms and their tremendous cumulative significance, but the public at large does not read what economists write.

The Israeli public has demonstrated that it can be mobilized to support systemic reform. This, then, places the onus of continued reform upon political leadership. It is up to political leaders to define issues sharply and make a match in the average voter's mind between a relatively simple label, such as 'electoral reform', and a much more complex reality. The more complex and fragmented the issue, the greater the task imposed upon political leadership: first, to grasp the essence behind the complexity and, second, to convey that essence to the voter and endow it with a sense of urgency. While the engine of systemic reform in Israel is, as in any democratic society, public support, the continuation of reform depends primarily upon the emergence of appropriate political leadership, one that is trusted by the public and has the ability to capture complex ideas simply. That is a tall order; merely to state the requirement goes far to explain why reform in most societies tends to be slow and halting. Israeli political elites can respond to crises when they emerge, but for the most part they have been followers rather than leaders. The continuation of the momentum of reform depends chiefly upon the emergence of leadership of a different type.

4. THE ISRAELI ECONOMY IN THE 1990s: BREAKOUT OR BREAKDOWN?

Pinchas Landau

The twin challenge facing the Israeli economy in the coming years seems easy enough to define: it must absorb into productive employment the influx of immigrants from the former Soviet Union, and it must itself be absorbed into the wider global economy. However, the only clear-cut aspect of the mammoth task involved in achieving these goals is that no one seriously disagrees that these overriding issues do indeed form the agenda. How the challenges are to be met and overcome is the basis for a much more complex discussion and often acute controversy.

Fortunately for Israel, the double challenge facing it is made achievable by the fact that the two challenges are so inter-related that they ultimately coalesce. In order to absorb successfully the immigration of some one million persons in the period 1990–95, Israel must open itself up to the international economy so as to achieve export-led growth. This is necessary because, to absorb the immigration, resources running into tens of billions of dollars will be required, and much of these funds will have to be borrowed from overseas. Only a massive expansion of exports, leading to the elimination of the chronic trade deficit that has been a feature of the Israeli economy since its creation, will enable these loans to be repaid. This kind of export-led growth can be achieved only by making Israeli firms, and the economy as a whole, competitive in world markets, and this in turn can be done only by eliminating the protectionist barriers and internal inefficiencies that have hitherto isolated the Israeli economy.

It must be stressed at the outset that there is no viable alternative to export-led growth. The option of absorbing the immigrants within the framework of a small and insulated domestic economy is not realistic, since it would entail a serious decline in the overall standard of living – a price which neither the immigrants, nor certainly the 'veteran' population are willing to pay. This assessment has very important ramifications for Israeli political life, and on the foreign and defence policy of any conceivable government – indeed, the 1992 election results were strongly influenced by these factors. The economic imperative is already a major factor in the peace process, and will outweigh many other factors, including some ideological and defence considerations, as the negotiations unfold.

The interaction between the domestic absorption of immigrants into the economy and the external absorption of the Israeli economy itself into the global economy may be viewed from the other direction as well. The goal of external integration was clearly identified long before the immigration wave began in late 1989. Indeed, had there been no immigration, that goal would still be the primary challenge facing the Israeli economy.

The pre-immigration economy was plagued by stagflation, which was engendered by lack of competition and deeply-rooted rigidity in many key economic structures. The huge immigration wave will inevitably overwhelm these rigidities over time, as is already apparent in many areas. Had it not emerged, a similar degree of shock treatment would have had to have been 'invented' to achieve this result. Whether any such 'treatment' would in fact have been applied is arguable, but it seems unlikely that any conceivable 'shock' that could have been administered could have had such immense potential as the incredibly rich human resources represented by the Soviet-Jewish immigration. The remarkable feature of this immigration is that not only does it make it essential, from the demand side, that Israel achieve its aim of integrating its economy into the wider world economy, but it also provides Israel, from the supply side, with the ideal tools – in the form of a flood of high-quality human capital – with which to achieve it.

The fact that over 400,000 immigrants have arrived over the past two and a half years, and that many more will continue to come, if only because of the on-going socio-economic disintegration of the former Soviet Union, makes the achievement of the twin goals defined above into a make-or-break issue for Israel. If these goals are to be reached, a number of far-reaching economic (and other) reforms need to be undertaken or, if already under way, completed. Conversely, if these reforms are not pursued, the goals will not be achieved, and Israel will be subject to severe social and economic strains, which would ultimately lead to an economic crisis whose severity would exceed that of anything seen in the past and result in dire social, political and geo-strategic consequences.

The reality of mass immigration makes it inevitable that all aspects of Israeli life will undergo far-reaching change in the coming years. With regard to the economy, which is commonly accepted as the crucial factor in the absorption process, the kind of change involved depends on a stark choice: either the pursuit of fundamental reforms that will allow the economy to break out of its largely self-imposed isolation and find a role on the global stage, or an attempt to maintain the outmoded system of a government-dominated, uncompetitive economy which will trigger growing unrest and lead to systemic breakdown.

Background to Reform in the Israeli Economy

The process of reform in the Israeli economy, meaning the pursuit of a long-term strategy aimed at reducing the extent of government involvement, and the initiation of a process of liberalization and deregulation of domestic markets, began in 1985 and has continued, albeit sporadically and often half-heartedly, ever since.

The key date in recent Israeli economic history is 1 July 1985, when the Economic Stabilization Programme (ESP) was put into place. In the same way as the Yom Kippur War of October 1973 marks clearly the point at which the Israeli economy moved away from the path of rapid growth that had characterized it for most of the previous 25 years from the founding of the state, so the ESP represents a watershed event. It brought an end to the period of deterioration, highlighted by ever-worsening inflation and balance of payments problems, and ushered in a period of rehabilitation and of significant, though partial, reform.

The ESP was a dramatic and drastic response to an emergency situation in which the economy was mired in deep crisis and faced imminent catastrophe. The roots of this crisis are to be found in the policies pursued from 1974 onward, in which government expenditure on defence and social welfare programmes grew rapidly, while private consumption moved steadily ahead on the back of rising real wages. All this was 'paid for' by – that is, came at the expense of – reduced investment in both the public and private sector, and by increased borrowing, both at home and abroad.

Fuelled by budget deficits which ran at levels of 10–14 per cent of

GDP in the early 1980s, inflation marched steadily higher, reaching triple-digit levels in 1979 and developing into fully-fledged hyper-inflation after 1983. Against this background of macroeconomic mismanagement, the abolition of exchange controls as part of a financial reform in 1977 led to large-scale flight of capital from the country and the depletion of foreign currency reserves to critical levels by mid-1985. A further blunder was the agreement to finance the withdrawal from Sinai in 1979–82 with loans rather than grants from the United States, resulting in the swelling of Israeli foreign borrowing and the balance of payments deficit becoming a separate focus of crisis in the early 1980s.

A series of attempts to tackle the worsening crisis, made during 1983–5, only succeeded in exacerbating matters because they were of a palliative nature, addressing symptoms rather than underlying causes. Only the revamping of the basis on which aid from the United States was given, so that from 1984 onwards this took the form of grants for both military and civilian aid instead of loans, represented a fundamental change for the better.

The ESP, which subsequently served as a model for similar attempts to tackle hyper-inflationary economies in South America and elsewhere, achieved its stunning success for two reasons: from the economic point of view, it simultaneously addressed all the key elements of the crisis, while, from the political viewpoint, it was introduced by a National Unity Government enjoying a massive parliamentary majority and won the support – or at least the acquiescence – of both manufacturers and unions.

It broke the price/wage rise/devaluation spiral by freezing all three, but only after the prices of government-subsidized goods and services, and the exchange rate, had been raised. The result was an unprecedentedly sharp drop in the value of real wages, of some 30 per cent in three months, but these were gradually restored in 1986/7. Meanwhile, inflation plummeted, from a rate of 15–20 per cent per month immediately preceding the introduction of ESP to a rate of 15–20 per cent per annum by the last quarter of 1985. This was to be maintained, despite interim fluctuations in the economic climate for the next six years and it was only in 1991/2 that significant progress was made in moving toward a single-digit inflation rate.

More importantly, the ESP eliminated the budget deficit. This was achieved, first, because the government itself was the greatest beneficiary from the reduction in inflation, in that the value of its tax revenues was no longer severely eroded by the time lag before they were collected; secondly, because subsidies were severely cut, either through price rises or by their direct elimination; thirdly, some government spending cuts were made and some tax increases introduced. For the fiscal years 1985 to 1988, the budget actually ran at a surplus before moving into deficit as the economy slowed down in 1988/9 and then, paradoxically, into a much larger deficit in the growth year 1990/91, this time under the impact of expenditures for immigration absorption.

Finally, the ESP had an enormous psychological impact, once the public grasped that it was going to work. Confidence returned, evidenced in the repatriation of flight money – attracted by very high interest rates, which were the result of an extremely tight monetary policy between 1985 and 1987 – and the changed pattern of behaviour of both households and firms.

However, the ESP was designed as a two-stage programme. The first stage, that of tackling the immediate crisis and achieving stability, worked better than even its planners had hoped. The second stage, of preparing the ground for a return to sustained growth, was far less successful – indeed, in the opinion of some analysts it proved to be a failure.[1]

Undoubtedly, the economy did not achieve a strong growth path – the boom of 1986/7 was led by consumer demand, fed by wage hikes and fizzled out by late 1987. The outbreak of the *intifada* applied further downward pressure, and 1988 and 1989 were years of low GDP growth and rising unemployment. Investment remained low throughout this period, in part because capital subsidies had encouraged over-investment in the first half of the decade, and also because many sectors found themselves in deep crisis, with bloated workforces, inadequate cost controls and equity bases that had been depleted or altogether wiped out by inflation. In fact, the key development in this period was the far-reaching shake-out of Israeli industry that took place, a development which stemmed from a new reality in which the government no longer stepped in to rescue corporate failures. However painful in the short term, this was an unavoidable element in making the economy competitive again.

Withdrawing support from corporate failures and withdrawing subsidies from staple foods and some state services were only the passive requirements of government policy in this period, although these were by no means politically easy to deliver. In addition, there was the need to move ahead with a series of reforms in virtually all areas of the economy, but here the results were generally disappointing.

In August 1986, the outlines of the capital market reform programme were announced, and the process began in earnest in 1987, and has continued to move slowly forward ever since. Simultaneously, the government announced a privatization programme, but despite sporadic sales both directly to investors and via the Tel Aviv stock exchange, this has never achieved any real momentum and, like the process of reselling the major banks into private ownership, has remained largely stuck in the mud. Tax rates on both companies and individuals were reduced in 1987 but more fundamental taxation reform has yet to be attempted, although committees have been appointed, sat, and produced reports but no real effect. The same is true of labour market reform, where a major study and accompanying recommendations by an official commission (the Sussman Report) has generated no practical outcome. Trade liberalization only started in 1990; until then, government policy was, if anything, more protectionist than ever. Deregulation and the opening up of sectors controlled by monopolies, cartels and guilds has also not been pursued with any great vigour, although this has now begun to change. To all these and other aspects of economic reform, we will return later.

The Challenge of Immigration
Notwithstanding Israelis' penchant for regarding their situation as unique, the foregoing analysis illustrates that both the type of problems that the Israeli economy experienced in the 1980s, and the solutions proposed and, to some degree, implemented, were not fundamentally different from those of many other countries. However, with regard to the 1990s, there can be no question that Israel has set itself a unique agenda, because it has committed itself to an open-door immigration policy that is likely to result in an increase in population, from immigration alone, of 20–25 per cent in a period of five to seven years. This policy is rooted in Zionist ideology and Jewish solidarity, and consciously defies economic logic in the crucial area of population and labour force. The starting point for economic policy is, therefore, entirely different from anything envisaged in any textbook. Whereas normally even a country positively disposed towards immigration will ensure that the influx is regulated in line with the economy's absorptive capacity, in Israel the basis for policy is that as many Jews as want to

may immigrate and the economy must seek to absorb them as best it can.

In practice, this approach has resulted in a situation characterized by several paradoxes. The first of these is that most of the immigrants and potential immigrants have and will come not out of choice but because they are leaving the former Soviet Union on account of the deterioration in general conditions, and the rise of anti-semitism in particular. (Given the growing general hostility to immigration on the part of most western countries, the only haven open to them is Israel.) However, the Israeli economy is unable to absorb either the quantity or the quality of the potential Soviet-Jewish exodus. What has happened, therefore, is that instead of the government intervening to prevent the labour market absorbing as many immigrants as it would like – which is the situation in most western countries today – the Israeli situation is the exact reverse: the market has intervened to prevent the government absorbing as many immigrants as it would like. The difficulty of finding employment, and especially jobs of a kind in which their professional and educational qualifications can be utilized, as became abundantly clear during 1991, is the single biggest factor deterring Soviet Jews from immigrating more quickly, and in larger numbers.

The pace, and indeed the overall extent, of immigration will therefore be determined not by the interplay of 'push' and 'pull' factors, in which the Jews are pushed out of the former Soviet Union itself and pulled to Israel, but by a much more subtle set of determinants: within the former Soviet Union itself there are 'push' factors – economic collapse and anti-semitism, and 'pull' factors – the fact that many Jews have prestigious jobs and positions, career advancement opportunities, family and cultural ties. Similarly, in terms of immigration to Israel, the immigrants face a mixed bag of 'pull' factors – the offer of a subsidized migration, a safe haven and a welcoming reception by the Israeli government and people, including support, subsidies, language and retraining courses, as well as a growing number of compatriots already in Israel; as against this, there are 'push' factors, including the difficulties attending any migration, but, above all, the fact that jobs are hard to come by and many immigrants will be forced to give up their professions and careers.

The challenge that mass immigration poses to the Israeli economy may, therefore, be simply defined: the economy needs to be capable of attracting and holding as many immigrants as possible. This is inherently extremely difficult, since even the best-managed economy is limited in its short-term absorptive capacities, as the example of the union of West and East Germany clearly shows. In the Israeli case, however, it verges on the impossible. The more successful the economy is in absorbing immigrants, so more will choose to come. However, the more immigrants that come the greater must be the short-term dislocation and the consequent difficulties in creating sufficient suitable jobs.

This paradox has only a partial answer as far as economic policy is concerned, given that the door must and will remain open. This answer is that policy should be designed to facilitate the absorption of the maximum possible number of immigrants. In simple terms, the economy should 'do its very best'. It is hard to ask for more than that, and if this were the only factor at work the economy's absorptive capacity would become the effective quota on immigration. However, as we have noted, many other factors are at work, and these may lead in the future, as they did in 1990, to a rate of immigration which is beyond any reasonable expectation of absorptive capacity.

In view of the national consensus that any and all Jewish immigration is desirable, the key issue in economic policy-making becomes how to achieve the goal defined above of absorbing the maximum possible number of immigrants. It is at this point that the debate over immigration absorption reverts back directly to the basic, underlying debate regarding the direction of economic policy and the need to lessen government involvement and control.

On one side is the free market school which, broadly defined, has been steadily growing since at least the late 1970s and in recent years has become easily the dominant approach to economic policy recommendations. It encompasses the overwhelming majority of academic economists, although there are, as in all countries, significant differences of approach and emphasis between them. The great majority of senior civil servants, not only in the 'economic' ministries but throughout the public sector, now espouse free market views. Businessmen, including industrialists, and the financial sector, especially the banking sector, have similarly become convinced in principle that free market policies are superior to the old approach of state intervention and subsidy. This school believes that the best way to make progress on the two challenges facing the Israeli economy – immigrant absorption and integration into world markets – is to press ahead with reforms, liberalization, deregulation and other measures, all of which are designed to reduce the degree of government involvement in the economy. By encouraging competition, opening up markets, reducing taxes and eliminating bureaucratic regulation, more and more productive jobs will be created. In short, the challenge of immigration, far from changing the thrust of economic policy from that in force before the influx began, actually serves to make it more urgent and necessary to move more rapidly along that self-same path.

On the other side there is a school comprised of those who all along had opposed the liberalization approach and, also, of others who, prior to the onset of mass immigration, had supported reform but who now believe that, in the face of a national emergency on this scale, there is no choice but to change course. This camp, despite having been whittled down over the years, is still a force to be reckoned with. It draws its strength from a range of deeply-rooted factors, political and ideological, populist and economic. The 'old guard' of most Israeli political parties, almost irrespective of the specific ideology they espouse, have always seen the state as the instrument through which their ideological goals are to be achieved. State intervention in the economy, in this view, is an essential element if Zionist ideological aims are to be realized, whether the ideology concerned is nationalist, socialist, religious or any other brand. The bitter lessons of the centrally-directed economies in the communist bloc have caused most of these 'true believers' to play down their real views, but they have not brought about fundamental changes in them.

Then the fact that structural change in the economy is sure to cause significant social and economic pain, especially in the 'development areas' on the country's periphery and in inner-city neighbourhoods makes it easy for politicians in the self-styled 'social lobby' to press for continued, or even increased, intervention through welfare programmes, subsidies and, of course, industrial policies aimed at preventing job losses. The policies are all based on the primacy of social policy goals over economic efficiency and free market criteria. As in every other country, businessmen tend to support liberal policies in every sector except their own. Vested interests, whose wellbeing and even whose very existence is dependent on continued government aid whether through protective trade policies, tax breaks, subsidies or other interventionist mechanisms, have fought bitterly to stop, or at least slow down, every free market initiative and may be relied on to continue to do so. On many occasions ad hoc alliances have been formed. The sense of being involved in a rearguard action, ultimately a losing battle, against worldwide socio-economic trends, has probably helped to spur, rather then depress, the interventionist camp. In the view of this camp, the massive task of absorbing the new immigrants can only be handled by the government. The national interest demands increased government intervention. Liberalization and reform will have to wait.

Today, after almost three years of mass immigration, a significant body of experience is available to serve as a basis for judging which of the two opposing policy approaches is preferable. As we shall see in the next section, the evidence points strongly to a clear-cut conclusion: government involvement is a recipe for delay and disaster. Although actual arrivals of Soviet Jews only began to mount rapidly in late 1989, the prospect of mass immigration emerged many months before. Despite the warnings of an impending exodus, the Israeli government did not engage in serious contingency planning and failed to take substantive measures to prepare for the human tidal wave that engulfed the country during 1990. Only when immigration became a firm reality did it begin to respond – and then mainly by panic and overkill. To make matters worse, at precisely the time the immigration swelled from a stream to a flood, in the early months of 1990, the government was paralysed by a political crisis that lasted from March to June. Only after a new, narrowly-based coalition was formed in mid-year did the focus of the leadership revert from political manoeuvring to national concerns, by which point immigrant absorption had become a pressingly urgent issue.

Immigration and Housing
From the very outset, it was clear that the two central concerns in handling immigration would be homes and jobs. The initial thinking was that, although jobs were ultimately more important, homes were a more urgent concern, because the housing shortage created a real threat that the immigrants would find themselves 'on the street'. Even then, the development of a coherent housing policy was held up, first by bureaucratic wrangling and then by the political crisis, so that not until the second half of 1990 did the government put into place an interventionist housing policy.

However a key decision made in 1989 proved to be of crucial importance to the resettlement of the almost 250,000 immigrants who arrived by the end of 1990. This was to adopt a policy of 'direct absorption', in which each immigrant was to be left to find his/her own accommodation, supported by a government rental subsidy but with no government officials directing the newcomers, on their arrival, to a particular apartment provided by the government at a location determined by bureaucrats, without reference to the needs and preferences of the persons involved. That had been the approach that had been used in the previous wave of Soviet-Jewish immigration during the 1970s, but it had since been discontinued and the government decided not to resurrect it (aside from the Ethiopian immigrations of 1984–5 and 1991 – when once again the system generated highly negative results in terms of social and economic adjustment).

The reasons for not adopting a paternalist approach were as much practical as ideological: low immigration coupled with budget cuts in the 1980s had resulted in a sharp contraction of the construction industry and, in particular, of public-sector financing of building. By 1988/9 total construction of new apartments was running at some 20,000 units per annum, hardly enough to cover current needs, and of these, the public sector was building only 2–3,000. The government simply had no apartments available for immigrants, and the scale of the influx made it impossible to send them to absorption centres for an extended period, as had been done in the 1980s, much less to utilize hotels and hostels for anything other than a brief stay in which the newcomers could orient themselves.

Since most of the immigrants had come with virtually nothing, the only option available to them was to rent and, to assist this process, the government gave them rental subsidies. Inevitably, however, the huge demand overwhelmed the insufficient supply of available apartments, so that rents soared by factors of up to three or four in some areas. However, despite predictions of disaster, with thousands of immigrants and Israeli young couples being left with nowhere to live – indeed, despite a rash of tent-camps in the summer of 1990, which highlighted the housing crisis – the real-estate market responded well enough to absorb all the immigrants into some kind of accommodation. It is true that this was only done through a great deal of duress, with many cases of two, three and even four immigrant families or one or two extended families cramming into small apartments, and many others paying high rents for sub-standard, and often totally inadequate, premises. Nevertheless, there were no riots or other overt signs of social strain. Freeing the housing market had led to higher prices, and this had triggered a textbook reaction in which a large increase of (hitherto unidentified) supply was called forth so that eventually everyone found a home of some sort.

Nevertheless, the imbalance of overall supply and demand, expressed in rapid price inflation for both purchase and rentals, persuaded the government that emergency measures were needed. This led to the appointment of Ariel Sharon as housing minister in June 1990, with a clear mandate to eliminate the housing shortage.[2] However, the long period of inaction and confused signals that had comprised government housing policy in the first half of 1990 meant that, even when contractors were offered government guarantees to buy unsold apartments, the private sector remained unpersuaded to undertake the kind of massive expansion needed. New building starts doubled in 1990, but even this was only half of what was necessary, and the solution eventually adopted was for the government to re-enter the housing market directly – in other words to undertake huge construction programmes that would be paid for directly from the state budget.

As a result of the panic over housing in 1990, by 1991 the housing shortage had been eliminated. Building starts had climbed to the 80–90,000 units that were needed to catch up with the needs of the immigrants. In addition, the amount of time needed in the planning, zoning and construction processes had all been sharply reduced, so that the time between deciding to build and the actual completion of the buildings was more than halved. The housing price boom, that peaked at a rate of 80–90 per cent per annum in mid-1991, had gone into reverse by the autumn. Yet the achievement was severely flawed. The distribution of the building programmes had been determined primarily by political considerations of directing population growth to the Negev, Galilee, the Jerusalem area and the West Bank. However, the immigrant population itself, utilizing its freedom to live wherever it pleased, had distributed itself primarily on the basis of where job opportunities were greater, not where housing was available. Thus, for example, 22 per cent of the new homes constructed under the Housing Ministry's programme were in the Negev, but only 7 per cent of the immigrants had moved there. The central area, where a large proportion of the newcomers resided, received less than 10 per cent of the new building.

The two potential solutions to this mismatch are obvious: either to facilitate some form of commuter network which would allow residents of far-flung towns to travel daily to the employment hubs in the central area, or to move some of the existing hubs to the new population. However, neither was a practical option in the short run, nor will either be for some time to come. The first option, of moving the people to the jobs, disregards the fact that Israel's road transport infrastructure is, by the early 1990s, suffering the cumulative effects of two decades of under-investment. In terms of road space available as against the number of vehicles on the road Israel has become the most crowded country on earth, with the possible exception of Hong Kong. The country's rail network is entirely under-developed and offers no commuter facilities of any practical value.

The second option, shifting jobs to people, was the focus of much discussion and grandiose plans were begun to move industries from the centre to the Negev in the south and to encourage the establish-ment of new industries. However, these plans must inevitably take years to realize, even in the best case. Furthermore, the diversion of resources to housing meant that the government was unable in 1990–92 to divert resources to encourage the relocating or creation of employment hubs. This is precisely the misallocation of resources and the 'cart before the horse' approach that made the housing programme a conceptual disaster even before its flaws in construction, financing and marketing became apparent.

In addition to spending large sums on caravans and other temporary dwellings, many of which proved physically unsuitable to Israeli conditions and most of which arrived after long delays, the Housing Ministry spent billions of shekels on infrastructure and in guaranteeing prices for apartments built in places where few jobs were to be found and where, in consequence, no one wanted to live. The way the programme developed also reflected bureaucratic factors: cheap land and rapid planning procedures were easier to come by in the sparsely populated Negev than in the crowded central areas, where residents harried planners and builders with objections and hearings. The programme's targets, once set, were met by following the path of least resistance, but this did not always prove to be the most effective.

The ill-conceived and poorly executed response to the housing crisis, which had been characterized by blithe disregard for budgetary controls and which had been motivated by political and ideological, rather than socio-economic considerations, led to another volte-face in government policy. After the jump from minimal involvement prior to 1990 to assuming the dominant role in the construction industry in 1990/1, the Likud government, under Treasury prodding, sharply reined in the publicly-financed building programme from 1992 onwards by cutting the budget provided to the Housing Ministry. At the same time, however, mortgages financed by the state were increased to boost demand from immigrants and thus prevent the need for the government to implement its guarantees to the contractors.

This retreat from direct intervention became absolute under the Labour government immediately on its assumption of office in mid-1992. It cancelled contracts under negotiation or in the earliest stages of implementation, covering thousands of apartments in the West Bank and in the Negev. The 1993 state budget, which would in any event have seen a sharp fall in the housing budget, contains an across-the-board cutback in an attempt to free resources for other needs. The Labour government is also talking of selling off the state-owned housing construction and ownership companies and ending government participation in the construction sector entirely. This somewhat ironic stance may in fact be one example where the Labour Party proves to be more liberal and free market-oriented than Likud.

Other instances, in the land and construction sector alone, could well be moves in the future to increase substantially the sale of state-owned land, both in the centre of the country and in the Negev, and firm measures to reduce the high level of taxation and levies on land, building and construction materials. These are estimated to account for as much 40 per cent of the total retail price of a typical urban dwelling, and their removal could not only reduce prices and bolster home ownership, but might well make the building of rented apart-ments economically viable for the first time in Israeli history. However, this long-sought-after development would also require the abolition or modification of rent controls – a political hot potato that may prove too hot to handle. However, the true extent of Labour's conversion to market solutions remains unclear, especially if a renewed surge of immigration were to threaten to create a new shortage.

Immigration and Employment
The sad saga of the government's mishandling of the housing problem has not been repeated, at least so far, in the handling of the other main issue, that of absorbing the immigrants into the workforce. Although the government has adopted various schemes aimed at promoting investments and has offered a variety of wage and training subsidies for employers willing to take on immigrants, it has stopped

short of seeking to 'create jobs', despite demands for it to do so. It would seem that ministers and senior officials understand that any such attempt would be counter-productive, involving a heavy budgetary expense which would bring only temporary benefits. Even the run-up to the 1992 election, against a background of record-high and steadily rising unemployment, saw no serious initiatives on this front, although several other very damaging populist pieces of legislation were passed by the Knesset in this period.

Given the size of the immigration wave, and the tendency of the immigrant population to seek work as quickly as possible, it was inevitable that the unemployment rate, however measured, would rise, even if employment also rose. This highlights another of the paradoxes generated by the immigration. Normally, a growing economy witnesses a decline in unemployment and, conversely, a rise in unemployment is a sign of a recessionary economy. In Israel in 1990/91, and for the foreseeable future, there has been and will be increases in both employment and unemployment simultaneously. As the economy grows, it creates new jobs and employment rises – but it cannot grow fast enough to enable all the new job-seekers to find jobs. The only question is how fast can the economy grow: the greater the rate of economic expansion, the more moderate the rise in unemployment. But, as we have noted already, economic growth will spur increased immigration, and hence the continued expansion of the labour force. Therefore there is no realistic scenario in which unemployment will not remain a central feature of the economy for years to come.

From late 1991, with the rate of immigration falling and the housing market moving into a state of large-scale excess supply, the issue that, from the outset, should have been the key to successful immigrant absorption – namely employment – was now the dominant item on the domestic political and economic agenda. From the point of view of economic analysis, 'real' jobs, meaning those with inherent justification (as distinct from make-work schemes) will be dependent in the coming years on investment.

It is important to stress that the debate about employment or, more correctly, the labour market as a whole involves two elements: quality and quantity. The main failure to date has been more to do with the former than with the latter because, as noted, most immigrants have sought to join the labour force as soon as possible, and the majority have, in a way, done so. However, the jobs they have been able to find, whether in the public or private sector, have been far below their capabilities and qualifications. The essential need is therefore for better jobs, which require large-scale investment and hence access to financing both at home and abroad. These higher quality jobs may be expected to generate large numbers of ancillary and supporting posts so that, overall, the immigration will create more employment than it itself takes up (this is the standard pattern of immigrations to all countries, and also conforms with past Israeli experience).

This highlights yet another paradox stemming from the immigration: if large numbers of high-quality jobs are created, the beneficiaries of the spin-off growth in employment, and ultimately in living standards, will be precisely those groups, such as the Palestinians and the Israeli blue-collar employees, who felt threatened (for national, ethnic or economic reasons) by the Russian influx. Conversely, if these better jobs are not forthcoming, the immigrants will vie for the lower-paid jobs held by members of these groups and, given their superior education, qualifications and work ethic, will displace them. In a scenario in which the Israeli economy is stagnant or barely growing, the Palestinian labour force, already under severe strain because of the impact of the Gulf War on Palestinian employment and income patterns, will be the primary loser if it has to compete against the immigrants for the jobs that are available.

The Agenda for Reform

The key areas in which reform is most necessary have long since been identified in the public debate, and the general outline of the measures needed is also the subject of widespread consensus. In fact, as we have seen, some progress has been made in all of these areas, but far more remains to be done. These target areas are:

Trade Liberalization

The protectionist sentiments that traditionally held sway in Israeli trade policy, and that reached their peak in 1984–90, when Ariel Sharon was industry minister, have now been reversed, and the thrust of trade policy is clearly towards liberalization. This change led to the formulation of a far-reaching package of trade liberalization measures, that took effect on 1 September 1991.

The two key elements in this package were the abolition of blanket trade restrictions on 'third countries' (those with which Israel has no formal trade agreement of the sort it has with the EC, USA and EFTA), and the replacement of non-tariff barriers such as licensing and quota restrictions with tariffs, themselves to be phased out over five to seven years. In principle, this is a bold initiative, offering great benefits for Israeli consumers and sounding the death-knell on several low-wage, 'low-tech' sectors of Israeli industry. Precisely because of this, the terms of the liberalization were the subject of a fierce struggle between the Treasury and the Federation of Chambers of Commerce on the one side, and the Industry and Trade Ministry and the Manufacturers' Association on the other.

However, the success of this liberalization programme is by no means assured. Vested interests in different industrial sectors, as well as the Manufacturers' Association as a whole, continue to lobby hard for delays, or for the exclusion of this or that item or branch from the process. While it seems inevitable that some tactical battles over specific products and industries may be lost, it is essential that the overall strategy be maintained and, indeed, intensified. In fact, the area of trade liberalization is one of the most encouraging in the context of overall reform, both because there has been significant movement recently, and because there is a clear understanding of the benefits of a liberal policy to the economy as a whole. The key requirement, therefore, is to ensure that the process is executed as planned and, as and where possible, speeded up.

Capital Market Liberalization and Deregulation
The degree of progress achieved in deregulating the Israeli capital markets since 1985 is probably greater than that in any other area of the economy. This process of reform is rooted in the July 1985 stabilization programme, and stems from the achievement of eliminating the budget deficit (until 1989). Freed of the need to borrow massively, the government began to withdraw from the markets, and to relax the rules governing the activity of all the other players. As a result of the deregulation measures in areas of direct government involvement and of tougher laws and regulatory procedures in the operations, management and overseeing of the markets, major improvements have taken place with respect to the markets' liquidity and smooth and fair functioning, while the range and sophistication of the instruments available has increased enormously over recent years. Simultaneously, a policy of slow and cautious deregulation of foreign exchange controls has removed many of the onerous restrictions that had been in place in 1985 on all aspects of foreign currency transactions.

Nevertheless, the pace of reform has slowed in recent years. This is due to a combination of political and economic factors. Political weakness has caused the Treasury to shy away from a show-down with the Histadrut over the need to extend the reform process to include the Histadrut-run pension funds. Economically, the move back to large budget deficits since 1990 under the impact of immigration and absorption spending has left the government with little budgetary leeway to pursue the deregulation policy that it had implemented in the markets in 1986–8. The result is that, on the one hand, the capital market is now important and independent enough to act as a constraint on government, through its response to whatever it perceives as negative government policies. The government can no longer dictate to the markets, but rather relies on them to provide cheap and plentiful funds – and must therefore cultivate their favour. But, on the other hand, the markets are not yet integrated into the global arena – although the degree of foreign interest is growing rapidly – and they remain narrow and shallow relative to their own, and the economy's, potential.

The goal here is clear enough. Israel must have a freely convertible currency, unencumbered by controls, and capital must be allowed to flow freely into and out of the country and between the different sectors of the domestic markets. Only in this environment will Israel be able to attract the enormous foreign capital it will need over the coming decade to realize its wider economic and national goals.

Labour Market Reform

It is common to put the blame for the extreme rigidity displayed by much of the Israeli labour market at the door of a monolithic and malevolent Histadrut. In fact, the problem is more to do with the weakness of the trade union umbrella organization than its supposed strength. For years the Histadrut has been dragged along in opposition to reforms needed at plant, sector and national levels of wage bargaining and to reforms in labour relations by powerful and rebellious unions, mostly in the public and semi-public sectors. Regrettably, it has been unable to deliver even on those promises of reform which it itself helped prepare, such as the Sussman Committee's recommendations on public-sector wage scales.

This situation is changing rapidly, under the impact of the heavy over-supply of labour that has characterized the market since 1990, an over-supply which is likely to continue for several more years.

Rigidity is increasingly giving way to a more pragmatic approach that interprets the rules more flexibly, and at times bends or simply ignores them. This process has grown out of the experience gained by labour market participants in the second half of the 1980s, when unions learnt to co-operate with a newly-realistic management in preserving jobs and seeking to maintain their members' real wages as far as possible.

These trends have been clearest in the private sector, but have not been absent in the public and semi-public sectors either. The examples of Koor Industries and Israel Aircraft Industries, the two largest industrial employers in the country, each of which laid off one-third of its workforce (at all levels) in a short space of time and eliminated numerous employee privileges and restrictive practices as part of its response to the crisis, illustrated that flexibility was obtainable in a supposedly rigid labour structure. But it was obtainable only on two conditions. The danger had to be obvious and immediate, and the rank and file had to be convinced that management was indeed working in the best interests of the firm and everyone employed by it. The influx of immigrants has created a new reality in which flexibility is becoming a more general and on-going requirement.

However, there is no alternative, ultimately, to overall reform. Key candidates for reform include the minimum wage law which clearly contributes to the elimination of low-paying jobs and hence creates unemployment; 'linkage' of salary scales and terms of employment between sectors that have nothing in common, and between firms in the same sector, irrespective of their relative success and state of health; the abolition of restrictions limiting mobility of workers within organizations and of lax regulations regarding sick and vacation compensation; and, in general, the acceptance of closer correlation between salary scales and pay rises on the one hand and personal or group achievements on the other – so that wage rises become less automatic and a flexible bonus system more commonplace. These ideas and practices are currently being implemented at plant or company level. At some point, they will have to be formally adopted and implemented by the Cabinet, the Knesset and the Histadrut itself.

Privatization and Deregulation

The government formally launched its privatization programme in 1986, but the achievements in this sphere to date can only be described as extremely disappointing. With privatization, more than in any other aspect of economic policy, the free market approach has carried the day to the extent that there is near total agreement that government ownership, control and involvement in management is negative and counter-productive. The issue is permanently on the public agenda, for many different reasons: the need to allow state-owned companies to operate freely and be managed on business lines; the need to reduce the political allocation of senior jobs and party influence; the need to encourage foreign investment; the need to develop the domestic capital market; and the need to raise funds for the budget by selling state assets.

A few state-owned companies have actually been either sold outright to investors, or floated on the Tel Aviv stock exchange. Prominent among the latter group are Bezek and Israel Chemicals Ltd, part of whose equity has been sold to the general public via the stock exchange. Even for the majority of state-owned firms, which have not yet been prepared for public sale, the prospect (or threat, as some of them perceive it) is becoming more real – they are psychologically readying themselves for what they know will occur sooner or later. Nevertheless, the pace of privatization has been gallingly, and needlessly, slow. There are many reasons for this, but the dominant one has been the lack of firm and determined leadership by the government, from the prime minister downwards. The new Labour government has made the same positive noises as its predecessor and has scattered promises in all directions; whether it will deliver the goods on privatization, however, remains to be seen.

Certainly, the pressure to sell state firms has been mounting from several quarters, and it is vital that this pressure be maintained and even stepped up. In this area, more than in any other, the issue is not whether to act, or how, but rather a basic failure to implement an agreed policy.

The issue of deregulation is more complex – if only because government regulation of economic activity in Israel is so widespread. But experience in the agricultural sector has demonstrated that the true power of the vested interests which prevent reformist initiatives is often much less than their monolithic image would lead one to believe. The partial deregulation of the energy sector has highlighted how even the most powerful vested interests can be attacked and forced onto the defensive. Furthermore, the piecemeal deregulation of the financial markets, noted above, illustrates that even a gradualist approach can achieve cumulatively impressive results, without the set-piece confrontations entailed in 'big-bang' initiatives.

As with privatization, therefore, what is needed is political leadership. Most of the deregulation initiatives to date have been led by younger politicians of all parties, ambitious to make their mark, and hence willing to take the lead in reform when given the opportunity. Here, too, the new Labour government has the opportunity to make a fundamental break with its own past and thereby remould the traditional, but now clearly outdated, pattern of Israeli socio-economic activity.

Budgetary and Fiscal Reform

These two issues, each of major importance in its own right, may be taken together since they are entirely interlinked, so that tax reform cannot be undertaken without regard to overall budget policy and, conversely, budgetary policy will not change substantially without tax reform being an intrinsic part of that change.

There is an underlying acceptance, among Treasury and other officials, and at Cabinet level, that both tax rates and the overall tax burden should be brought down. But increased government intervention in the economy, both in terms of spending programmes in housing and in subsidies to industry for investment and to promote employment, combined with the need to embark on new weapons programmes in the wake of the Gulf War, have combined to stall, and indeed partially reverse, the progress made in 1987–8 in cutting both the budget and taxes.

However, the combination of lower-than-expected immigration in 1991–2, the end of the massive outlays on government-financed housing and the achievement of lower inflation have created the prospect of reduced pressures on the budget in the coming years. The government has adopted a multi-year plan aimed at eliminating the budget deficit by 1995, and this goal is achievable if the political will is found to stand firm against lobbyists and spending ministries. But even the elimination of the deficit does not represent a basic reform in budgetary and tax policy, while there is little doubt that sooner or later fundamental changes will have to be made in both the budgetary framework and the tax system.

The direction and general substance of these changes are fairly clear. With regard to the tax system, it is widely recognized that the needed reform is one that raises tax thresholds, lowers marginal rates and eliminates exemptions and privileges, which are even more distortive in the personal tax system than in the corporate one. In addition, quasi-taxes raised through the National Insurance Institute (NII) must also be reduced. Employers' contributions to the NII have been cut in recent years, but those of employees must also be reduced, and replaced by user charges and by rationalization and competition in the areas that receive these funds, notably education and social welfare.

Reform on this scale will inevitably have major budgetary implications, and significant reductions in the tax burden can only be achieved by cutting expenditures. The two main thrusts of any such programme must be to eliminate subsidies and to end direct government involvement in various areas of the economy.

The list of possible areas of budgetary savings is almost as long as the list of government ministries, many of which are recognized to be unnecessary, doing more harm than good, and often overlapping with each other. Although the entire political structure militates against wholesale reform, even a gradualist approach could generate very significant benefits within a short space of time. As in so many areas, the Labour government's promise of changed priorities has raised hopes and the government's progress on these fronts will be carefully monitored. But underlying short-term political manoeuvring, the pressures building up from within and outside the economy will force any Israeli government to move in the general direction outlined above. The pace, and the panache, with which the government responds to these pressures remains in its own hands.

Conclusion

The Israeli economy has been presented with an extraordinary opportunity to break decisively out of the pattern of flawed achievements that has characterized it since the implementation of the Economic Stabilization Plan of July 1985. In addition to being well placed to reap the benefits of its own painful but effective restructuring in the second half of the 1980s, the economy has been handed 'on a silver platter' the greatest boon possible, namely a massive infusion of top-quality human capital. The high levels of education and qualifications that characterize the wave of immigration from the former USSR, together with their sheer numbers and strong motivation to succeed, make it almost certain that the Israeli economy will undergo major structural changes in the coming years, in the direction of export-led growth stemming from the rapid expansion of science- and technology-based industries and services. This process, if accompanied by domestic reform will allow the achievement of both the key goals of the economy in the 1990s, namely the successful absorption of as many immigrants as possible and the full integration of the Israeli economy into the wider global markets for goods, services, and capital.

However, the harnessing of this human capital requires a commensurate infusion of financial capital, with which to create physical capital. Fortunately for Israel, the external circumstances, at both the global and regional level, have changed in its favour. As a result, not only is it able to move forward in the search for political and military accommodation with its neighbours, but the combination of political and economic change should make it attractive to the money, know-how and other resources of multinational companies, all of which are essential for Israel to realize its aspirations, whether at the national, corporate or personal levels.

That a positive external environment is merely a necessary, but far from sufficient condition for economic growth has been brought home to Israelis through the damage inflicted on these goals, as a result of mistaken government policies or failure to implement correct policies in the years from 1989 to 1992.

On the one hand, this record shows that the attainment of the twin goals is neither inevitable nor assured. On the other, it highlights the fact that their attainment is possible, and that the single greatest impediment to this happening is the role of domestic policy. Yet, what needs to be done is known, in outline if not in fine detail. Given an unprecedentedly favourable external background, there can be no more excuses for the Israeli economy not to realize its potential. The probability is that this time it will deliver.

PART TWO
The Israeli Political System

5. THE ISRAELI POLITICAL SYSTEM: A PROFILE

Itzhak Galnoor

For quite some time the prevalent mood in Israel has been that the political system is not functioning well. Some even maintain that it is suffering a crisis of legitimacy. One manifestation of this is the strong support among both the general public and many politicians for the introduction of far-reaching reforms into the electoral system. Another indication is the low level of political efficacy among the general public. A survey conducted before the general election in June 1992 asked the following question: To what extent can you and people like you influence government policy? Fifty-one per cent of the respondents felt that they possessed some degree of influence.[1] On first reading, this figure may appear rather high, but in Israel, where citizens are very alert politically, this should be considered an indication of dissatisfaction. Yet, one week later, almost 80 per cent of the population showed up to vote in the elections and turned the ruling party out of office. How can one explain the discrepancy between the sense of powerlessness and the high rate of participation in Israeli democracy?[2] Is the political system suffering from a crisis of legitimacy?

Main Features of Israeli Polity

Israel is a new state whose political system has been shaped by various influences: the heritage of the pre-state institutions, the era of the British Mandate (1920–48), and – above all – the turbulent history since its establishment in 1948. Israel has remained a democracy, one of the few stable democracies among the new states established after the Second World War. The significant milestones in Israel's collective chronology are the frequent wars. Consequently, the most import-

87

ant factor is the preoccupation with security and other external challenges, from which internal developments cannot be detached. This preoccupation has had a crucial impact on the evolution of the Israeli political system and the nature of its democracy, particularly since 1967, when military rule was established over a million and a half Palestinians in the administered territories.

Before discussing the changes that have taken place, some underlying features of Israeli society and politics deserve to be noted. First, Israeli Jewish society is still a community of newcomers. In the late 1980s, 45 out of 100 Jewish citizens were born outside the country. In the 1990s, immigrants became a majority within the Jewish population, due to the new waves of immigration from Ethiopia and the former Soviet Union. Secondly, Israeli society is heterogeneous. Social scientists describe the main internal divisions in terms of cleavages between Jews and Arabs, observant and non-observant Jews, 'Oriental' Jews (originating from Asia or Africa) and 'Occidental' Jews (originating from Europe or North America). In addition, there is the complicated relationship between Israeli and Diaspora Jews as well as 'normal' social distinctions based on education, employment or income. Thirdly, as in other new states, the Israeli political system is overburdened. Israelis have high expectations from politics, not only as a means for safeguarding collective security, but also as a vehicle for social and economic development. As a consequence, the political system is highly centralized and politics permeate all aspects of life. Through various agents, but in particular the political parties, society is highly politicized and the extent of government involvement in daily life is probably among the highest in democratic societies.

Finally, the political institutions have been based on a rather pure system of proportional representation. The whole country is in fact one constituency and parties are represented in the Knesset roughly according to the percentage of votes they receive in the elections. Hence, Israel has always had a multi-party system, with no party ever receiving a majority of the votes. In the 1992 elections, for instance, ten parties were elected to the Knesset, a considerable decrease from the fifteen parties elected in the previous 1988 elections. As a result, Israeli governments have always been based on coalitions, the Labour Party dominating these coalitions until 1977, and the Likud Party from 1977 to 1992, with intervals of national unity governments in 1967–70 and 1984–90.

As of 1993, a few constitutional reforms have taken place with respect to the formal structure of the political institutions. However, Israeli 'politics' – as a democratic process of translating collective needs and interests into policy-making – has undergone remarkable changes in the period under review.

Society and Politics: The First Two Decades, 1948–67

Several approaches can be taken to analyse the functioning of the Israeli political system during the first two decades of its existence. There are those who place particular emphasis on the regulation of conflicts and on alliances among elite groups; while others stress the functioning of political parties as coordinating agencies closely linked to other channels, notably bureaucracy and the mass media.[3] In all the above studies, there is broad agreement on two issues. First, there is a clear functional connection between the structure of the political system and its way of 'doing politics'. Second, despite the immense challenges, the system has demonstrated a highly developed capacity for both overcoming crises and ensuring stability. Let us examine first the way the political system coped with the main internal cleavages mentioned above.

In Israel, social conflicts are frequently 'elevated' to the attention of the political system, thereby undergoing an intense process of politicization. Thus they cease to be 'just' social, cultural, or economic issues. It can be argued that religious faith or immigrant absorption are issues of concern to the individual or to the community, and that the intervention of the political system in such issues should be minimal. However, as new countries engage in the process of nation-building, their political system usually plays a central role. Success here depends on the degree to which the political system can penetrate social structures and mobilize citizens. In Israel, too, the state has assumed a dominant position.

Yet the ability of the Israeli political system to bring about permanent solutions to deep-rooted social schisms has been quite limited. For example, politics can offer no solution that would satisfy the diametrically opposed aspirations of those who advocate a state based on Jewish religious law, and those who call for the separation of religion and state. Thus, political handling of such matters by the state will perforce lead to ad hoc solutions and to arrangements founded on compromise and tactical concessions. An example is the religious status quo agreement which has granted jurisdiction to the religious on such matters as family law, marriage and divorce. This is the type of solution in which political systems specialize.

Such arrangements carry a social price tag. The attempt to wrest controversial issues from the deadlock of incessant social rivalry requires an unusually high degree of politicization, as well as a high level of political institutionalization. Political institutions and organizations have therefore played a dominant role while the coordination of the activities of these institutions was ensured by the mediating role of the powerful political parties.

Accordingly, it can be readily understood why the principle of proportional representation – in the electoral system, in coalition governments, and in the distribution of benefits – has been of such vital importance in the Israeli political system. The logic of this principle derives from the fact that it enables coexistence between, on the one hand, wide-based representation, and, on the other hand, structured aggregation of interests by the political parties.[4] Moreover, it gives relatively small groups an opportunity to attain representation in the Knesset, and, at the same time, it used to create rather stable coalition governments. During the period 1948–67, proportionality not only faithfully reflected the political way of life, it also strengthened and perpetuated those political arrangements. For nearly 20 years, Israel's coalition governments refuted the assumption that proportional representation and stability cannot go hand in hand. Furthermore, the 'party key' – according to which public jobs were distributed and resources allocated – was essential for the functioning of this political system.

In practical terms, autonomy was granted to the various political parties with regard to the internal management of their affairs. There was also a tacit understanding that matters that were considered of paramount importance to the agenda of a political party, especially in the case of the religious camp, would not be concluded against its will. The prevailing pattern required that major decisions be hammered out through a process of negotiation and mutual concessions at the elite level. The political system was therefore always in need of relatively broad-based coalitions (70–80 seats out of the 120-seat Knesset) and could not rely merely on a simple majority. Finally, despite its centralized nature, the political system operated in accordance with democratic rules. The legitimation accorded to the above patterns of political activity was attained in free elections, and was based on a high level of citizens' participation.

What follows is a summary of the main factors that enabled the political system to cope with the major internal challenges during the first period.

Religious groups: The numerous religious groups coalesced around three religious parties – the Zionist and dominant National Religious Party (NRP), and the two non-Zionist ultra-Orthodox parties. Together these parties arrived at political arrangements with the dominant Labour Party, the so-called 'status quo' agreements on religious affairs. The NRP became a constant partner in the coalition governments, whereas the special interests of the ultra-Orthodox parties were accommodated through other arrangements. Consequently, the religious groups had reinforced representation in the political system which ensured their control over religious legislation. Thus, religious affairs were dealt with at an elite level through alliances among political parties. This did not, however, prevent many coalition crises arising over religious matters.

Ethnic groups: During this period, there were neither autonomous ethnic organizations with political clout, nor direct ethnic representation in the Knesset. Immigrant organizations were controlled by the political parties, or by the labour union. Accordingly, the most prevalent political arrangement was co-option of ethnic and communal leaders by the political parties. This was carried out through symbolic appointments to the Cabinet and to other public positions, while immigrant absorption was handled by government ministries, the Jewish Agency, and the political parties. Consequently, there was no legitimation for separate political organizations of ethnic (mainly Oriental) groups. The ethnic gaps in Israeli society were defined as temporary educational or economic problems, which the government preferred to handle on a case-by-case basis.

Israeli Arabs
Similarly, there were no autonomous Arab political organizations with political clout, nor any independent Arab parties represented in the Knesset. Arab parties were affiliated with and controlled by Jewish parties, with the exception of the Communist Party, which expressed the aspiration of a segment of the Israeli Arab population. The prevailing political arrangement was the co-option of clan, communal and religious leaders by the government and the political parties.

Central control was exercised through military government in the Arab regions, until 1966, and through the separation of the Druze and Circassian communities. There was, however, recognition of Arab autonomy in religion, language and, to a lesser extent, education and local government; and in the existence of separate newspapers and radio programmes in Arabic. The problem was predominantly defined as a security issue, and policy was implemented through the military government and special advisers on Arab affairs in key government ministries. There was no symbolic appointment of Arabs to important public positions and the government preferred the case-by-case handling of crises, causing the cleavage to remain an open and somewhat intensified issue.

The dominant presence of Israel's political parties in the above three areas in fact determined the way the issue was handled through the political process at that time. Whereas party politics was recognized as legitimate for religious interests, it was camouflaged and indirect for ethnic and Arab interests. The basic aim was to prevent autonomous organization in Israel along ethnic or national (Jewish/Arab) lines, and this goal was almost completely attained. The centralized nature of the political system enabled the prominent use of co-option in those areas not characterized by direct representation. In other words, ethnic and Arab leaders were appointed or 'elected' by political parties.

More generally, the parties contributed to reducing the impact of the social cleavages, serving as shock absorbers, particularly in periods of crises. The parties in power also managed to segregate decisions on foreign and security affairs from inner politics. This was no small achievement, from their point of view, given the bitter ideological rivalries and the intensity of the political process.

It would therefore not be an exaggeration to say that, in the first 20 years of the state, domestic affairs were based on the functioning of the parties. Parties were not merely involved in the classic political function of interest aggregation and articulation, since their activities extended into most aspects of social and economic life. Israeli political culture was shaped by the fact that the parties, notably Mapai (the Labour Party), served as exclusive mediators between society and its political system. In time, this structure proved not to be as rigid as was commonly assumed. It did not prevent changes in the political system. The shifting fortunes of the various political forces that were in

political system has tried to cope with internal challenges during the second period.

Religious Groups

The main changes have been the organizational disintegration of the previous religious camp; the decline of the NRP, and the rise of ultra-Orthodox parties. The religious parties went through many internal splits, and, for the first time, ethnic-religious parties appeared, such as Tami and Shas. The previous political arrangements collapsed, resulting in the re-opening of the status quo agreements on religious affairs. From 1977, all the religious parties joined the Likud-led coalitions, but Shas alone joined the first Labour-led coalition in 1992. As a consequence, fragile coalition agreements became a substitute for the previous binding arrangements. The increased representation of the ultra-Orthodox parties in government coalitions exacerbated the tension surrounding religious affairs in Israeli society, causing further polarization. Furthermore, religious confrontations became closely linked to the ethnic cleavage within Israel and to the internal debate over the future of the territories.

Ethnic Groups

The first change was the increased assertiveness of Oriental groups in municipal governments, workers' committees, labour councils, etc. Later, protest and interest groups appeared with ethnic messages, and political parties with ethnic platforms, resulting in much greater mobility of Oriental leaders in the political system. It also meant the collapse of most previous arrangements (co-option, token appointments), and the emergence of a strong ethnic identity within party politics. The number of Oriental Jews appointed to important public positions increased dramatically, even though there are still demands for affirmative action to promote ethnic groups. Consequently, the opening-up of the political system meant greater accessibility of Oriental Jews to centres of power. The situation in low-income neighbourhoods and development towns became part of the national agenda, and strong demands are now heard for equality in education, employment and housing. It has also intensified other tensions, setting the need to help distressed ethnic groups against absorption of new immigrants or the funding of Jewish settlement in the territories.

Israeli Arabs

The main change has been the increased political independence of
Israeli Arabs in local authorities; attempts to establish umbrella frameworks (National Committee of Heads of Arab Local Authorities); the
creation of voluntary Arab organizations; and, since 1984, the appearance of independent Arab parties. Some of the previous methods of
co-option and token appointments have survived, despite the disappearance of Arab parties affiliated with Jewish parties. Similarly,
despite increased autonomy in certain areas, there is still a lack of
Jewish legitimation for Arab organizations, and continuation of separate treatment of 'Arab affairs' in government ministries. The situation
is fluid, internal splits have resulted in the under-representation of
Israeli Arabs in the Knesset and other institutions. Formally, Israeli
Arabs have equal rights, but in the distribution of government services
they are far from equal, and while Arab parties are represented in the
Knesset, they lack general support from Arab voters. Furthermore,
tensions between Jews and Arabs have been exacerbated by the
Palestinian problem, the new wave of Jewish immigration, and the
lack of equality.

As the above demonstrates, there have been considerable changes in
the way the political system has coped with the internal challenges
during the second period. Although some of the previous arrangements, such as the status quo religious agreements, still remain, many
are no longer in existence. The political parties, the key coordinating
factor during the first phase, are unable to carry out this function,
social cleavages are now finding different outlets within the political
system. Oriental Jews, Israeli Arabs, ultra-Orthodox Jews, and even
some Diaspora Jews have created their own organizational frameworks. Although such frameworks have not yet been accorded general
legitimation, they are supported by their respective constituencies. For
example, two Oriental parties, Tami and Shas, in turn presented a
clear ethnic message. Moreover, the overlap between ethnic identity
and voting behaviour has increased, with Labour/Likud receiving
about two thirds of the Occidental/Oriental votes, respectively. New
parties have also appeared on the right and on the left, in the Arab
sector and in the ultra-Orthodox community.[6]

While these developments have helped create a more pluralistic and
open society, social tensions have become more tangible and less
manageable politically. In other words, the inability of the parties to

perform their mediating roles discreetly contributes to political instability. Furthermore, political energy has become invested in interpersonal conflicts and in the establishment of ad hoc coalitions. As a result, the ability of the political leadership to make decisions has been adversely affected. The fact that the previous political arrangements are now obsolete tends to sharpen inner conflicts, and the social cleavages may become so great that they threaten to split society.

Consequently, there has been a marked decline in the ability of the system to do what it does best, namely, coming up with ad hoc political solutions. Because the current arrangements have become increasingly temporary in nature, they are not only unable to settle conflicts, but are actually contributing to the instability of the political system. For example, whereas the participation of the religious parties in coalition governments was once a stabilizing factor, it has now become a disruptive element. One result of the current situation is the growing use of the courts to resolve problems which, in the past, were settled within the political system.[7] This fluid situation has also affected government performance in external affairs. The controversy within Israeli society over foreign and defence issues is now directly reflected in the difficulty of the political leadership to arrive at binding decisions. Ever since the Israeli victory in 1967, the political system has been unable to point to any consensus-backed achievements in the areas of foreign affairs and defence, with the notable exception of the Israeli–Egyptian peace treaty. It can be maintained that the external challenges have become more formidable and that, correspondingly, the decision-making process has become more difficult, and the chances for success more remote. Another line of argument, however, is that social and economic changes have weakened the relatively exclusive or elitist nature of Israeli politics.

As noted above, the most obvious change during the second period has been the decline of the political parties. Even though Israeli society is still very 'political', the level of politicization has, in fact, dropped, while there has been an increase in the relative power of other groups. Once the primary channels for coordination, the parties now exert far less influence, and their role has diminished as the key modifying mechanism between society and the political system. Indeed, coalition negotiations between the parties have become an ugly affair, engendering lack of public confidence in the political leadership. Aside from serving as an arena for internal and interpersonal squabbling and, more significantly, providing a potential organizational infrastructure for the eventual creation or toppling of a government, the parties are essentially inactive between national election campaigns.

Proportional representation once served as an effective means for distributing political power and for allocating resources in accordance with the 'party key'. However, since the 1970s this system has produced its fair share of surprises: the Likud victory in 1977; the stalemate between the two large parties in the elections of 1981, 1984 and 1988; the split in the religious camp; the rise of the ultra-Orthodox parties; and the Labour victory in 1992. At the same time, it contributed to growing public dissatisfaction with the entire system of government and with the democratic rules of the game.

As a result of the decline of the previous 'establishment', primarily the political parties, new independent interest groups have sprung up.[8] Extra-parliamentary groups, such as Gush and Emunim Peace Now, have provided a new framework for citizens who cannot find expression for their goals within the present array of political parties. In the democratic sense, this development can be viewed as positive since these groups operate with a large measure of organizational autonomy and have helped reduce the special privileges enjoyed by the political parties. Another positive aspect is the opening up of the previous political elite. For example, it is now much more difficult to mobilize Oriental Jews or Arab leaders by using the antiquated methods of political co-option. However, the new groups have also weakened the parties and the performance of their essential democratic roles. Some of these groups have had a negative effect on Israeli democracy because of their willingness to engage in violent and unlawful activity.

Between 1977 and 1992, there was no dominant political party in Israel.[9] Furthermore, no single party controlled the 'pivotal position' as far as coalition-formation is concerned. A party situated in the pivotal position can prevent other parties, on its right or on its left, from attaining a majority and thus from forming a coalition. The Labour victory in the 1992 election does, however, place it in the pivotal position and, with the parties to its left, it can block a right-wing coalition. However, this majority is very narrow (61 seats out of 120) and it has forced the Labour Party to include a religious party in the coalition formed in July 1992.[10]

Moreover, ever since 1967, coalition governments have been either too narrow or too broad. The negotiation process no longer leads to stable agreements or binding decisions. One reason for this is that even internal party decisions do not carry sufficient weight to last long. Another is that citizens' participation has become more autonomous, as can be seen in their shifting voting patterns and in their intensified activities, through pressure groups, demonstrations, strikes, etc. This new situation during the second period has limited the element of manoeuvre of the political leaders, who are no longer able to control information sources, or to prepare the ground for acceptable decisions.

Steering Capacity
The viability of a political system can be evaluated according to its capacity to ensure the survival of the state, to adapt to changes, and to invest in development. The steering mechanism aims at guiding society towards the attainment of collective goals, while maintaining stability, and preventing crises from turning into breakdowns. It is thus vital that the steering mechanism establishes a firm link between the helm and the ship, that is, between the political system and society. To ensure the attainment of the collective goals, steering also means the ability to make acceptable and binding decisions. In a democratic political system, it must also be representative and accountable to the citizens. It is an aggregate of leadership, institutions, political processes and decision-making. In the light of the above, we can offer a portrait of the changes in Israel's steering capacity during the two periods.

During the first period (1948–67) politics in Israel was highly 'autonomous', that is, serving as a separate, differentiated social function. Social divisions were regulated by political arrangements, there was little 'street politics', and the political elite was strong and rather independent in performing the steering roles, through the mediating services of the political parties. Thus the political system acquired almost monopolistic control over the representation of society and state, including its official symbols. Most importantly, there was no serious competition to the state's political leadership by other elites. Monopoly was coupled with exclusiveness, that is to say there was no serious competition to the elected political leaders by rival political centres of power. In retrospect, we also know that there was no real attempt to question the legitimacy of the elected government. After 1948, the bitter ideological and personal rivalries of the pre-state era were channelled democratically into the Knesset.

The efficacy of a political system requires a shared language of politics and an internal communication network capable of reaching most parts of society. In these respects the steering score of the Israeli political system during the first period was about average. The system was rather inclusive and managed to penetrate society, but towards the weaker groups, as already noted, the methods of communication were often paternalistic, while information flowed from below only through centrally controlled channels. Finally, the steering mechanism of the system displayed a high capacity to cope with a multitude of shocks and to overcome crises of near collapse. It proved capable of making difficult decisions about domestic and foreign affairs, while maintaining the democratic rules of the game. In those senses, the steering capacity of the system during the first period scores a high mark. It avoided not only the characteristic revolutions, internal violence, and military takeovers of new states, but also political instability and deterioration. The Israeli political system in the first period was rather stable and effective, and enjoyed a high degree of both public support and legitimation. The citizens' loyalty to the state was never in doubt, and the rate of economic growth was one of the highest in the world. It was also democratic, even though it was a rather well-organized democracy from above.

During the second period under consideration many aspects of the previous political structure survived, such as the formal division of functions among the institutions in the system. However, in terms of the actual political processes, almost everything has changed. The autonomy of the political process decreased considerably and the social divisions, especially around religious issues, have produced recurring crises. The waning of the previous political establishment and the weakening of the political parties further contributed to instability and also to deviations from some democratic rules of the game. Perhaps more menacing, from the point of view of the political centre, has been the appearance of competing definitions of the goals of the state, and of a powerful opposition to government decisions (for example, the evacuation of Sinai in 1982). This was also manifested in rival symbols (Judaism, the Land of Israel), questioning the monopoly of the state and its political leadership.

Central government has weakened since 1967, due to the fact that a separate mechanism for administering the occupied territories gradually appeared. The discovery of a Jewish underground among the settlers was the most threatening indication of this phenomenon. On a different level, public dissatisfaction with government has

Rabin. This transfer of loyalties arose because almost all the signs indicated clearly that only Rabin would be able to win the election convincingly and beat the Likud. The results of the election appear fully to justify this move.

The primaries served Labour well. They displayed openly that it is in the business of democratizing itself. The best proof of their success was the announcement by the Likud, shortly after the Labour primaries, that it, too, would select its candidates in the future by a similar process. They also scored high for Labour in the public opinion. More importantly, they also settled in an orderly and reasonable fashion the leadership question, especially since both Peres and Rabin had fully endorsed this new procedure. Lastly, for Labour the primaries were a stepping stone to the newly passed Basic Law which provides for the direct election of the prime minister by popular nationwide choice separate from the regular parliamentary election. This unique electoral system has been adopted after a lengthy and turbulent legislative, as well as extra-parliamentary, passage. It had been supported all along by a majority of Labour leaders and parliamentarians, including Rabin and Peres. The latter was in fact one of its prime initiators. As with the primaries, Labour's continuous and persistent support of the direct election of the prime minister has provided ample proof of its commitment to constitutional reform. Although the implementation of this new law will not occur until the next election, scheduled for 1996, Rabin conducted Labour's election campaign as if it were already in force. Likewise, he conducted the coalition negotiations after the election in a similar manner.

After years of unsuccessful attempts to reform the parliamentary electoral system, and in particular to introduce a system of constituency representation in order to counterbalance the less positive effects of proportional representation, the success of these two reforms is bound to strengthen renewed attempts in this area. As well as primaries for the selection of their candidate for the prime ministership, in 1992 the Labour Party also introduced primary elections for all parliamentary candidates. The existing proportional representation system with rigid lists in one 120-member national constituency had led in all parties to the extreme centralization of the selection process and had given additional power to the parties' central bodies. Indeed, this may be one reason why in the past the party bureaucracies have been unwilling to consider electoral reforms which would include the introduction of local or regional constituencies.

Labour's use of primaries for the selection of its parliamentary candidates was in general, a successful experiment. The actual method of selection may have been too biased in the direction of decentralization and localization inasmuch as those who were chosen in local districts needed only a fraction of the support of the rest who were elected nationwide.[15] If there is to be a new electoral law, providing for a proportion of Knesset members to be elected from constituencies, the primaries will have to be modified to fit that system.

It remains to be seen if and to what extent candidates selected by the open, democratic system of primaries will be more representative and more accountable to the electorate than hitherto. Central control over local party chapters must necessarily be diminished by this decentralization, but what effect this is going to have on Labour is as yet unclear.

The Fourth Generation

Yitzhak Rabin and Shimon Peres are the last of Labour's third generation of leaders since independence. Once they depart from active politics, presumably in 1996, the fourth generation will have taken over. The question is, how will this new generation differ from the previous ones? We can perhaps risk a few informed guesses. Labour MKs (Members of the Knesset) today have a much higher formal education than in the past, and this is likely to increase. Yet in the past there were many learned men without much formal education, and who is to say which is preferable? In the early years the standard of parliamentary discourse and debate was much more impressive than nowadays. Will that return? The leaders are getting younger, or more precisely the number of the older ones (say, those over 67) is declining. The number of women in the leadership group may actually be on the decline and, most probably, will not rise. Sephardi/Orientals comprise almost 40 per cent of Labour's Knesset members in 1992, an all-time high, a situation which has been influenced by the primaries. This figure is unlikely to rise in the future, since it is slightly larger than the percentage of registered party members of this background.

Much more important than any of these are the attractiveness, the trustworthiness, the selflessness, the humanity of the leaders. By and large, the newer generation of Labour leaders seem to be competent and effective. Though they may not be paragons of virtue or intellect, we do not know how to find better people by better systems. However, that should not be an argument against change and reform. Labour can and does attract as good a reservoir for potential leaders as any other party.

The questions for Labour do not revolve around personalities, but rather what is to be done and what can be achieved. Rabin, as prime minister, has proclaimed an agenda, without so far being too specific about it. As far as foreign policy is concerned, this new agenda very clearly indicates the avoidance, at almost any cost, of a collision course with the United States. The immediate consequence of this new approach was the turnabout in the policy towards the building of Jewish settlements in the occupied territories, namely the cessation of all government-supported development schemes there. This policy, which is being decried by its opponents as the 'drying up' of Jewish existence on the West Bank, will test Labour's governing talents and its legitimation to the utmost.

On the economic front Labour will have to attract substantial foreign resources for capital investments in order to restart economic growth in a serious way, after almost 20 years of stagnation. To achieve this goal a whole series of measures will have to be introduced in business management and labour relations, in governmental procedures, including central economic planning, and in fiscal and monetary policies. Past experience casts serious doubts on the likelihood of success in all these areas. These efforts are not only essential for the long-term development of the Israeli economy. There is the immediate need to alleviate the worsening unemployment situation, which heavily effects not only young people as they finish their army service but also the large numbers of new immigrants.

In the realm of social policies, the Labour government is aware of the need to increase substantially the resources at the disposal of the educational system at almost every level, as well as to adjust the allocations to the various educational sectors. This will include considerable increases in the allocations for Arab schools, but it will also mean stricter control over financing of the entire system. The purpose of this administrative reform is not to create greater equity in the educational system, but to correct serious deficiencies which have recently been discovered in the standards of elementary and secondary schools.

Labour is committed, and will be prodded by its main coalition partner, Meretz, to enhance substantially legal, civil and social rights, both by new legislation and law enforcement. On the relation between religion and state Labour appears to be divided between radicals and conservatives. It is doubtful, therefore, whether Labour will introduce any far-reaching changes to the traditional *status quo* but efforts will be made to undo at least some of the measures adopted by the previous government which have come under wide criticism.

For Labour, whose collective morale has been low since 1977, winning the 1992 election should prove sufficient to revive its spirits. Nothing succeeds like success, and Labour can be assured of winning the next election provided it can show substantial progress in the peace process or, failing that, that it has done everything humanly possible in that direction; and that it has achieved growth in the Israeli economy. It must raise Israel's standard of living, particularly for the many who live under the poverty line. To achieve all this the Labour government will require a bit of luck – though dissension and internal squabbles within the Likud would also help, as would the continuing splinterings of the right and the religious camps.

Jews who have succeeded in Israel's public life. Together with the somewhat older David Levy, they are Likud's greatest vote-getters among Israel's numerous Oriental Jews, and the key to the party's political success. Shamir believed that with the support of these two groups he could take over the party, assert his authority, and change it at will.

What resulted in January 1989 was an undeclared coup from above. Skilfully pushing aside Ariel Sharon and David Levy, two of the main contenders for the leadership, Shamir promoted Meridor, Olmert, Milo, and Katzav to the rank of full Cabinet ministers, thereby gaining supremacy within the party's top ranks. Netanyahu was appointed Israel's deputy foreign minister, affording him unlimited access to the national and international media. Shamir's choice of young, open-minded and pragmatic ministers indicated that he wanted to provide his party with a centrist image and a new moderate look.

The operation started with Shamir's surprising decision to form another national unity coalition with the Labour Party. Given the bad faith between Likud and Labour during the first unity coalition (1984–8), and Shamir's total mistrust of Peres, then Labour's leader, this was an unexpected development. Having initially negotiated coalition agreements with the small right wing and ultra-Orthodox parties, Shamir turned to Labour instead. He had became convinced that the *intifada* could not be put down by military means. Moreover, he also did not wish to become dependent on the radical right, or have Ariel Sharon as his minister of defence.

By mid-1989 it was clear that the major axis in Israeli national politics was the personal alliance across party lines between Yitzhak Shamir and his Labour minister of defence Yitzhak Rabin. This strange covenant communicated pragmatism, and unwillingness to use excessive force against the *intifada*. The main product of the new axis was the Rabin–Shamir Peace Plan, under which the Palestinians of the West Bank were to elect representatives to negotiate a permanent solution with Israel. The radical right regarded Shamir's peace initiative as disastrous, a sure recipe for future Jewish concessions in the occupied territories and leading to the potential creation of a Palestinian state.

Had he been successful, Shamir might have significantly changed the shape of Israeli politics, curbing Likud's growing radicalism, and working with Labour towards achieving peace. But Shamir has never been an imaginative strategist, and his grand move was lost by a series of miscalculations. Over-confident of his control of the party, Shamir moved too fast and too carelessly. In addition to Sharon, he also alienated David Levy, the party's most popular vote-getter, and Yitzhak Modai, the ambitious leader of the Liberals. Shamir disliked this trio, doubting either their competence or their lack of integrity and personal loyalty. Had Shamir taken on Sharon and Modai and not Levy as well, he would probably have been successful, since Levy's cooperation would have assured him of wide support within the party. Levy was neither a true radical nor a menace to Shamir. Levy, however, coveted the post of foreign minister, a job which the prime minister did not think he could handle. For Shamir, Levy proved to be 'a bridge too far'.

The Shamir–Rabin peace plan of May 1989 offered the three ministers the opportunity for revenge. What followed was a classical Sharon manoeuvre, a slow galvanization of internal party opposition, an appeal to the 'sacred principles' of Herut concerning 'no talks with the PLO', and a surprise attack at the right moment. The isolated radical right in the Knesset and the lobbyists of the settlers in Judea, Samaria and Gaza were more than happy to step in. In the face of a sustained attack on his readiness to talk to the Palestinians, his ambiguity about the status of Jerusalem and his amiable relationship with Yitzhak Rabin, Shamir began to back off. Outflanked by the three 'constraint ministers', Shamir started to stall. He sent mixed messages to the American administration, greatly irritating President Bush and Secretary of State James Baker. The inevitable coalition crisis with the Labour Party took place in March 1990 when Shimon Peres, hopeful of forming an alternative government, brought down the Cabinet with a vote of no confidence.

The collapse of the unity coalition undermined Yitzhak Shamir's authority. Though remaining at the helm, he lost much of his power and prestige. His silent revolution within the Likud had failed miserably. The 'princes' and the young Sephardi leaders could not secure him enough votes in the central committee to overcome the combined power of Sharon, Levy and Modai. It took an unprecedented three months to form a new coalition with humiliating consequences. In addition to incorporating the ideologically demanding partners of the radical right (whom he had rejected in 1988), Shamir had to make substantial concessions to the ultra-Orthodox religious parties, who were also indispensable for his brittle coalition. Three out of his four senior ministers – Levy (Foreign Affairs), Modai

(Finance), Sharon (Construction and Immigration) – were forced upon him against his better judgement. No Israeli premier has ever been constrained in this way.

Shamir's tactical failure to isolate the radical right was only one reason for the apparent radicalization of the Likud. A more substantial reason involved the changing nature of the *intifada*. What had begun in 1988 as a popular uprising, highlighted by daily demonstrations of hundreds of women, children, and ordinary residents all over the occupied territories, was reduced a year and a half later to scattered eruptions of a few dozen rock-throwing kids and to occasional sabotage by a handful of individuals organized in small underground cells. Much of the killing took place within the Palestinian community itself and involved the execution of Arab 'collaborators', individuals who were suspected of helping the Israelis. Continuous reports of the brutal execution of collaborators by their own kin damaged the Palestinian cause significantly, giving some credence to the Israeli right's argument that the Palestinians were nothing but terrorists.

As Israel regained its control over the area, mobilizing its military, political and economic resources against the uprising, it was clear that the end of the occupation was still far away. The conviction of Arab radicals that a Palestinian state was just around the corner proved unsubstantiated. The new circumstances reduced the external pressure on Israel to come up with a credible peace plan and convinced many Likud members that the risky Shamir–Rabin plan should be shelved.

There was an additional fact which the radicals, both in and out of the Likud did not fail to notice, namely their continued popularity among ordinary Israelis. Though the political developments since the end of 1987 appeared to have constituted a setback to the Israeli extreme right, they had not affected its immediate popularity and appeal.

The Right and the War in the Gulf

It was clear in the summer of 1990 that, in order to survive, the new Cabinet would have to adopt extreme nationalist positions. Indicative of this was the decision to authorize the building of the controversial Tomb of Yosef Yeshiva in the middle of the Arab city of Nablus. No previous Israeli government had ever approved such a provocative act. Yitzhak Shamir, who had little difficulty in resorting to the rhetoric of the radical right, repeatedly announced that he would never negotiate

with the PLO, bow to American pressure or return any of the
'liberated' territories to the Arabs. Official declarations involving the
possible settling of Russian immigrants in the West Bank, though later
retracted, only succeeded in angering President Bush, and brought
US–Israel relations to an all-time low.

When Saddam Hussein invaded Kuwait on 2 August 1990, he
inadvertently did a great service to the Israeli right by diverting world
camp attention away from the West Bank and the *intifada*. President
Bush and Secretary of State Baker, who were about to exert heavy
pressure on Israel to advance the peace process, lost interest in the
question, as did the rest of the world. Even the October 1990
demonstration on Jerusalem's Temple Mount, in which 19 Palestinians were killed by Israeli police, and the violent eruption which
followed the assassination of Rabbi Meir Kahane a month later, did
not succeed in returning the Palestinian problem to the headlines for
more than a few days.

Like most Israelis, the right viewed the outbreak of the war in the
Gulf with great satisfaction. The long-held Israeli contention that
Saddam Hussein posed a threat to the entire region was finally shared
by most of the civilized world, which was now prepared to counter the
danger. The real breakthrough for Israel came two days into the war,
when Iraq fired Scud missiles on Tel Aviv. The attack triggered
widespread solidarity with Israel notably in America and western
Europe. All previous criticism directed at the radical right for being
responsible for the government's extremist positions on the Palestinians quietly died out. Israel's agreement to bear the brunt of the
attacks and to delay its retaliation magnified this support. The bitter
disagreement between Shamir's government and the American
administration disappeared overnight. Cordiality and co-operation
took their place. Israel was immediately supplied with state-of-the-art
Patriot anti-missile missile systems, and was promised a positive
hearing for its new military and economic needs.

The crisis in the Gulf also had a dramatic effect on the domestic
standing of the Israeli right, and on its relationship with its adversaries
on the left. The PLO's Algiers Resolution in 1988 in which it
accepted UN Resolution 242 and its willingness to co-exist with Israel
had been a great boost for the Israeli left. For the first time since 1967
the 'peace camp' could argue that there was a Palestinian counterpart
which was willing to coexist with Israel. These new facts could not be
ignored by the right whose positions had already been damaged by the

intifada. It found worrisome the possibility of an Israeli–Palestinian rapprochement, with its implication of a potential territorial compromise for fear that this would attract many Israelis weary of the Palestinian uprising. The Labour Party was clearly tilting in this direction.

The crisis in the Gulf removed the anxieties of the right overnight. The immediate identification of the Palestinian community with Saddam Hussein, who had overrun the Kuwaiti state within a few hours and who had promised to do the same to Israel, pulled the rug from under the peace camp's feet. The emotional identification with Saddam Hussein expressed by even the most liberal Palestinians, shocked Israeli peace activists. Many felt that they had been deceived, and admitted that the right's refusal to trust the Palestinians was not baseless. The Labour Party, already torn apart by internal dissensions lost whatever momentum it had previously achieved.

By March 1991 it appeared that a new political consensus had emerged in Israel: a wide agreement that the Arabs had not changed, and that a peace process involving significant territorial concessions was out of the question. The barrage of Iraqi Scud missiles, and the arrival in huge numbers of Russian immigrants united the Israelis in the conviction that the immediate tasks facing the nation were the continued fortification of the state and the quick absorption of the new immigrants. Israelis continued to be divided about the desired peace, but they were in agreement that the question had to be postponed. While the entire Israeli right gained comfort by this development, the radical right was thrilled. As a full partner in the government they envisaged a period of expanding the Jewish presence in Judea and Samaria, thereby creating an almost insurmountable obstacle to any future territorial compromise.

How the Likud Lost the 1992 Election

The most important conclusion that may be drawn from the 1992 election, albeit tentatively, is that it was the Likud, not the radical right, which was defeated so badly. The parties of the radical right which ended the twelfth Knesset with seven seats, returned to the thirteenth with 11. Though Tehiya lost its three seats, Tzomet gained six (quadrupling its strength), and Moledet one. In addition, the National Religious Party, which has recently undergone a conversion to the radical right, also gained one new seat. The power transformation of Israeli politics has been caused primarily by the Likud's loss of eight Knesset seats and Labour's gain of five.

A preliminary analysis of the Likud defeat does not reveal any broad socio-political shift from right to left. Instead, it reveals a combination of a significant decline in the emotional attachment of former Likud voters to their party, and a series of blunders and mistakes committed by the party's leadership in the year prior to the elections. Much of the blame appears to belong to Yitzhak Shamir.

At the end of the Gulf War Yitzhak Shamir, like President Bush, was at the height of his popularity. His decision to refrain from retaliating against Iraq had paid handsome rewards. Israel's most dangerous enemy had been crushed by the coalition forces, and without a single Israeli war casualty. Moreover, Shamir's shaky international reputation had improved immensely. By the spring of 1991 Shamir was electorally unbeatable. Having re-established himself as a judicious defender of the Jewish state, and a world statesman in his own right, Shamir had dwarfed all his potential rivals.

A further reason for Shamir and the Likud's post-Gulf war popularity was the prospect of generous international financial support. Israel's brittle economy was badly hurt by the Iraqi invasion of Kuwait and by the Scud attacks on Tel Aviv. The absorption of hundreds of thousands of Jewish immigrants from the former Soviet Union had increased the burden on the economy considerably. Now, there was a widespread expectation that Shamir's responsible behaviour would reap financial rewards. Indeed, immediately after the war, Israel received $650 million from America as a compensation for all its war-related expenses. A further $100 million came from the Federal Republic of Germany as a special humanitarian grant to cover the damages caused by the Scud attacks. Russian immigration to Israel, the fulfilment of one of Zionism's most cherished dreams quickly resumed at the pace of over 10,000 a month, and a spectacular two-day operation brought to Israel almost 15,000 Ethiopian Jews. Israel was on the point of receiving the large loan guarantees, needed for the absorption of Russian Jews, from the Americans and Europeans. The agreement of all the Arab states to attend the Madrid peace conference, in accordance with the conditions set by Shamir, seemed to underline his claim of Israel's strength and independence. All these developments strengthened Shamir's popularity.

Yitzhak Shamir's 'march of folly' started in the summer of 1991, with his decision to support Ariel Sharon's ambitious settlement plans.

Sharon publicly questioned the American peace initiative and asserted bluntly that his ministry was about to embark on a massive settlement drive in Judea and Samaria to demonstrate Israel's determination to keep the occupied territories. Sharon's statements were soon followed by deeds. The building of new settlements, roads and infrastructure was tripled, even quadrupled. The scope and the intensity of the building was unprecedented.

There were some indications that Shamir felt uneasy at these independent initiatives of Sharon. But everyone was aware that a clash between Shamir and Sharon over the settlements could have brought down the government. Shamir's decision to back Sharon rather than openly challenging him reflected the prime minister's confidence in his own popularity at home and in America.

President Bush's decision to link his response to Israel's request for $10 billion in loan guarantees in connection with the costs of absorbing the massive Russian immigration loan guarantees to a settlement freeze surprised Shamir, but failed to produce a policy change. Israel's prime minister was deceived by the lack of vocal opposition at home to his intransigent stand. Furthermore, he failed to detect the growing anxiety within the country over the unexpected crisis with the United States. Shamir ignored the iron law of Israeli politics; never go to the polls with strained relations with the nation's greatest friend.

Perhaps the most serious consequence of Shamir's failure to secure the loan guarantees was its impact on the Russian immigrants. The guarantees became a symbol, a code word for successful absorption, indicating hope for economic recovery and new employment opportunities. By the autumn of 1991 the issue of employment had become the most pressing on the agenda of the Russian immigrants. Failure to secure the guarantees signalled a dead end and a hopeless future. Russian immigrants who seemed to have been massively pro-Likud upon arrival in Israel was already puzzled by the clerical nature of the Shamir government and its dependence on the ultra-Orthodox parties. Highly educated and secular, they had started to ask hard questions even before the crisis with the United States. Shamir's decision to sacrifice the loan guarantees for the sake of settlements appears to have tipped the scales. It led the majority of the immigrants to reject the Likud.

The term 'political settlement' was coined by Labour's leader, Yitzhak Rabin, in a rare moment of inspiration and it proved to be the explosive phrase of the campaign. 'Political settlements', he stressed to the Israeli public, were different from the 'strategic settlements' that were necessary for Israel's security, and it had been for the sake of the former, including settlements established purely for mystical reasons and irrelevant attachment to biblical lands, that the Likud had sacrificed the loan guarantees.

Rabin's 'political settlements' was a direct hit. It touched a raw nerve among the 250,000 adult Russian immigrants (equivalent to 12 Knesset seats), who felt deserted by the government. It also had an impact on many of the Likud's Sephardi supporters, the poor residents of development towns, and municipal slums. These voters turned to the Likud in the 1970s for social, psychological, and economic reasons. They have never been fully committed to the idea of the Greater Land of Israel. They, too, had been waiting for Israel's post-Gulf War recovery. Instead they were faced with a national unemployment rate of 11.5 per cent and a rate which was much higher in their towns and neighbourhoods.

The loss of the loan guarantees made it impossible for the Likud to minimize the significance of three additional pre-election blunders: the vicious struggle within the party for safe Knesset seats; the charges of corruption levelled by the State Comptroller; and the refusal to support electoral reform. The intra-Likud conflicts among the party's three camps (Shamir/Arens, Sharon, and Levy) started long before 1992, and had already produced a negative effect on the party's public image. But the situation deteriorated significantly in March 1992 with the selection of the party's Knesset candidates. The selection was made in a secret ballot in the party's 3300-member central committee. It was dominated by an open alliance between the Shamir/Arens and Sharon camps, which managed to exclude most of David Levy's supporters. Hurt and humiliated, Levy, Likud's most popular vote-getter among the Sephardi Jews, did not keep silent. Openly charging his colleagues with ethnic discrimination, Levy told his supporters all over the country that Likud had become a 'white' elitist party in which Sephardim did not have a chance. It took the sluggish Shamir three precious weeks to pacify Levy, by which time it was too late to extinguish the ethnic fire.

Likud corruption was also not a new issue and was no secret. Likud contenders even tried to recruit members of the central committee to their camps by advertising their ability to provide better jobs and lucrative positions. Likud corruption came under unprecedented fire, however, in the March 1992 report of Israel's highly respected State

Comptroller, Judge Miriam Ben-Porat. The devastating report, published just three months before the elections, charged several Likud officials with misuse of public funds and corruption. In certain cases the state attorney-general was asked to press criminal charges. For many supporters, the report was the final nail in the Likud coffin.

Likud's refusal to support electoral reform in Israel and the popular bill for the direct election of the prime minister also hurt the party. Hundreds of thousands of Israelis had demonstrated in the spring of 1990 against what they termed the 'blackmail politics' of the nation's small religious parties in selling their support for subsidies and other favours, and the refusal of the secular politicians to reform the electoral system. The bill for direct election of the prime minister became, irrespective of its controversial nature, a symbol of the struggle against corruption and for good government. The Labour Party challenged Shamir to compete against Rabin in direct elections. Shamir's rejection of the bill was nourished by many considerations, some of which were not personal. Indeed, several of the nation's top political scientists campaigned against the new bill, arguing that it could tear apart the delicate fabric of the state. But the public refused to be persuaded. Shamir's opposition was read as support of the corrupt status quo, and also as fear to confront the popular Rabin. Prominent Likud supporters of the bill, such as Binyamin Netanyahu and David Magen, failed to convince Shamir of its popularity. By the time the bill was finally passed in an amended version, with a provision that it would only be implemented in 1996, Shamir's image as a do-nothing, arch-conservative was firmly rooted. By the spring of 1992, within a year of his unprecedented popularity, Yitzhak Shamir had become Likud's greatest liability. There was no way he could win the election.

Out of Power: the Future of the Israeli Right

The 1992 electoral debacle of the Israeli right and Labour's return to power, have placed a large question mark over the future of the Israeli Right and the dream of Eretz Yisrael. If Yitzhak Rabin succeeds in making significant progress in the peace process, including a settlement freeze and the implementation of the Autonomy Plan for the Palestinians in the occupied territories, what will remain of the dream? Viewed from this perspective, Labour's victory is more than just a change in government. It may turn out to be a turning point, and lead to the marginalization of the Israeli right, similar to its experience between 1948 and 1967. To what extent is this likely to occur?

The first question we must address is: what kind of agreement with the Palestinians are the majority of Israelis ready to support? Three alternative answers can be forwarded. The first, offered by Labour and its left-wing ally Meretz, is that the Israelis have finally come to their senses and have decided to reject the mirage of Eretz Yisrael. Israelis may not be ready to return to the 1967 borders and accept a fully sovereign Palestinian state, but they would be willing to support a significant territorial compromise and accept the establishment of a Jordanian–Palestinian confederation, whereby the West Bank would be demilitarized. This has long been the position of the Labour Party and its acceptance by the Israeli public would mean the death knell for the Israeli right.

The second answer, advanced by the pragmatic right, is based on the belief that the Likud lost the election because of its corruption and internal divisions and not over the question of Eretz Yisrael. The pragmatists argue that Yitzhak Shamir should have been more flexible over the settlements, but they reject the idea of a territorial compromise and question the view that the majority of Israelis have adopted this stance. For them, any territorial compromise endangers the very survival of the State of Israel, and when the people return to their senses they will reject it categorically. The idea of Eretz Yisrael, according to this interpretation, is not dead, and if the Likud undergoes meaningful internal reform, it could easily regain power in 1996. Likud pragmatists, such as Binyamin Netanyahu, are already mobilizing to replace the old guard with this aim in mind.

The most extreme answer is provided by the radical right. For them the idea of Eretz Yisrael was not defeated in 1992, but, on the contrary, enhanced. Despite the failure of the Tehiya, the parties of the radical right, Moledet, Tzomet, and the National Religious Party (running on an extreme right-wing platform) increased their Knesset representation. It was the pragmatic right, not they, who lost the elections due to internal divisions and corruption on the one hand, and a diluted commitment to Eretz Yisrael on the other. The implementation of territorial compromise is not feasible. Jews and Arabs alike will ultimately reject it. The religious settlers are, of course, convinced that God would not permit an evacuation of Eretz Yisrael regardless of what the politicians might decide.

The future of the Israeli right depends to a large extent upon the

Rabin government. For, if the government makes significant headway in the peace process, the Likud and radical right have only limited means to halt its progress. The extreme right will undoubtedly try to subvert the process by extra-parliamentary, and even violent means, and will probably be supported by radical elements within the Likud. But success would make the government popular and difficult to defeat.

The elections left the Israeli right bruised and deeply divided, with the Likud in grave financial difficulties and facing a divisive contest for the party's leadership. The radical right emerged shocked psychologically, with internal schisms developing between radical and pragmatic settlers. This internal damage, to be sure, is not irreparable, but its healing requires time. This is to Rabin's advantage. If the prime minister acts decisively, he may succeed in achieving the peace treaty Israel has been seeking for 45 years, and thereby ensure another long stay in opposition for Israel's political right.

8. STRATEGIES OF MOBILIZATION AMONG THE ARABS IN ISRAEL

Majid Al-Haj

After the Arab–Israeli war of 1948 only 156,000 Arabs remained in Israel, amounting to 13 per cent of the total Israeli population. Those who did remain were a weak group, cut off from their kith and kin, who had become refugees in the Arab countries. Nearly all of the Palestinian Arab middle and upper classes – the urban land-owning mercantile, professional and religious elite – had left Israel. The vast majority, or 80 per cent of the Arab citizens, were villagers. The Arab urban population was almost totally evacuated as a result of war and the exodus. Only 6 per cent of the 200,000 Arabs who had formerly lived in cities remained after the war. In addition, some 20 per cent of the total Arab population of Israel had become 'internal refugees' having been forcibly moved to new communities after the destruction of their original villages during and immediately after the war.[1] Although Arabs are dispersed throughout Israel in seven cities, three towns and 148 villages, they are largely concentrated in three geo-cultural areas: Galilee, the Little Triangle and the Negev. About 85 per cent of them live in homogeneous Arab villages and towns with 15 per cent in seven mixed Jewish-Arab cities. However, even in those mixed localities, Arabs live in segregated neighbourhoods.

Since the 1950s the Arabs have undergone deep changes. Their number has quadrupled because of high fertility and decreasing mortality rates. In 1990 there were 710,000 Arabs in Israel (excluding East Jerusalem) constituting some 15.6 per cent of the country's total population. Of the Arabs 75 per cent are Sunni Muslims, 15 per cent Christians of several denominations and 10 per cent Druze. The Arabs in Israel have experienced a conspicuous modernization process in different areas. It is reflected in the rise in the level of education, improvements in the standard of living, the intensive politicization process, and social modernization in terms of attitudes and lifestyles.

While modernization has increased Arab aspirations for socio-economic mobility, the ethnic stratification in Israel has placed a mobility ceiling on them. The educational gap between Arabs and Jews, although it has decreased, is still wide. In 1990 the median length of schooling among the Arab population was 9.0 years as compared to 11.9 among Jews. While the proportion of Arabs in Israeli population is one in six, only one Arab in 60 occupies a senior government position.[2] Arabs are situated in the lower and middle classes. The rise in Arab standards of living has not diminished the gap between them and the Jewish population, which still exists in several areas and in some cases has widened.

The modernization process among Arabs in Israel has been interrupted by both internal and external factors. Arabs started from a very low point of development. The fact that Israel was created by Jews and for Jews placed Arabs outside of the process of modern nation-state building. The bond between the Israeli Arabs and the Arab world, particularly the Palestinians, seen against the background of a continuous state of war, has placed Arabs in Israel in a status of 'hostile minority'. This has strongly affected relations between Jews and Arabs, which one commentator has characterized as formal, asymmetric and leading to estrangement and tension.[3]

The national awakening, termed by some scholars as the 'Palestinization'[4], has been accompanied by an increasing tendency among Arab citizens to seek integration into Israeli society. The growing perception of the Arabs in Israel of their future as firmly linked to the State of Israel has in turn increased their attempts to participate in decision-making in regard to their own affairs, including the allocation of resources and the shaping of their political future.

The Palestinian *intifada* in the occupied territories has placed Israeli Arabs in a very disadvantageous position. It has highlighted their status as being on the periphery of both Israeli and Palestinian society alike. Expression of their support and identification with the *intifada*, albeit within the confines of law, is perceived by large segments of the Jewish public as anti-Israeli since they find it difficult to reconcile the divided loyalties of the Israeli Arabs – to their national group and to the state of Israel. However the Arabs in Israel have not actively participated in the *intifada*. They have rather emphasized the citizenship component in their identity, asserting that, even if a Palestinian state were established, they would not move to live there. This has shaken their national commitment in the eyes of their Palestinian brethren and further marginalized them in the Israeli–Palestinian conflict. They are perceived as a support group, with almost no say in the decision-making of the Palestinian National Movement.[5] Taking into consideration this background, what are the main forms of political organization among Arabs in Israel? What are the main factors that have affected over time the Arabs' political behaviour? Has social localization also resulted in political localization?

Mobilization through Parliamentary Politics
As citizens of Israel, the Arabs were from the outset granted the right to vote free, democratic elections for the Knesset. Nevertheless their share in the centre of national power has been restricted. The circumstances that prevailed among the Arab population in the aftermath of Israeli statehood facilitated the political localization of the Arab minority. At that time the lack of national leadership combined with low political consciousness among Arabs to furnish the base for traditional local leadership. The government's goal was to gain control over the entire population via a few key people, while simultaneously preserving internal divisions among Arabs so as to counteract the formation of a collective national identity or any affiliation with the left-wing parties.[6]

The military administration in the Arab-populated areas was used to suppress any nationalist trend among Arabs and help in the revival of the traditional leadership. The fact that Mapai (Labour Party) was the ruling party and controlled the military apparatus gave it a strong hold over Arab communities and a tremendous influence with Arab local authorities. The military administration excluded any local leadership which showed resistance to the establishment. In many cases new *mukhtars* (community leaders) were created in addition to those already serving, so as to foster a new leadership and in turn increase the competition between the various factions and reinforce the trend of co-operation with the authorities.[7]

At the national level, the Arabs' participation in party politics were minimal. They were not eager to join existing parties and to enter nationwide politics but the main reason was the lack of any political organization which could have appealed to Arab citizens. Arabs were not accepted as members in the Zionist parties nor could they identify with the basic ideology of those parties. Arab-affiliated lists were one of the most efficient instruments of channelling Arab votes, in particular until the late 1960s. These lists were initiated and backed by Zionist parties, mainly the Labour Party which was the principal force in the Israeli establishment until 1977. The purpose of these lists was not the political mobilization of the Arab population, but rather the catching of Arab votes through traditional means of persuasion. The structure of the Arab-affiliated lists was tailored to fit the deep social territorialization of the Arab population and its traditional character. They were designed to include candidates who represented the main divisions among the Arab population: by geographic region, religious group, prominent *hamulas* (extended kinship groups) and large Arab localities.[8]

Until the Knesset elections in 1969 the affiliated lists with the Labour Party were the main political framework for Israel's Arab minority. In the 1951 election they received 55 per cent of the Arab votes cast and even in 1969 as much as 40 per cent (see Table 1).

In the early 1970s the Arab-affiliated lists within the Labour Party decreased in strength and by the tenth Knesset election in 1981 none of them was represented in the Knesset. Since then the affiliated lists have disappeared from the national political scene and the Zionist parties have, without exception, sought to compete in their own right for the Arab vote. Their approach toward the Arab population has been paternalistic and based on individual interests. Hence, they sought to gain influence through local *hamula* heads and notables. By doing so, they minimized their costs and maximized their gains.

Initially, the Zionist parties sought Arab votes without accepting them as party members. It was not until 1954 that Mapam became the first party to open its doors to Arabs and integrate them into its activities. However, the fact that Mapam, through its partnership in the Labour Alignment until 1984, was identified with the establishment impeded its activities among the Arab minority.

Maki, the Israeli Communist Party, was the only non-Zionist party with which the Arabs could identify. Indeed, this party began its activities among the Arabs during the British rule, earlier than any other party. Voting for the Communist Party has been a symbol of protest at two levels. At national level it has for a long time channelled the feelings of frustration and resentment of the Arab population against the government's policies.[9] At local level it has absorbed the protest of the younger generation and peripheral groups in the Arab

Table 1 Arab vote for the Knesset 1949–92

	ARAB VOTERS (percentage)		BREAKDOWN OF ARAB VOTE (percentage)				
Knesset	Arab voters as percentage of total	Voting turnout	Communist Party		Arab Lists Affiliated with Labour	Labour	Total of Zionist Parties
First 1949	6.6	79	22	—	28	10	—
Second 1951	7.5	86	16	—	55	11	26
Third 1955	8.2	90	15	—	48	14	23
Fourth 1959	7.9	85	11	—	42	10	26
Fifth 1961	8.3	83	22	—	40	20	29
Sixth 1965	8.6	82	23	—	38	13	27
Seventh 1969	8.4	80	28	—	40	17	27
Eighth 1973	8.5	77	37	—	27	13	29
Ninth 1977	8.9	74	*DFPE* 50	—	16	11	21
Tenth 1981	9.8	68	37	—	12	29	45
Eleventh 1984	10.4	72	32	*PLP* 18		26	50.4
Twelfth 1988	12.0	74	34	*ADP* 14	11	17	42
Thirteenth 1992	11.8	69.7	23.2	9.2	15.2	20.3	52.3

The 1992 results are based on Sarah Ozacky-Lazar, The 13th Knesset Elections among the Arabs in Israel, Review no 9, Givaat Haviva: The Institute for Arab Studies. Source: Based on Majid Al-Haj and Henry Rosenfeld. 1990. *Arab Local Government in Israel*. Boulder: Westview Press, p. 71.

villages against the traditional local leadership and the prominent *hamulas*.

Since the early 1970s several factors have intensified the Arabs' politicization and increased their tendency to take part in the competition over the national power system. The modernization process experienced by Arabs in Israel has increased their political consciousness, including an awareness of their potential power and of the democratic means available to them for the promotion of their interests. The growing proportion of Arabs in the electorate as a result of high fertility and changes in the age structure, has increased their political value. In the 1992 Knesset elections Israeli Arabs constituted some 12 per cent of the total number of eligible voters, thereby attracting intense competition between the right and left wings for their support.

The abolition of the military government and the growing accessibility of the Jewish population have facilitated contact between Arabs and the Jewish centre. Improved levels of education and the growing number of the younger generation have increased the awareness of the Arabs of the rules of the 'political game' and have reduced the power of traditional methods of persuasion. In the early 1970s a strong national awakening was observed among the Arab minority in Israel, which was brought about by the renewed contact between the Arabs in Israel and their brethren in the West Bank and Gaza after the Six Day War of 1967; the rise of the Palestinian National Movement and the increasing international recognition of the PLO; and the outcome of the Yom Kippur War in 1973, which boosted the feelings of dignity among the Arab minority.

The government and the political parties alike have attempted to absorb and utilize this new trend among the Arab population. Israeli officials view it as worrisome and have sought to localize national feelings and to channel them into questions of citizenship and daily life. The Israeli government declared its intentions to improve the conditions of the Arab population and to speed up its integration. To achieve this, several ministerial committees were set up to investigate the services offered to the Arab population. The Ministry of Education formed the Peled Committee for the planning of Arab education towards the 1980s, the Ministry of Interior established the Geraisy Committee to investigate local services and municipal budgets in the Arab localities; the prime minister's adviser for Arab Affairs initiated research into the situation of Arab university graduates and their possible absorption into government offices; and a policy-oriented research body examined the planning of housing aid for Arab villages. In the aftermath of the Land Day strike on 3 March 1976, when Arab demonstrators were killed in clashes, a special ministerial committee was formed to deal with the needs of Arab citizens.

The Communist Party sought to utilize the new changes in the orientation of Arab citizens to expand its own base. It tried to fill the gap resulting from the diminishing power of the traditional Arab leadership, with the object of becoming the sole representative of the Arab population. In this sense the party started to establish itself as the 'informal establishment' among the Arab minority in Israel. For this purpose the Communist Party initiated a number of extra-parliamentary Arab organizations, and in 1977 it established a wider Arab-Jewish party called the Democratic Front for Peace and Equality (DFPE). In addition to the Communist party leadership, the DFPE included non-communist Arab and Jewish public figures. Backed by the PLO and Palestinian national leadership in the West Bank and Gaza, the DFPE gained a sweeping victory in the 1977 Knesset elections, receiving about 50 per cent of all the Arab votes cast.[10]

The structure of the DFPE has been repeatedly criticized by some of its non-communist Arab partners. The first signs of split occurred in Nazareth when some of the university graduates broke away after a dispute with the communists over the control of the party. This breakaway faction, the Progressive Movement in Nazareth, ran in the 1983 municipal elections and won 20 per cent of the vote.[11] Encouraged, it sought to increase its effect on a national scale. It established the Progressive List for Peace (PLP) together with a Jewish group called 'Alternative'. This list was the main competitor for the DFPE in the 1984 Knesset elections and won 18 per cent of the Arab vote. Since then, however, its popularity has been in decline. Its support fell to 14 per cent in 1988 and to 9.2 per cent in the 1992 election.

The main competition among the Arab population in the 1988 Knesset election was between the three predominantly Arab parties: the DFPE, PLP and the newly formed Arab Democratic Party (ADP). Having similar political platforms, they based their dispute, to a large extent, on issues of personality. Although, altogether, they secured about 60 per cent of the Arab votes, they may well have thrown away two seats by failing to form an agreement between them for the division of the residual votes.[12] This outcome outraged many Arab voters, who demanded that the parties minimize their disputes and establish a framework for cooperation. This pressure accelerated the formation of the joint Jewish-Arab list for the 1989 Histadrut elections. However, the list, which for the first time included representatives from all three predominantly Arab parties, was limited in its appeal and received the support of only 35 per cent of Arab members.

The Zionist parties' traditional tactic was to argue that only through the mainstream parties would the Arabs be able to promote their case. This approach was mainly adopted by the Labour Party. The National Religious Party (*Mafdal*) was able to exploit its long-standing control of the Ministry of the Interior and the Ministry of Religious Affairs to pick up some support in the Arab communities because of their administration of subsidies and favours through the channels of the traditional leadership.[13] The Likud, unlike the other Zionist parties, sought from the outset to focus its efforts on two particular groups: the Druze and the Bedouin. The Labour Party maintained its position as the central Zionist party among the Arabs, despite its gradual decline after the 1981 Knesset elections. In 1981 it received 29 per cent of the Arab votes, in 1984 this figure fell to 26 per cent and by 1988 it was as low as 17 per cent. The 1988 election was held in the shadow of the Palestinian *intifada*, and, in particular, the role of the Labour Minister of Defence, Yitzhak Rabin, in repressing the *intifada* severely weakened the standing of the Labour Party in the Arab sector. Despite this, the party has been able to regain its power among the Arab population. In the 1989 Histadrut elections it received 43.3 per cent and in the 1992 Knesset election just over a fifth (20.3 per cent) of the Arab vote.

As a result of the gradual decline of the Arab-affiliated lists, Labour has sought since the early 1980s to include Arab candidates directly in its list for the Knesset elections. Indeed, two Arab Knesset members were elected through the Labour slate in the 1981 and 1984 elections, and one in 1988. In the recent Knesset election the Labour Party attempted to satisfy all religious groups among the Arabs. For this purpose it placed a Muslim candidate in position number 20, a Druze in number 30 and a Christian Arab in number 46, the latter missing election since the Labour Party received only 44 mandates.

In the 1988 election, the left-wing Zionist party, Ratz (the Civil Rights Movement), quadrupled its support among Arab voters from 1 to 4 per cent, and Mapam, now running as a separate list from Labour, received nearly 4 per cent of the Arab vote. In the 1989 Histadrut elections Ratz received 7.2 per cent and Mapam 8.6 per cent of the Arab votes. In the last Knesset election Ratz, Mapam and Shinui forming a joint Zionist-Left bloc under the name of Meretz, received about 10 per cent of the Arab vote, which was roughly equivalent to the total that the three lists received in 1988.

In the 1992 election over 50 per cent of the Arab vote was given directly to Jewish-Zionist parties, mostly to the Labour Party and to Meretz, its future coalition partner. This pattern of voting displays strong evidence that Arab citizens sought to affect directly the political system in Israel and to replace the Likud as the governing party. Among the predominantly Arab parties only the Arab Democratic Party increased its vote, rising from 11 per cent in 1988 to 15 per cent in 1992. The DFPE dropped from 34 to 23 per cent and the PLP from 14 per cent to about 9 per cent. As a result the DFPE fell from four to three seats and the PLP failed to gain any seats. Despite the politicization of the Arab miniority and its eagerness for political integration in the national political system, the Arabs remain without a share of national power. This has led to a growing process of political localization.

It has been repeatedly emphasized that formal policy towards the Arabs in Israel is directed by three main considerations: the democratic principle, the Jewish-Zionist principle, and security concerns. While the first drives towards equality and integration of Arabs, the other two pull in the opposite direction. When these features are juxtaposed, it is clear that Jewish-Zionist and security considerations have gained the upper hand. As a result, Arabs have only 'partial membership' in Israeli society.[14] They are excluded from the main national organizations in Israel and from its core political culture. While the non-Zionist ultra-Orthodox parties are considered legitimate partners in the government coalition, the Arab parties are not.[15]

In 1988 the predominantly Arab parties took an unprecedented step towards becoming a legitimate partner in the establishment. They declared their willingness to participate in a coalition formed by Labour and the other leftist Zionist parties under certain conditions. The required conditions, such as a commitment to the promotion of the peace process with the Palestinians and equality for Arab citizens in Israel, were not specific, and were subscribed to by the leftist Zionist parties during their electoral campaign among the Arab population. Darawshe, the head of the ADP, had gone further in his pragmatic approach. Throughout his electoral campaign he emphasized his intention of being included in the political consensus in Israel as a legitimate partner with Zionist parties.

In response to the pragmatic tendency of the predominantly Arab parties, the Zionist parties, including Labour and its allies, have never offered them any chance of becoming a legitimate partner in a coalition government. Instead, Labour has counted on their support in blocking the possibility that the Likud might form a coalition. The formation of the National Unity governments (1984–90), bringing together Labour and Likud, further weakened the bargaining power of the predominantly Arab parties. The manoeuvring power of these parties is very limited. Unlike the Jewish Orthodox parties, their potential partnership is limited to the left-wing parties led by Labour. After the fall of the unity government in March 1990, small parties proved to be of crucial importance in deciding the balance between the Likud and Labour. This situation should have given the Arab parties a boost, but once again Labour counted on their support 'from the outside', and not as integral partners. The religious parties with whom Labour were negotiating expressed opposition to a coalition dependent on the Arab parties. The same trend continued after the 1992 election. Neither the DFPE nor the ADP was asked to participate in the government led by the Labour party, although both have supported it in the Knesset from outside the coalition.

Political localization of the Arab minority is also affected by the nature of Arab–Jewish relations in Israel. Most of the interpersonal relations between Arabs and Jews are formal, technical, and of a minority–majority character. This asymmetry is also reflected in the political sphere. While large-scale well-organized Jewish parties and associations have continuously penetrated the Arab minority, there has been no corresponding effective penetration of the Jewish majority by the predominantly Arab parties. Despite the fact that the leadership of the DFPE and the PLP has been almost equally divided between Jews and Arabs, the support they have received from the Jewish population has been negligible. Upon the formation of the joint list in the 1989 Histadrut elections, the DFPE insisted that a Jewish member of the Communist Party chair the list. This decreased the list's popularity among the Arab population without bearing any fruit from Jewish voters.

Since the Likud came to power in 1977, a more pragmatic approach may be noted among the leadership of the predominantly Arab parties. The fear from the expansion of the right-wing parties has driven the

DFPE and later the PLP into co-operation with Labour to support its candidates against those nominated by the Likud or other right-wing parties. Such was the case of the election of Shlomo Hillel, the Labour candidate, as Speaker of the Knesset in 1984.

Although political localization is mainly imposed on the Arab minority in Israel, some Arab political groups have voluntarily refrained from participation in parliamentary politics and have established themselves as extra-parliamentary organizations. Most prominent among them are *Abna el-Balad* (the Sons of the Land) and the Islamic Movement. Having rejected the right of Israel to exist as a Zionist-Jewish state, Abna el-Balad has repeatedly declared that the Israeli parliament and its elections are considered illegitimate. But it has not succeeded yet in expanding its base and, for the time being, it has been a marginal group even in local Arab politics.[16] Unlike Abna el-Balad, the Islamic Movement has been much more powerful among the Arab population. While participating in local politics, the Islamic Movement has refused so far to take part in the parliamentary elections. Its stand towards the Histadrut elections of 1989 was initially vague. Eventually, the Movement made it clear that Muslims should not vote for non-Muslim candidates. Thus, while abstaining from voting from the general assembly of the Histadrut, they did vote for the Muslim slates which competed for the local Labour councils in Taibe and Nazareth.

The behaviour of the Islamic Movement only a month before the 1992 Knesset election reflected its ill-defined stand towards Israeli parliamentary politics. It declared that it would not run or support a specific list, but at the same time it called upon its followers to utilize their right to vote.[17] Despite this statement some leaders of the Islamic Movement had clear doubts about the efficacy of parliamentary politics for Arabs, and in most localities controlled by the Islamic Movement, the turn-out at the polls was lower than for other Arab localities.

Mobilization through Local Politics

Upon the establishment of Israel in 1948 there were only three Arab localities with local councils that originated in the British Mandate. During the next decade, the Israeli authorities took the first steps towards establishing local authorities in the Arab settlements. Mandatory Arab local authorities were reactivated. In addition, eight local authorities were set up in the large Arab villages in the northern and central regions. The request of Arab communities for municipalization increased steadily to the point where today two-thirds of Arab settlements are administered by local authorities.[18] This includes three municipalities (towns), 58 local councils, and 38 regional councils.

According to Israeli policy-makers the purpose of these authorities is to improve the level of services and to give the Arab population an opportunity to increase their involvement in running their internal affairs. But there was the further intention of establishing relations between the Arab population and the central government, as well as creating a 'safety valve' for the feelings of frustration aroused by the sudden transformation from the status of majority to that of minority.[19]

The importance of local government for the Arab population has gradually increased. It has now become the central political mechanism and the most important means of mobilizing the Arab minority in Israel. Several factors have contributed to this. Taking the political localization of the Arab population into consideration, local government has become the only political framework in which Arabs appear to have a direct impact. The legal impossibility of establishing openly Arab nationalist political parties increases the value of local politics as a means for organizing on a nationalist basis. Many localized Arab political organizations view the municipal system as the only official framework which does not contradict their ideology, while, for the parliamentary parties, involvement in local politics has a major impact on the votes that they may receive in the Knesset elections. Party links with local leadership have proved to be of major importance for political recruitment.

The paucity of local economic resources among the Arab population, as a result of its dependency on the Jewish centre, further increases the importance of local government as a channel for the allocation of resources and benefits. The failure of government ministries to hire Arab university graduates forces them to compete for jobs in their own communities. Local government is a main employer and the projects carried out by the municipalities are an important source of livelihood for Arab contractors and entrepreneurs.

Since the mid-1960s conspicuous changes have occurred in local politics. The system has become politicized and local concerns have been coupled simultaneously with national issues. The political campaign in the local elections of 1989 was of special interest. Many of the slates in those elections were directly backed by parliamentary parties or Arab extra-parliamentary organizations. As a result the

Table 2   Results of the Local Election for Mayor in the Arab Settlements by Party Affiliation of 1983 and 1989.*

Political Affiliation	1983	1989
DFPE	20	14
Labour Party	14	4
Likud	3	1
Islamic Movement	1	5
Arab Democratic Party	—	3
PLP	—	2
Civil Rights Movement (Ratz)	—	2
Independent	12	14
	50	45

* The table relates only to the settlements in which elections were conducted, including Druze local authorities.

disputes among the political parties in the Knesset elections were transferred to local politics.

The rise in the power of the Islamic Movement may be one of the most salient features of recent local elections. While in the 1983 elections only one of the elected mayors was affiliated with the Islamic Movement, in the 1989 elections it gained the mayoralty in five local authorities and was represented in the local councils of another nine settlements. One of its most important achievements was in Umm el-Fahim, the second largest Arab town in Israel. The former mayor, affiliated with the communist DFPE, was replaced by the candidate of the Islamic Movement who received 75 per cent of the vote (see Table 2).

While in 1983, 20 of the elected mayors were affiliated with the DFPE, this number declined to 14 in the 1989 elections. As a result, the status of the DFPE among the Arab population was shaken. The impetus gained by the Islamic Movement has turned it into the main competitor of the DFPE in the Arab sector. Indeed, in the municipal elections held in Kabul, in Galilee, in 1991, the Islamic Movement came to power beating the two candidates from the Labour Party and the DFPE. These elections are significant since Kabul was the first locality in the Galilee to be controlled by the Islamic Movement. The elections which took place in Baqa el-Ghabiych in May 1992 provide another example of the power of this movement. In the first round none of the candidates achieved the 40 per cent of the vote needed to win the mayoralty, which gave the Islamic Movement the chance of determining the contest by throwing its support to the eventual winner.

The PLP ran in the 1989 elections and gained the mayoralty of Arabi, one of the largest Arab villages in Galilee. It also has seats in a number of official councils. Encouraged by its success in the Knesset elections, the Arab Democratic Party now sought to penetrate Arab local politics and won the three mayoralties.

The main loser in the 1989 elections was the Labour Party. Only four mayors affiliated with the party were elected, as opposed to 14 in the 1983 elections. These results are consistent with the dramatic decrease in the power of the Labour Party among the Arab population in the twelfth Knesset elections of 1988. On the other hand, two of the Zionist parties further to the left, Mapam and the Ratz, used the momentum gained in the same parliamentary elections to increase their holding in Arab settlements. Ratz candidates captured the mayoralties in two Arab villages while Mapam candidates were elected as members in a couple of Arab local councils.

The partisan identification of Arab mayors, however, is not always straightforward. Those affiliated with the DFPE are usually more committed to their party and well-organized as a distinct group. Some of the so-called independent mayors are informally linked to one party or another. The 'independent' status allows them to manoeuvre and, if needed, to shift alliances in order to maximize their gains. Therefore the results of the local and the national elections do not necessarily coincide, though they are interrelated. In the former, local factors such as the kinship affiliation of the candidates and intergroup competition are important, whereas in parliamentary elections they are more limited.[20]

Mobilization through Extra-Parliamentary National Organizations

Since the mid-1970s the Arabs in Israel have started to develop an important network of extra-parliamentary organizations. The National Committee for Heads of Arab Local Authorities has become the major representative of the Arabs in Israel. Interestingly, upon its foundation in 1974, it gained the sympathy and even the support of the central government. By encouraging the creation of this committee, it is reasonable to assume that the authorities aimed at channelling the national awakening among Arabs into local issues as well as creating a counter-balance to the growing power of the Communist Party.

However, the co-operation between the National Committee and the authorities did not last. Whereas originally, the founders of the committee focused solely on local services, after the first Land Day Strike in 1976 they shifted their emphasis to citizenship and national questions, recognizing that these issues are inseparable.

Aside from budget allocations, the National Committee was involved in issues such as planning, construction and land in the Arab settlements, industralization of the Arab sector, and the development of local services. Several times, differences over these issues led to serious confrontations with governmental agencies, which were sometimes prolonged and accompanied by strikes. Only in rare instances did these strikes meet with understanding on the part of the government. In most cases the latter insisted that these actions were unjustified and politically motivated.

As a way of building its struggle on a more sophisticated basis, the National Committee established a network of professional committees for specific areas. The first was the Follow-up Committee for Arab Education composed of Arab academics, educationalists, students, mayors, and representatives of several public bodies dealing with education. Since its foundation in 1984, this committee has been in charge of the negotiations with the ministry of education and the other official bodies concerned for the promotion of the Arab education system. It has focused on changes in the aims and the curriculum of Arab education, which has been deprived of any Arab-Palestinian national content. In 1986 a special conference was held in Nazareth to deal with the situation of health services in the Arab settlements. A Follow-up Committee of Arab physicians, professionals and public figures was set up in its wake to trace the implementation of its recommendations and to lobby for the improvement of medical and health services for Arab citizens. In 1987 a third professional committee was founded by the National Committee to deal with social services in Arab localities. Since its formation it has led the negotiations with government officials for the improvement of the welfare services and has organized the campaign among Arab citizens against drug abuse and youth delinquency.

Since the mid-1980s there has been a process of semi-institutionalization of the National Committee. In 1984 it issued its political guidelines, which have become the cornerstone of the consensus among the Arabs in Israel regarding the national and citizenship issues.

The Arab masses in Israel are an integral part of the Palestinian Arab nation, and it is important for them that to realize their legitimate national rights ... At the same time, the conference emphasizes that the masses of Arabs in Israel are an integral part of the state, that they share a common fate with the Jewish masses in Israel in a common homeland . . .[21]

The National Committee, aided by the Follow-up committees, made tangible achievements concerning services and budget allocations to Arab communities. While in the 1970s the average ratio between the budgets of the Jewish and the Arab localities was 13:1, this decreased to 2.5:1 in the 1980s. Educational, health and social services have been also improved, although they still do not meet the expectations of the Arab population.[22] Equally important, these committees have emerged as a unifying power among the Arab population. Furthermore, the National Committee has become the only body capable of speaking in the name of the Arab citizens and authorized to decide on their nationwide policies. This, in turn, has created considerable competition among the different Arab political groups over its control. Some groups, in particular Abna el-Balad and the Islamic Movement, complained of their non-representation. In order to overcome these disputes, the National Committee was expanded in 1987 to become the 'Supreme Surveillance Committee of Arab Affairs', composed of all representatives of the public bodies and political parties including Arabs affiliated to Zionist parties.

The Supreme Committee and the bodies participating in it are often described as the 'parliament of the Arabs in Israel' and the 'institutions of autonomy'. Since its formation the Supreme Committee has led a number of demonstrations and general strikes as a means of mobilizing the Arab population over citizenship and national issues. Central among them are: the 'Day of Equality' (24 June 1987); the 'Day of Peace' (21 December 1987); the 'Day of Housing' (15 November 1988), in addition to the annual commemoration of the 'Land Day'.

Conclusion
The Arabs in Israel are a disadvantaged national minority confronted with contradictory agencies of citzenship and national identification. Over time they have experienced a conspicuous modernization process accompanied by deep politicization. This has brought a shift in the

political behaviour of the Arab population: from passive participation and the politics of protest to a sophisticated organization guided by pragmatic considerations. The political organization of the Arabs has reflected a competition between a strategy of integration and a strategy of segregation. The first expresses itself in parliamentary politics, while the second is embodied in local politics and extra-parliamentary organizations.

Parliamentary politics has the advantage of being the only political framework shared by Jews and Arabs in Israel, on an apparently equal basis. It offers the Arabs the potential to translate their demographic size into political power and affect the distribution of national power. The balance between the right-wing and left-wing blocks increases the importance of the Arab vote in determining this distribution. However, several internal and external factors have combined to block the potential power of Israel's Arabs and marginalize their status in the national political scene. The Arabs are politically fragmented. They have failed so far to form a united Arab list. In addition, some Arab political movements, such as the Islamic Movement and Abna-el-Balad, have ideological objections to participating in parliamentary politics. The asymmetry of Jewish–Arab relations is also reflected in national politics, where Arabs are excluded from the national consensus and not considered a legitimate partner in government coalition. As a result, the returns from parliamentary politics have so far been negligible for Arabs.

This has increased the importance of the strategy of segregation, reflected by local politics and extra-parliamentary organizations. Here, the Arabs have several advantages. Arabs do not have to compete with the Jewish majority in local elections, since, except for mixed Jewish-Arab cities (where only 10 per cent of Arabs live), all other localities where Arabs live are homogeneous and therefore controlled by them. Local government has thus become the only political system which Arabs control directly. Through extra-parliamentary organizations, Arabs have been able to utilize their increasing politicization and overcome their political fragmentation to form an efficient pressure group for citizens' rights and national issues. As a flexible framework, these organizations have given Arabs the chance to maximize their bargaining power and minimize Jewish control.

On this analysis it is reasonable to suppose that the importance of the strategy of segregation will increase. The parliamentary elections of 1992 have given an impetus to this trend. Once again Arab parties have been excluded from the government, even though it is a coalition led by the Labour Party with the participation of the Zionist left. But this does not mean that parliamentary politics have been exhausted in the eyes of the Arabs. It is safe to say that, precisely because of this marginalization, the Arab public will increase the pressure on its leadership to form a united Arab list so as to participate in future Knesset elections from a position of strength. But, at the same time, it seems certain that the Arabs in Israel will want to reorganize and reinforce their extra-parliamentary organizations.

PART THREE
Issues in Israeli Society

9. JEWISH ETHNICITY IN ISRAEL

Sammy Smooha

At its forty-fourth birthday – 14 May 1992 – Israel's Jewish population numbered 4.2 million, hailing from over one hundred countries. This considerable ethnic diversity reflects two thousand years of dispersion of the Jewish people. Zionism set forth the vision of the amalgamation of exiles after their ingathering in the land of Israel. Yet, despite one hundred years of Jewish settlement and integration, ethnicity has not vanished and Israel is still facing a Jewish ethnic problem.

The main ethnic division is between Jews originating from Muslim and Christian lands. Lumped together as 'Orientals' or 'Sephardim' (Spanish) the former include Jews from the Near East, North Africa, Yemen, Ethiopia, the Balkans, Iran, India and the Muslim republics of the former Soviet Union.[1] The latter, known as 'Ashkenazim', tracing their roots to Germany and to the Yiddish language which developed there, include most of the Jews of Europe and America (who themselves came mainly from Eastern Europe).

In 1992 Orientals and Ashkenazim were, thanks to the strengthening of the Ashkenazim by the large immigration from the former Soviet Union, divided roughly 50:50 in Israel, but abroad the proportion is 5:95 (only 500,000 of the 9.5 million Jews in the Diaspora are Oriental or Sephardi). Ashkenazim have enjoyed clear dominance among the Jewish people in the modern era. They constituted 92 per cent of world Jewry at the turn of the century, 90 per cent of the immigrants to Palestine during the 1919–47 period and around 80 per cent of the Jews in Palestine in 1947. They established the Zionist movement, settled Palestine and founded the State of Israel. Their dominance was ideological, political and socio-economic. On the other hand, the Orientals' mass immigration during the 1950s and their high birthrate won them a numerical majority by the mid-1960s. It is the contrast between demographic strength and social disadvantage that has made Oriental status problematic in Israel and drawn attention to it as an unrelenting source of internal conflict.[2]

Class

There is ample evidence to document the wide ethnic inequalities. To begin with, Ashkenazim have a decided advantage in education. In 1990 they had on average 1.4 more years of schooling than Orientals. More telling are the disparities at the extremes of the educational scale: Orientals are clearly disadvantaged, in their relatively high rate of illiteracy and in their relatively low rate of college education.[3] The discrepancy in college education is staggering. Only 16.5 per cent of Oriental *sabras* (Jews born in Israel), as compared with as many as 56.0 per cent of the Ashkenazi sabras, have received a college education.[4]

The gap has somewhat narrowed over the years as a result of the attrition of 'the generation of the desert' and compulsory education up to the tenth grade. School attendance in 1981/2 of youth aged 14–17 was as high as 79.2 per cent among Orientals and 84.2 per cent among Ashkenazim.[5] The ethnic gap in education has passed on to the Israeli-born generation. It is evident that while Ashkenazi *sabras* overtake their parents, Oriental *sabras* do as badly as theirs did. Despite the doubling of the student population at the universities after 1967 and all the programmes to boost Oriental attendance, Ashkenazim have maintained a lead of four to one.

The ethnic educational gap will be greater than shown in these figures because of the lower quality of Oriental education. There is a substantial discrepancy in the performance of Oriental and Ashkenazi schoolchildren on various achievement tests, including IQ.[6] High-school education for two-thirds of the Ashkenazi graduates means an academic track leading to college, whereas for two-thirds of their Oriental counterparts it is terminal vocational schooling. The best summary measure reflecting the cumulative ethnic inequality in the educational system is the proportion of recipients of matriculation diplomas from among a certain year of first-graders. Of pupils who attended the first grade in 1977/8, only 25 per cent of the Orientals as compared to 46 per cent of Ashkenazim went on to receive matriculation diplomas in 1988/9. Of even greater significance is the persistent disparity in higher education which determines the future position of the two ethnic groups in the economy. Studies show that the chances of Orientals completing an academic high school and attending university are lower than those of Christian or even Muslim Arabs.[7]

The failure of the educational system to close the ethnic gap in the quantity and quality of education is caused partly by cultural differences but mostly by class discrepancies. Despite all the efforts to advance the Oriental schoolchildren, the curriculum is still not really geared to serve them. Although special budgets are invested in schools for 'the culturally disadvantaged,' the pupils in these schools are still lacking the quality of teachers and enrichment programmes received by Ashkenazim in better-off areas. Poor and working-class children get much less by way of educational resources from the family, peer group and neighbourhood than middle- and upper-class children.

These divergences in education are manifested in the occupational structure. Among the foreign-born, Ashkenazim were twice as likely as Orientals (40.5 per cent to 20.3 per cent) to reach the three top occupational categories (professionals, managers and technicians) in 1990; among the Israeli-born, the disparity was even wider (49.4 per cent to 20.8 per cent). Since high-school education expanded dramatically in the 1960s to include the majority of youth from both communities, it was greatly devalued as a preparation for white-collar jobs and hence its spread failed to close the ethnic gap.[8] The upgrading of educational qualifications for high-status jobs has had the effect of pushing some Orientals into alternative, less structured but more lucrative channels, such as sports, entertainment, and small businesses (such as subcontractors, taxicabs, small garages and popular restaurants).

There is also considerable ethnic inequality in the standard of living, but the disparity is less than in education and employment. In Israel in 1988, an average Asian-African household head earned 82 per cent of the income of a European-American one, but only 67 per cent per capita.[9] Ashkenazim also live much more comfortably.[10] On the other hand, durable goods have become standard and the ethnic differences can be seen only in brands and models.

The most crucial material gulf between the two ethnic groups lies in the quantity and accumulation of wealth. Although research is lacking on this key point, it is reasonable to assume that the reasons why Ashkenazim enjoy a decided advantage include their head start as old-timers, their benefit from German reparations, their residence in the better neighbourhoods where the value of property has gone up sharply, and their smaller families which are conducive to a greater capital-accumulation per capita.

These diverse ethnic gaps taken together create a system of ethnic stratification. In the Jewish population the poor and working classes are predominantly Oriental, the middle stratum is ethnically mixed with some Ashkenazi over-representation, and the upper-middle class and elite are predominantly Ashkenazi. This structure is stable and self-perpetuating as implied by the passing on of ethnic inequality from the foreign- to the Israeli-born generation.

What are the factors accounting for the persistence of ethnic stratification in Israel? Looming largest among them are the normal class mechanisms of perpetuation found in any industrial society. Although social mobility is common in industrial societies, it is normal for most families to manage, through upbringing and inheritance, to bequeath their status to their offspring. Despite the openness of the society, the selection of friends, neighbours, classmates and marital partners is largely determined by social class. Given the historical overlap in Israel between class and ethnicity, the persistence of the ethno-class structure there should be considered a normal phenomenon.

Secondly, ethnic differences in family background reinforce ethnically structured inequality. The present young generation of Orientals were raised in large and not well-to-do families, where parents did not have much to offer their children. The opposite is true for the Ashkenazi *sabra* who enjoy, throughout their lives, the better resources of the smaller families in which they were brought up. Since the norm in Israel is life-long support by parents of their children, Orientals are thereby at a continuing disadvantage. This factor is expected to diminish in the future because family size among the Israeli-born varies only slightly according to ethnicity, but for the time being it carries a strong impact.

Thirdly, ethnic inequality persists simply by default because the numerous programmes aimed at closing the ethnic gap fall short of effective intervention. The more universalist among them are welfare policies designed to help large families, the needy and distressed neighbourhoods. More specific programmes are in the area of compensatory education for Orientals (who are referred to as 'culturally disadvantaged'). These measures are effective in preventing ethnic inequality from increasing but not in reducing it over time. Nor are they a substitute for a comprehensive social policy or a programme of affirmative action.[11]

How did the present ethnic stratification arise? By the time of the proclamation of the state, Ashkenazim were firmly established as the dominant group. They constituted the majority and mainstay of society from the working class through to the elite. On the other hand, the Orientals were a small, weak and poor community with a tiny Sephardi elite. During Israel's first decade there was mass immigration, almost equally divided between Jews from Eastern Europe and Jews from the Middle East. The government was faced at the time with a host of equally urgent problems: increasing the size of the army, industrializing the economy and tying it to the world market, settling the areas seized during the 1948 war so as to curb international pressure to withdraw from them, and expanding services (education, health and welfare) to cater to the needs of the swelling population. The state's efforts to deal with these exigencies affected differently the old-timers, the Ashkenazi immigrants and the Oriental immigrants. The old-timers experienced a sudden mass mobility. A large proportion of them moved up from the working to the middle class. Some became professionals, managers and small businessmen, while others took advantage of state subsidies to become entrepreneurs and industrialists or to expand their existing enterprises. They were able to seize upon the new openings due to their special strengths: knowledge of Hebrew, better education, accumulated assets and affinity to the elite and decision-makers.

The Ashkenazi new arrivals did not at first fare especially well, but after a transition period they managed to escape their initial dire conditions, and succeeded in entering the middle and higher classes thanks to their advantageous social networks, small families, personal reparations from Germany and self and public image as Europeans.

The mobility of Ashkenazim was, however, to a large extent predicated on the channelling of Oriental newcomers to the lower rungs of society. Most were housed in temporary accommodation in localities where services were bad. A good many were sent to new development towns in remote areas, with dead-end jobs and where unemployment ran high. Those who were assigned to build new *moshavim* (co-operative farms) received insufficient means and quotas of production and could not compete on an equal footing with the prosperous veteran *moshavim*. New Oriental immigrants were too weak politically and socially to resist streamlining into the lower strata and vast discrimination in the allocation of resources. Among their weaknesses were low formal education, large families, lack of assets, no other country to go to, the absence of any network of kin or friends among the old-timers or power-holders and limited experience of modern organizations and politics.

It was the Labour establishment, dominating all centres of power at the time, that engineered the policies which resulted in ethnic stratification. It also propagated the ideology that the Oriental immigrants were 'a lost generation of the desert', and posed a threat to democracy and to Israeli culture. It was said that their needs were fewer and that they should be grateful for whatever they were accorded. While it was not certain whether Oriental adults could be de-cultured and re-cultured, their children were expected to assimilate completely into Israeli life. To the great injury inflicted by discriminatory policies was added the grave insult of a paternalistic ideology and humiliating stereotyping.

This special combination of the urgency of the state's needs, its discriminatory policies and the vulnerability of the Orientals crystallized into an ethnic stratification. It also engendered the immense resentment Orientals feel toward the Labour Party and explained the shifting in the 1970s of their political support to the right-wing camp. Seen from Labour's perspective, the state policies of the 1950s were inevitable and their implementation succeeded in executing Israel's national goals and in averting the threat to its culture and democracy.

Clearly, the origins, magnitude and persistence of ethnic stratification among Jews present a serious problem for Israel. It stands as a mark of failure for Zionism and for the Jewish state, which are both officially committed to full ethnic quality, integration and fusion. Oriental Jews expect the state to bring them to a par with their Ashkenazi brothers and feel disgruntled when facing continuing discrimination.

Culture

Orientals and Ashkenazim share a core culture composed of Jewish faith, Jewish nationality, Hebrew language and writings, Israeli local patterns, a version of the Protestant ethic (the values of merit, achievement, hard work, investment, profit and competition) and some other western influences (the democratic ethos, the legal system, materialism, middle-class lifestyle and mass culture). This Israeli culture is semi-western. It is less western in its strong emphasis on the family, its stress on collectivist and nationalistic considerations, the importance of human and neighbourly relations, the attitude towards the law as a not-too-binding restriction and the permeation of personal and public life by religion.

Although the two communities share Israeli culture, they still differ in their subcultures. The most crucial difference lies in the practice of religion. Orientals have a religious style and liturgy of their own; they are found less among the ultra-Orthodox and the true secularists, and tend to be over-represented among the middle categories of the traditional (*Masorati*) religious. Although religious tradition is a way of life for many of them, it is common to find Orientals watching television or going to the beach after attending synagogue on the Sabbath. Far from being fundamentalist they are pragmatic and conciliatory in their interpretation and observance of strict prohibitions. The average Oriental family is larger than the average Ashkenazi family. Traditional gender roles and strong ties with the extended family are more common among Orientals than among Ashkenazim. Yet these ethnic differences in the family area have become considerably blurred among the Israeli-born young generation. The Oriental use of Hebrew is more authentic, closer to Arabic and less formal. Since a larger proportion of Orientals are in the poor and working classes, they have developed over the years proletarian and poverty patterns of adaptation which mark them off from Ashkenazim who belong to the middle and higher classes.[12]

Such differences in ethnic subculture are common and non-controversial in other societies but tend to cause tensions in Israel. At least until the mid-1960s, Oriental Jews were viewed as culturally inferior and threatening and were strongly pressured to assimilate. But later on, in reaction to the cultural change Orientals had undergone, to their own protests and to the revival of ethnic pluralism in the United States, Ashkenazi attitudes have softened. The Ministry of Education and Culture introduced a programme of Oriental and Sephardic Heritage aimed at enriching the curriculum with Oriental history, literature and folklore. The national television and radio channels were opened to Oriental folk culture which had formerly been considered as low and to be kept underground.

This shift from cultural exclusivity and superiority to partial openness on the part of Ashkenazim has created constructive ambiguity over the cultural issue. Rather than basically changing, the Ashkenazi position has become more subtle, sophisticated, disguised and flexible.

Oriental Jews are still perceived as not having rid themselves of backward Arab thinking and behaviour, their ability is still seen as limited and they are supposed to be in need of cultural refinement. For instance, in 1978 the then army chief of staff said in a public interview, 'It will take years and years before Oriental Jews, even those acquiring full education, will manage to cope with the mentality of the West.'[13] Ashkenazim still continue to stereotype themselves as superior Westerners and to project Orientals as inferior, arabized Middle Easterners.[14] They allow the expressions of a Judaeo-Oriental heritage only because they regard these as harmless elements of a dead historical culture.

Today the cultural issue is dormant. Oriental Jews do not demand a right to be different, with a separate identity, culture and education. Rather they want to be recognized and have an impact on the national culture. They neither claim to have an Arab culture nor do they advocate it for Israel.[15]

Culture may, however, become a bone of contention once the Palestinian question is settled. Peace may open Israel to Arab culture and may make relevant the Oriental Jews' cultural affinity with the Arabs. In the event of peace, Israel's cultural orientation may become a real issue which could divide Israeli Jews ethnically, the Ashkenazim tending to consolidate Israel's western orientation in order to prevent the danger of 'Levantization', or assimilation into the Arab world, and some of the Oriental Jews wanting possibly to benefit from fostering cultural and other ties with the Arabs.

Politics

Orientals have made more headway in politics than in the areas of class and culture. Between 1965 and 1990 the status of a numerical majority in a multi-party, highly competitive democracy has favoured Orientals and steadily reduced ethnic inequality in political representation. The main trends are the following:

Firstly, Ashkenazim are in control of all the national power centres (the government, the Knesset, the top echelons of the civil service, the Supreme Court, Israel Defence Forces, the executive of the Jewish Agency and the central committee of the Histadrut). Yet Orientals have reached appreciable representation in these ruling positions. By 1992 they have already at one time held the posts of state president (Yitzhak Navon), deputy prime minister (Moshe Nissim and David Levy), ministry for foreign affairs (David Levy), army chief of staff

(Moshe Levy), secretary-general of the Histadrut (Yisrael Kessar) and treasurer of the Jewish Agency (Meir Shitrit) and they have been competed for the role of party leader and potential prime minister (Levy for Likud and Kessar for Labour). It is highly significant that one-third of the 120 members in the Knesset elected in 1992 and five of the 17 cabinet ministers in the Labour-led government of that year were of Oriental (or Sephardi) origin.

Secondly, all the political parties, except Shas (Torah Observing Sephardim) are led by Ashkenazim, but Oriental representation in their governing bodies is substantial and has reached one-third in the Labour Party and one-half in the Likud Party.

Thirdly, representation in junior public positions, and particularly in areas where Orientals constitute a demographic majority, is proportional and high. This is true for the leadership of local authorities and workers' councils. Thousands of Orientals also serve as councillors, heads of workers' committees, board members of voluntary associations and members of local steering committees.

Fourthly, Ashkenazim still maintain a monopoly over economic power. They fill in power positions in the top economic institutions, where Oriental representation is minimal. These include the economic ministries of the government, government corporations, the industrial complex of the Histadrut and the political bodies of the private sector (the Industrialists' Union and the Coordinating Committee of the Economic Organizations).

And fifthly, the rising trend in Oriental representation is clear-cut and evident in all areas but is more impressive in elected rather than appointed and in junior rather than senior roles. In general, the noticeable participation of Orientals in various spheres of power in the 1990s contrasts sharply with their conspicuous absence during the 1950s.

Another source of Orientals' political strength is the concentration of their vote in the Likud camp. It is estimated that about 80 per cent of Orientals voted in the 1988 elections for the Likud, Shas, the National Religious Party, Moledet and other small parties on the right, whereas a similar proportion of Ashkenazim voted for Labour and smaller parties on the left. This block voting makes the Likud dependent on Orientals and forces Labour to court them. The 1992 election results indicate a significant tendency for the middle class, both Oriental and Ashkenazi, to defect from the Likud to Labour, making the Likud increasingly dependent on poor and working-class Orientals.

Shas is also a power base for Oriental Jews. It succeeded the ethnic Tami Party in 1984 to survive as the only party directly representing Orientals and as such carrying a special weight. Its Sephardi leaders rose from the ambience of the ultra-Orthodox (*Haredi*) Ashkenazi community but its constituents are mostly traditionally religious Orientals. From 1990 to 1992, Shas gradually liberated itself from Ashkenazi hegemony. It won six seats in the 1992 election and even joined Yitzhak Rabin in the Labour-led coalition in defiance of its aged Ashkenazi mentor, Rabbi Schach, who went so far as to declare that Sephardim did not deserve to lead the Haredi community or the state.

The rise in Oriental representation and the linkage between voting and ethnicity have led some scholars to advance one view that is worth a brief mention. It is argued that the Ashkenazi dominance in politics has now come to an end and that the Orientals are Israel's new majority. They put Likud in power from 1977 to 1992 and they helped to institute a new political culture, which draws on a diluted version of Revisionist Zionism, stressing the importance of power, military force, land, nation, Jewish blood and fundamental mistrust of Gentiles.[16] It is said that this new ideological Zionism converges with the Oriental political folk culture which is allegedly authoritarian, ethnocentric, fanatical, pre-modern, religious and irrational. According to this view, two processes coincided: veteran Ashkenazim lost their universalist values of labour and egalitarianism, and at the same time immigrant Orientals asserted their particularist Judaism. Hence the scale tipped in favour of nationalism and religion.[17] The rise of a new nationalist political culture is made to account for Likud's success in capturing the Oriental vote, thereby marking Labour's failure to instil its humanistic, pragmatic and conciliatory political culture into Oriental immigrants of the 1950s and their children.[18]

The validity of this view, which is popular among Ashkenazim and leftists, is doubtful. The Oriental rise in politics has not terminated Ashkenazi political dominance. Most national policy-makers are still Ashkenazim and they determine the national issues with little regard to Oriental needs. The Likud did not pursue a policy that favoured Orientals and does not possess a social policy that differs significantly from that of the Labour Party. Orientals make only a limited imprint on the national agenda and on the considerations that go into decision-making. It is also wrong to portray the Oriental political culture as nationalistic, extremist and anti-Arab. It is, rather, non-ideological and pragmatic. Orientals prefer the Likud camp because they see in it a means for social mobility and attainment of status. For them Labour is responsible for their predicament and it stands for the Ashkenazim who enjoy status and privilege and harbour feelings of paternalism and rejection towards Orientals. Contrary to the Ashkenazi left, they believe that the Likud is more able to negotiate peace with the Arabs and they would endorse any compromise settlement that it endorses, as already shown by their unrelenting backing of the peace treaty with Egypt. This pragmatism is the more remarkable in view of the hard-line messages conveyed to the Orientals by the Likud.[19]

The overlap between the political and ethnic divisions augments ethnic intolerance. The Ashkenazim's stereotyping of Orientals as backward and irrational is reinforced by their confrontation with them in an opposing political camp, to which they attribute intransigence and intolerance. Similarly, Orientals' resentment and stereotyping of Ashkenazim as pseudo-liberals feeds on their appearance as a partisan adversary.

The Resilience of Ethnicity as a Submerged Issue

Many feel that ethnicity is being slowly but steadily phased out as a cleavage in Israeli society and hence should not be counted as an issue for those concerned with the ills of the Jewish state. There is much evidence to substantiate this common feeling: cultural and social assimilation is progressing rapidly; the common mass culture makes all alike; cross-ethnic friendships and neighbourhoods multiply; mixed marriages are nearly a quarter of all new marriages;[20] fertility rates have evened out; and, more generally, Israelis on the same socio-economic level think and behave in the same way irrespective of their ethnic origin. Orientals differ considerably among themselves in their rates of mobility and class interests. The success of certain sectors among them is disguised by the lowering of the Oriental average by a large poor stratum. There is no significant ethnic discrimination or prejudice to hinder those Orientals who have high motivation, work hard and invest in long-term careers. Ethnic integration is quite advanced in the middle, upper-middle and elite levels.

Furthermore, it is claimed that Orientals themselves do not feel ethnic deprivation, do not have ethnic identity and do not support ethnic movements and ethnic election lists. Findings from the 1988 survey show how weak ethnic identity is in Israel. Jews were asked to indicate whether each of the following eight identities was important to them or not: residence in the homeland, nationality, socio-economic status, minority/majority (Israeli Arab/Jewish) status, citizenship, religion, religious observance and ethnicity (Oriental/Ashkenazi). With the exception of ethnicity, large majorities considered all identities as important, ranging from 44.0 per cent for residence in the homeland to 68.6 per cent for religious observance. Only a minority of 28.8 per cent (32.6 per cent of Orientals and 26.4 per cent of Ashkenazim) regarded ethnicity as important. When they had to choose three of the eight identities, less than 3 per cent of either Orientals or Ashkenazim selected ethnicity.[21]

Public opinion surveys also show that Orientals believe in the efficiency of the stock solutions to the ethnic problem – investment in and integration of education; urban renewal; and mixed marriages. Only a few endorse affirmative action as a means to boost Oriental representation in the universities and in top posts and only a negligible minority supports radical steps that would hurt Ashkenazim, like mass protest, cessation of immigration from Europe and America and the use of violence. Many Orientals feel that the ethnic situation has improved and expect further improvement. The potential for ethnic protest and unrest is reputedly being steadily depleted by the basic belief that Orientals can get along and integrate in Israeli society, the prevalence of visible social mobility of able and ambitious Orientals and the widespread co-option of Oriental leaders.

The view that stresses the decline of ethnicity also points to the relative absence of ethnic unrest as a test of its ultimate validity. Israel has not had ethnic riots with losses of property and lives. Ethnic protest movements have been short-lived and not separatist in their goals. No Israeli government has ever fallen over an ethnic issue.

Yet one is struck by the resilience of ethnicity and its resurgence from time to time. The shock and fear aroused by the Wadi Salib riots of 1959, the Black Power Movement of 1971, the manipulation of ethnicity in the 1981 Knesset election campaign and the disturbances occasioned by the Abu-Hatzeira Affair in 1984–5,[22] to mention only some of the ethnic disruptions, were quite disproportionate to the modest scale of these events. It seems that the intensity of the submerged ethnic tension runs much deeper than one can discover in ordinary public opinion polls or in daily life.

The ties between Orientals and the main right-wing party are indicative of the complexity and resilience of ethnicity. Since the mid-1950s Herut and, in its later form, the Likud party served Orientals as a legitimate outlet for ethnic protest. Headed by its charismatic leader, Menachem Begin, Herut conveyed to them the message of the commonality of fate of the 'the excluded' (Revisionists and Orientals were both historically rejected by the elitist and discriminatory Labour Party), self-respect and full acceptance as equal Jews and Israelis. After the ascendance of the Likud to power many Oriental activists in the Likud developed expectations for political mobility and clout. David Levy, who is of Moroccan origin, has led them, established a faction in the party and even striven to become the leader of the Likud. The continuous succession fight, under way since Begin left office in 1983 had a distinct ethnic dimension. Although Orientals can be found in all the Likud factions, almost all the party followers of Levy are North Africans and other Orientals. The representation of Orientals among the party elite and nominees to the Knesset and government is significantly lower than among the party members and voters. The opposition to Levy stems from lack of appreciation of his leadership capability, his insufficient commitment to the ideology of Greater Israel and a sense of ethnic superiority that the Likud is the patrimony of the Ashkenazi Revisionist family and its descendants.

Ethnic unrest among members of Levy's faction surfaced during early 1992 when some of them called, for the first time and publicly, for breaking away from the Likud. The threat to split the party followed the apparent contrast between the gain by Levy of a third of the votes in the central committee in the contst for the leadership of the Likud and his faction's modst showing in the subsequent nominations for the Knesset.[23] In order to prevent defection, Prime Minister Shamir was forced to sign an agreement recognizing Levy's special status in the party. The calls for defection had pointed to widespread disillusionment among Orientals with the Likud. The hopes of some ambitious Orientals to take over party and to reorder its priorities was shattered. As a result the Likud suffered a setback in the June 1992 Knesset election among its Oriental constituents: many middle-class Orientals defected to labour and a significant number of lower- or working-class Orientals simply abstained. Many of the Oriental youth under 30, the Likud hard core, voted for Tzomet.[24] The Oriental desertion of the Likud weakened it in the predominantly Oriental urban slums and development towns where Labour campaigned without the disruption it has encountered in some previous elections.

Contrary to popular misconceptions and despite improvements in ethnic relations over the years, the potential for ethnic conflict has remained appreciable because Ashkenazim have continued to maintain their dominance. They it was who formed the Zionist Movement to resolve the Jewish question in Europe, founded the *Yishuv* (the pre-state Jewish settlement in Palestine), cast its institutions and norms and led it. The mass immigration of Orientals in the 1950s changed the demographic balance and partly eroded Ashkenazi dominance. However, Oriental numerical preponderance (until the arrival of the latest wave of mass immigration) was unable to undermine the foundations of Israeli society which were laid down by Ashkenazim and are still bolstered by their class, political and cultural superiority. Their dominance in Israel is further solidified by their clear-cut prominence in the Diaspora which, through Zionism, serves as Israel's hinterland and reservoir of manpower and other resources.

Holding in abeyance this potential for ethnic conflict is itself a measure of Ashkenazi dominance. Ashkenazi control of the sources of legitimacy and the continuing delegitimization of the issue of ethnicity inhibit Oriental mobilization. Although they make ethnic appeals to harness partisan loyalties, the largest two parties, which are controlled by Ashkenazim, suppress ethnicity as a political or ideological issue.

Yet ethnic inequality is a continuous source of deprivation for Orientals in Israel. Its political potency stems precisely from the combination of a national consensus against ethnic inequality and the failure to eliminate it. Orientals feel relative deprivation and witness the inability of the system to satisfy their needs and to bring them up to par with their Ashkenazi brothers. Continued ethnic inequality is a potentially solid and legitimate ground for Oriental disaffection, mobilization and struggle even though these do not take separatist or exclusively ethnic forms.

The unfulfilled promises of ethnic equality and integration legitimize and reinforce Oriental grievances. Orientals face the unpleasant contradiction between their numerical strength and non-dominant status. The knowledge that their children do not fare better than they have is a growing and unsettling realization. The fact that, of all Oriental and Sephardi Jewish communities in the world today, Israeli Oriental Jews enjoy the worst socio-economic achievements may also add to their discontent.

Impact of New Russian Immigration

Ethnic cleavage and Ashkenazi dominance in Israel will persist for years to come. Contrary to the common belief that Zionism is the grand ideological and political force that fuses all Israeli Jews into a melting pot, it can reasonably be argued that the Jewish-Zionist character of the state, set forth by Zionism, both facilitates and impedes the bridging of the ethnic gap. It is obvious that the Zionist ideology of national unity negates ethnic differences and enshrines ethnic amalgamation, yet it also militates against full ethnic equality and integration. Two obstacles stand in the way. Continued ingathering of exiles constantly creates a new population in need of attention and resources and it also changes the ethnic balance. Zionism also requires that a large Jewish majority be maintained, at least part of whom must, therefore, be in the lower echelons of society.

The current ethnic division will probably be exacerbated by the mass immigration in the 1990s of Jews from the former Soviet Union to Israel. 340,000 Russian Jews came between September 1989 and early 1992 and one to two million more are expected to arrive during this decade. Such large-scale immigration will proceed only if sustained economic growth, which ceased in 1974, is resumed. The historical experience of the 1930s and 1950s shows that rapid economic growth, generated by massive influx of immigrants, benefits the entire population. Yet it is reasonable to assume that the absorption of mass immigration will hit Orientals hard. A new Russian ethnic problem will emerge that will overshadow the Oriental ethnic problem. Orientals will be hurt by losing their numerical strength in Israel as a whole and in many particular localities (like development towns) and by an appreciable decrease in their electoral power. Immigrant absorption will further undermine the welfare state which was already weakened in the 1980s. Transfer of budgets from present welfare services to new immigrants will directly squeeze the lower strata. The greatest damage will, however, be the reduction in Orientals' chances for occupational and class mobility. The new Russian arrivals have high levels of education and occupational skills, but due to the downward mobility caused by immigration they will find themselves in direct competition with Orientals who are in the process of entering the same jobs (for instance, Russian engineers will look for jobs as practical engineers or even as technicians and hence will be competing with Orientals who work or seek employment in these occupations).[25]

Since 95 per cent of Jews abroad are Ashkenazi, any appreciable immigration to Israel implies a demographic, cultural and political change detrimental to Oriental interests. Whether or not the forecast of a mass immigration from Russia and the other republics formerly in the Soviet Union materializes, as long as Israel remains committed to the absorption of Jewish immigration it is only a matter of time before Orientals will be reduced once again to a minority in Israeli society as in world Jewry and the improvement in their status and their calls for equality will continue to receive a low priority.

Zionism's other requirement – to maintain a state with a Jewish majority – means that there will always be a Jewish working class, a Jewish poor stratum, a restricted absolute number of Jewish professionals (like doctors and lawyers), limited numbers of Jewish students and professors in universities, and relatively large numbers on the lower rungs of the social ladder. In contrast to Jews in western societies where they constitute a negligible minority (for instance, Jews in the United States number only 2.5 per cent of the population) and where therefore most of them can reach the higher strata, most Jews in Israel cannot be in top positions as long as Jews make up 85 per cent or more of the population. Since the competition for the limited supply of high-demand jobs and roles occurs in Israel among Jews, most of the losers in this competition are also, perforce, Jews. Under these circumstances Oriental Jews and their offspring who are presently located at the lower levels have a slim chance to compete successfully with Ashkenazi Jews and their offspring who start off by being better placed. The alternative is to staff the lower strata with non-Jews (as is the case in the West), but Israel would then become much less Jewish or even non-Jewish.

These structural impediments for accomplishing ethnic equality and fusion will not necessarily cause ethnic disruptions. It is quite likely that low-status Orientals will not develop a distinctly ethnic consciousness and will not wage a radical ethnic struggle. Sporadic ethnic eruptions will continue but there is no real danger of political instability or a civil war. Since Jews in Israel have much in common, concessions and improvements will continue to dull the sting of the ethnic conflict.

10. THE ULTRA-ORTHODOX AND ISRAELI SOCIETY

Menachem Friedman

Introduction

The results of the elections to the twelfth Knesset in 1988 reflected a dramatic rise in the political power of the Haredi (or ultra-Orthodox) parties. For much of the Israeli public, the elections marked a second political upheaval, following the one that brought the Likud to power after the ninth Knesset elections of 1977. *Agudat Israel*, the veteran Haredi party, tripled its electoral power, even after losing 40 per cent of its constituency to a rival splinter party established by its 'Lithuanian'[1] faction *Degel Hatorah*. The Sephardi Haredi party, Shas, participating in elections for the second time, obtained 60 per cent more votes than before. The Haredi parties, which together had previously secured about 5 per cent of the overall vote, doubled their share to about 11 per cent in the twelfth Knesset elections. The Haredim had apparently succeeded in breaking through the traditional boundaries of their society, gaining increasing influence in certain sectors of the Israeli public.

Coalition negotiations for establishment of the new government were overshadowed and largely influenced by the accumulated Haredi political clout. Although the two major parties – Likud and Labour – eventually agreed to establish a national unity government, each retained the option of forming a narrow coalition. The Haredim constituted the only factor that was not identified with either of the two large political blocks; in principle, it could join a coalition with either of them. The Haredim had thus become an essential component of any coalition, thereby gaining significant positions of influence (the

Ministry of the Interior, chairmanship of the Knesset Finance Committee and de facto control of the Ministry of Labour and Social Welfare). However, the power of the Haredim in the Israeli political system was most strongly sensed during the cabinet crisis that followed the attempt by Labour party leader Shimon Peres to bring down the national unity government and establish a Labour-led coalition that would include the Haredim. This attempt failed primarily because of the objection of two aged Haredi rabbis: Rabbi Menachem Mendel Schneerson, leader of the Lubavitcher *Hasidim* (*Chabad*)[2], who resides in Brooklyn, New York, and Rabbi Menachem Eliezer Schach, head of the *Ponevezh Yeshiva* in Bnei Brak (in the Tel Aviv metropolitan area). At the height of the crisis (26 March, 1990), the latter convened an assembly at Yad Eliyahu Stadium in Tel Aviv. Before thousands of followers and admirers and millions of astounded television viewers throughout the world, he negated the Labour Party's legitimacy and essentially compelled the Haredi parties to join a narrow right-wing coalition headed by the Likud.

As fundamentalist-religious movements began to gain power elsewhere in the world, many observers – in Israel and abroad – tended to view the rise in Haredi strength as a genuine threat to liberal-secular culture. Secular anxiety over the 'Khomeinization' of Israel has been fuelled by Haredi involvement in politics and the exploitation of power for advancement of sectarian economic interests; by an increase in the 'return to Judaism', wherein young Israelis undergo a kind of intra-religious conversion, abandoning their secular way of life and joining one of the Haredi communities,[3] by the growing popularity of saint-worship and ritual practices at tombs of the righteous and by the emergence of active messianism among the Chabad Hasidim and the reinforcement of the Gush Emunim movement, whose messianic-religious ideology is linked with a nationalistic political conception.[4]

Even if there is some measure of paranoia in these attitudes towards Haredim, there is no doubt that a significant change has taken place in the position of Haredim on the political map and within the overall social system of Jewish society in general and Israeli society in particular. In the early 1950s, many people still believed that traditional Judaism, of which the Haredim consider themselves the epitome, was doomed to rapid disappearance. The Holocaust virtually destroyed Eastern European Jewry, the main human reservoir of traditional-religious Judaism and the source on which Haredi society drew. At that time, few could imagine that modern western society, the secular and permissive city and the Zionist-secular State of Israel would constitute fertile soil for Haredi rehabilitation, where the ideal of Torah study would flourish with unparalleled intensity and scope.

Sources of Haredi Judaism

Haredi Judaism developed as a part of and as a reaction to the crisis of Eastern European Jewry's survival in the latter half of the nineteenth century. During this period, the processes of modernization and secularization and the accompanying economic and political crises attacked the very foundations of survival for the Jewish masses and challenged the validity and applicability of traditional ways of life. Many Jews, particularly those of the growing younger generation who migrated from small villages to large cities and western countries, had abandoned the faith of their fathers. The correlation between modernity and the economic-political crisis made secularization and the move away from Jewish religion and tradition not only an issue of high level significance to the Jewish public but also one of religious-ideological importance, linked essentially with the questions of the uniqueness of Jewish history and the meaning of Jewish identity. Two fundamental positions of traditional Jewish society should be emphasized; first, that legitimate Jewish identity can be manifested only by fulfilling a way of life based on both public and private observance of religious law (*Halacha*), as interpreted by recognized authorities; and secondly, that the Jewish people are above history, and their political and spiritual destiny is determined directly by God, according to their fulfilment of *Halacha*. Jewish life on the existential, everyday level, as a minority without sovereignty, subject to constant humiliation and persecution, was defined as a situation of both cosmological and political exile, considered as the degree of fate and the purpose of the Jewish people. This situation could only be changed by Divine will, through Redemption and the coming of the Messiah, who would restore sovereignty to the Jewish people in its land, the Land of Israel. Most of the outstanding rabbis perceived the mass abandonment of religion and tradition – particularly by the younger generation – and the attempt to cope with existential questions concerning the Jewish people by direct confrontation and involvement with history – whether through participation in Jewish and non-Jewish revolutionary movements or in the endeavour to establish a modern, independent and sovereign (Zionist) Jewish society – as a denial of the religious-historical destiny of the

Jewish people and as an unprecedented rebellion against the God of Israel.

On the other hand, traditional solutions to the severe political and economic crisis did not suffice to instil hope and comfort in the masses. Rank-and-file Jews, including many still faithful to religion and tradition, no longer believed that their religious authorities were capable of leading the nation to a more secure future. Instead, they tended to accept alternative solutions, within the historical process, as more legitimate and realistic. This crisis of faith between the religious-traditional Jewish public and its rabbinic leadership, resulting in the expulsion of rabbis from politics, was a highly significant phenomenon in the development of Jewish society. It enabled movements of change (Zionism) and revolution (the *Bund*) to operate within traditional Jewish society in Eastern Europe.

The conflict between the traditional rabbinate and Zionism is the clearest and most outstanding reflection of the tension within traditional Jewish society, which constituted the majority of Eastern European Jewry until the Holocaust. For most traditional religious authorities, Zionism was the quintessential expression of what Haredi religious-political jargon calls 'rebellion' against the God of Israel. Zionism sought to establish a sovereign, modern and secular Jewish society in the Land of Israel, the Holy Land, as part of a historical process, ignoring religious-cosmological concepts such as exile and redemption or 'a nation that dwelleth alone' (Numbers 9: 23). Moreover, Zionism was a secular movement whose quest for a Jewish society in the Land of Israel laid the foundations for a fully secular Jewish culture as an alternative to traditional Jewish culture and identity.[5]

Relations between Zionism as a national movement and traditional-religious Jewish society were by no means one-dimensional. It was precisely the complex and problematic affinity of secular Zionism for Jewish religion, tradition, history and identity that enabled a minority of the religious-traditional public, the religious Zionists (the *Mizrachi* Movement), to identify with some of its objectives. These religious Zionists considered the secular-Zionist Jewish identity to be an essentially positive phenomenon, as it restored and reinforced the unity of Jewish society, which had begun to deteriorate because of secularization. Moreover, much of the traditional Jewish public in Eastern Europe that did not formally join Zionism still found it difficult to reject the movement outright or deny its accomplishments in Palestine. The Zionist enterprise in the Land of Israel appealed to deep internal sentiments and aroused feelings of sympathy, identification and partnership, even if not always expressed publicly and openly. This dialectic attitude, reflected in relationships of love-hate, envy and rejection, inferiority and superiority, identification and isolation, characterized the attitudes of the religious-traditional Jews of that time – as it does of the Haredim of the present day – to Zionism and the State of Israel.

The secularization process reached a peak after the First World War. The horrors of war, the weakening of the traditional Jewish leadership, the rise of nationalism and anti-semitism, the communist revolution in Russia and the Balfour Declaration (2 November, 1917), which promised the establishment of a Jewish national home in Palestine, led many religious-traditional Jews to believe that history and the future tended to favour the rebels against religion and tradition. Moreover, the continued challenge to the status of Jews in Eastern and Central Europe forced many religious-traditional Jews to seek the very solutions proposed by Zionism and the new Zionist-secular Jewish community in Palestine (the *Yishuv*). Paradoxically, this dependence on historical enemies, along with confusion and frustration over the secularization of the Land of Israel, intensified Haredi opposition to Zionism, which it saw as responsible for this erosion and for the development of an overtly secular Jewish society in the Holy Land. These developments and the attendant historical experience helped shape the present overall outlook of Haredi Jewry and its leaders in contemporary Israel.

The most outstanding political manifestation of Haredi tradition is the Agudat Israel Movement, founded in Katowice (then part of eastern Prussia) in 1912. The history of this movement, described and analysed elsewhere,[6] reflects the complexity of relations between the Haredi world and Zionism and the Zionist-secular community that was developing in Palestine. Nevertheless, it should be recalled that even though Agudat Israel represented the majority of Haredim, it always constituted a kind of confederation, comprising representatives of various shades of tradition, different geographic and social landscapes in Eastern and Central Europe[7] and a broad spectrum of religious outlooks on everyday life and the constantly changing surrounding world, Jewish and non-Jewish alike.[8]

The other face of Haredi Judaism is characterized by fear of the surrounding modern secular world which threatens to engulf it. From this point of view, Haredi Judaism represents an outstanding example of defensive tactics. It has developed as a reaction to the schism in traditional society and the deterioration of the traditional Jewish community. Furthermore, it underscores the cleavage within the nuclear family and its increasing difficulty in functioning as a social unit capable of ensuring continuity of its heritage in the next generation.

The traditional process of socialization was based primarily on study of the Talmud and its commentaries, followed either by the acquisition of a trade in commerce or crafts – depending on one's talents, financial skills, abilities and environmental conditions – or, alternatively, advanced study of Halachic literature at the community *Beit Midrash* (study hall), in pursuit of the 'crown of Torah' and rabbinic ordination. This process, however, did not conform with the new economic and technological realities. Talented young people in search of success now required a broader education, including the study of languages, classical literature and the sciences, enabling them to attend universities and polytechnic institutes. The issue of earning a livelihood (*Tachlith*)[9] began to undermine traditional Jewish society and may have been the factor most responsible for the change in its nature.

The correlation between modernity and education on the one hand and secularization and abandonment of the traditional way of life on the other, the fear that exposure to modern culture would engender total rejection of traditional religious authority and accelerate the assimilation process, led the religious traditional leadership to oppose any change in educational patterns for the younger generation that were based on religious works alone, that is the study of the Talmud and its commentaries. But the world was changing rapidly: railway and telegraph were followed by books and newspapers, and consequently even small-town youth had unmediated contact with sources of information that contradicted and sometimes explicitly rejected the traditional knowledge represented by religious fathers and authorities. Hence it became necessary to develop new means and methods of coping with the challenges the traditional world now had to face. The Volozhin-type[10] ('Lithuanian') *yeshivot* were prepared to face this challenge.

The Lithuanian *yeshivot* were the embryonic cells of the Haredi society-in-formation that became institutionalized as a 'society of scholars,' in Israel and in the western world after the Second World

War. The original *yeshiva*, as an academy of Talmudic study, is an ancient institution in Jewish history in general and in Ashkenazi tradition in particular.[11] The traditional Ashkenazi *yeshiva* was generally a community institution, supported by working people and intended primarily for local students. The community rabbi served as the *Rosh Yeshiva* (head of the *yeshiva*).[12] Most students were local residents, living at home and involved in family and community life. Study discipline was generally rather lax. The Lithuanian *yeshiva*, in contrast, was a super-communal institution. The local community did not underwrite the *yeshiva's* expenses – which were met by contributions from individual benefactors – but provided services, for a fee, to the *yeshiva* and its students. The vast majority of students came from other communities and the *yeshiva* supplied their basic needs – room and board. For most of the year, they remained within the confines of the *yeshiva*, generally returning home only twice annually, during the spring and autumn recess (the Hebrew months of Nisan and Tishrei, respectively). The *yeshiva* selected its students carefully; not all applicants were accepted. Most were unmarried young men aged 15–24, charged with a single mission: to devote all their time to the study of the Talmud and its commentaries. Strict order was maintained at the *yeshiva*: far from home and isolated from their families, the only way the students could obtain status in this society of scholars was through scholastic and personal achievement. The instructors, too, had to defend their own status through constant direct intellectual confrontation with their students. The Lithuanian *yeshiva* was thus a semi-monastic institution, comprising scores and sometimes hundreds of talented young men who devoted themselves to Torah study with all the enthusiasm and intellectual fervour of youth. It is hardly surprising that these *yeshivot* became centres of Talmudic creativity, achievement and innovation, earning appreciation not only among scholars but throughout the traditional Jewish world.

As the traditional communities in the villages of Lithuania and White Russia began to erode and deteriorate, the *yeshivot* began to perceive themselves not only as educational and intellectual institutions but also – perhaps even primarily – as havens preserving the values of the Jewish religion and unconditional commitment to Halacha as basic norms to be imparted to the next generation. They based their religious status with the public and socio-economic relations with the Jewish world on an ideology that can be stated briefly as follows: the study of the Talmud and its commentaries

(Torah study) is considered an absolute value on which the continuity and survival of the Jewish people is dependent in both the spiritual and actual physical sense. In modern secular society, the Torah – and consequently the Jewish people – cannot survive without the *yeshivot*. Moreover, the *yeshivot* themselves cannot survive without great Torah scholars who devote all their time and efforts to Torah study. Such absolute dedication is possible only within an institution that does not allow secular studies. Therefore, a *yeshiva* seeking to fulfil its national mission must be a sacred *yeshiva* that rejects all practical considerations. These axioms became the basic principles of Haredi religiosity and any deviation from them represented a denial of Haredi identity.

Life within the *yeshiva* environment was an intense experience, leaving an indelible mark on all who participated in it. In the final analysis, *yeshiva* students were an elite group of vibrant young people, living within an intensive environment and maintaining a system of social relations based on lofty norms of personal ethics and mutual assistance. It is not surprising, therefore, that the *yeshivot* produced outstanding Torah scholars and religious personalities, the next generation of *Roshei Yeshiva*, attracting masses of students and followers. This was the greatest success of the Lithuanian *yeshivot*: despite their failure to stem erosion, they succeeded in creating a new elite of top-level religious leaders who bore the *yeshiva*'s message, rendering it the basis of the new Haredi society emerging in Israel and in the West.

The Socio-Economic Background of the Haredi Society of Scholars

After nearly a hundred years of erosion, during which traditional-religious Jewish society declined from majority to minority status among Jews, and suffered a mighty blow during the awesome European Holocaust, a historic turning point took place in the secular-Zionist State of Israel during the 1950s. Not only did the Haredim succeed in halting the move away from their ranks but their entire society became consolidated as a 'society of scholars'. For many Haredim, this was seen as a miracle, a kind of compensation for the horrible losses they sustained in the Holocaust. However, closer analysis reveals that the main reasons were socio-economic, connected, rather paradoxically, with the establishment of the Zionist State of Israel and the development of Western economy in the post-Second World War era.

Before the establishment of the State of Israel, Haredi leaders were convinced that the secular-Zionist state would deny religious Jews the opportunity to educate their children as they wished; *yeshivot* would be closed and it would be difficult to observe the sabbath and dietary laws, as had been the case in the Soviet Union.[13] Their historical experience, however, did not include western liberal democracy. The establishment of the State of Israel as a western welfare state created nearly ideal economic and social conditions for the flourishing of special Haredi educational institutions. The state financed nearly all the expenses of elementary education and health insurance, while pension rights freed parents of financial dependence on their children in case of illness or old age. The rise in the standard of living and government involvement in housing enabled many middle-class parents to allocate far more resources for their children's education at the more advanced stages of the socialization process (secondary school and higher education). These developments laid the foundations for the establishment and institutionalization of the Haredi ghetto,[14] in which the Haredim were not a small minority but a decisive majority, exercising their power in moulding the public according to their own conceptions. The Haredi ghetto became a protected territorial entity in which the Haredim could institute an efficient system of social supervision to prevent deviation from their way of life. Furthermore, Israel's commitment to the principles of western democracy and to Jewish history precluded enactment or enforcement of discriminatory laws of an anti-religious nature. The Haredim soon realized that, in a western-style democracy, a determined minority has the power to prevent the government from passing laws that ostensibly threaten their sacred principles. For example, the Haredim succeeded in 1953 in preventing the enforcement of a law drafting all women into national service. If carried out, the law would have led to a civil rebellion with religious women preferring imprisonment to conscription.

For many Jews, in Israel and the Diaspora alike, the Holocaust confirmed the Zionist prognosis and signified the tragic failure of Haredi-traditional Judaism under the leadership of rabbis and scholars.[15] On the other hand, the Holocaust and the tragic loss of Eastern European Jewry also led, paradoxically, to a new, more tolerant and even supportive attitude towards the remnants of the traditional heritage of Eastern European Jewry, of which the Haredim, the *yeshivot* and the Torah sages were the most faithful representatives.

These revised attitudes were reflected in several spheres of activity. Firstly, Zionist socialist leaders, headed by Ben-Gurion, felt some guilt about their attitude towards the traditional Judaism of their childhood and responsibility for preservation of the remnants of the traditional Jewish heritage. This was the background for Ben-Gurion's consent to exempt *yeshiva* students from the draft. Secondly, after the Holocaust, Diaspora Jews, especially those in the United States, were more willing to contribute to the maintenance of *yeshivot* and other traditional-religious institutions. Beyond the feeling of financial obligation to the Jewish past, many sought to perpetuate the memories of their loved ones who would never have a proper gravestone, turning to institutions reflecting traditional Jewish identity in their nature and often also their name. For example, the Ponevezh *Yeshiva* continues and perpetuates the name and traditions of the town after which it was named. The vast resources pouring into the *yeshiva* world constituted the primary economic basis for the development of the Haredi society of scholars. Finally, when Israelis began delving into the history of the Holocaust, they revealed its complex nature, whereas, immediately after the tragedy, they pointed an accusing finger at the Haredim for proceeding 'as lambs to the slaughter'.[16] From the 1960s on, such accusations were rarely voiced, having been replaced by counterclaims regarding the activity – or inactivity – of the Zionist leadership during the Holocaust itself. With this background, the Haredim achieved recognition as equal partners/victims in the terrible tragedy that had befallen the Jewish people.

Agudat Israel joined the government coalition after the establishment of the State of Israel, signalling at least *de facto* recognition of the Zionist Jewish state by the mainstream of Haredi Jewry. Within the framework of coalition agreements, Agudat Israel established a wholly separate educational system, financed by the government, within the framework of the Compulsory Education Law. The institutionalization of this educational system constituted a true revolution in the status and functioning of Haredi education. For the first time in history, Agudat Israel had an entire educational system of its own, with separate facilities for boys and girls, financed almost entirely by public funds. This enabled the system to expand substantially and penetrate various population groups, including the new immigrants arriving from Arab countries.[17] Furthermore, this network of schools offered teaching positions, primarily for graduates of the Agudat Israel's teaching seminaries. This last development may have had the most significant long-term result since it gave Haredi women the opportunity to play a key role in shaping the emerging Haredi society of scholars. The exemption of *yeshiva* students from military service was the second indispensable condition for the institutionalization of the Haredi society of scholars, since it ensured a closed and undisturbed process of socialization, within a system of total institutions, from early adolescence until several years after marriage.

The Haredi society of scholars began to develop in the late 1950s. Under the influence of Rabbi A. I. Karelitz (the *Hazon Ish*),[18] who resided in Bnei Brak, *yeshiva* students sought to realize the ideal of devotion to Torah study by continuing their studies after marriage in the post-*yeshiva* institution called the *kollel*. There had been various attempts at institutionalizing the *kollel* as an academy for talented married *yeshiva* students (*avrechim*),[19] but until the 1950s, the *kollel* was not a significant factor in the Haredi world. Its golden age began under the economic and social circumstances prevailing after the establishment of the State of Israel. More and more *yeshiva* graduates began to consider *kollel* studies as a viable option, postponing departure to the working world by several years.[20] Several economic developments facilitated *kollel* study: parents were now able to buy a home and furniture for their children; support from western countries for the establishment and maintenance of *yeshivot* and *kollels* allowed for disbursement of large stipends to students; *kollel* students' wives could work as teachers and serve as the main breadwinners of their families during the first few years after marriage. By the mid-1960s, the *kollel* had opened its doors to all *yeshiva* students, not only the brightest among them. The *yeshivot*, too, took in all youngsters brought up in Haredi society, without exception. Within a relatively short time all males in Haredi society became *yeshiva* students and, after they married, continued studying in *kollels*. This social change, unparalleled in Jewish history, is of appreciable significance in all other areas of life. From the late 1960s on, Haredi society as a whole has become a society of scholars.

One immediate result of this dramatic social-religious change was an almost total halt in erosion from Haredi society to secular or modern-religious Jewish life. The principal factors responsible for this achievement are that in the first place secondary and higher education have become an inseparable part of the socialization process for the middle class. Hence Haredi society's failure to impart secular education to its sons renders it difficult, if not utterly impossible, for

Haredi youth, nearly all of whom study at *yeshivot* and live in boarding school environments, to integrate within non-Haredi society, even if they desired to do so. Secondly, the relatively early age of marriage (19–22 for men, 18–21 for women) in Haredi society and the birth of the first child within the first year of marriage render the young Haredi family almost totally financially and socially dependent on their extended families, who are obliged to purchase a home and supply other basic needs, so virtually preventing the couple from abandoning the Haredi way of life, either jointly or separately. Finally, against a background of the crisis in modern society, social alienation and the development since the Second World War of a permissive-hedonistic culture, *Roshei Yeshiva* succeeded in offering their students the ideal of a model Haredi society, outstanding for its commitment to mutual assistance, concern for its weaker members and a total devotion to Torah study, in contrast to the achievement-oriented 'rat race' of the outside world.

The Haredim perceived this surprising achievement as a miracle and as incontrovertible proof – if such were required – that the *yeshivot* were the only institution capable of tackling the challenge of erosion. Hence all means of maintaining *yeshivot* and *kollel*s are considered worthwhile and appropriate. Consequently, the nature of Agudat Israel changed as well. Its focus of activity now shifted to protection of the society of scholars and acquisition of the resources required for its maintenance and development. The party became the political representative of the *yeshivot* and *kollel*s, committed to their well-being and exploiting political circumstances to the maximum for this purpose.

At the same time, the image of Haredi society changed as well, primarily among the Haredim themselves but also among much of Jewish society in general, in Israel and elsewhere. Some caution should be exercised in assessing the legitimacy now accorded to Haredi society, especially in Israel. Nevertheless, one should acknowledge that the change in its status is exerting an influence on political life in Israel. The new-found admiration enjoyed by Haredim originates from certain changes in Jewish society in the Diaspora. The rapid assimilation of western Jews has aroused deep anxiety among both Diaspora Jewish leaders and Israeli public opinion regarding the future of Jewish identity. Assimilation, and not anti-semitism or physical danger, is now perceived as the most serious problem threatening the future of the Jewish people. The intensification of a

Jewish consciousness among young western Jews is considered a top priority of Zionism and the State of Israel. From this standpoint, the Haredim, who represent traditional Jewish identity to the secular majority and are fighting assimilation and intermarriage, are seen as allies. The relative success of the Haredim in educating their children merits admiration today. Furthermore, their work in preventing assimilation is seen as contributing to the advancement and reinforcement of the State of Israel.

Moreover, the crisis of Zionism – the loss of idealism among young Israelis and the decline in the status of the kibbutz as the model society of social justice and an overt reflection of Zionist fulfilment – accords the Haredim a sense of victory in their historic battle against secular Zionism. In their eyes, secular Zionism has failed in its attempt to establish an ideal society in the Land of Israel. Haredi society, in turn, with all its charitable institutions, represents a deep-rooted Jewish alternative to the secular Israeli society that appears steeped in permissiveness. 'Ours,' say the Haredim, 'is better than yours.' Some secular Israelis were convinced by these arguments and 'returned to Judaism', namely became Haredi. However limited in scope this phenomenon may be, it confirms that Haredi society is no longer seen by the Israeli public, as it was by secular Zionism in the past, as a corrupt and withering society destined to disappear from the face of the earth. Rather it is perceived as an alternative to permissive western culture. The increase in the crime rate, narcotics abuse and sexual permissiveness, as well as alienation and lack of communication between parents and children, undermine the self-confidence of the middle class in the large modern city. In contrast, even non-Haredim often regard the Haredi ghetto as a model society, with its system of social security, mutual assistance and concern for the weak, an atmosphere of law and order, an island of stability in family life and respect for parents.[21]

This development was reflected in the political upheaval following the Likud's rise to power in 1977. Prime Minister Menachem Begin hastened to co-opt Agudat Israel to the ruling coalition, after an absence from it of 24 years. In return, he agreed to institute significant changes in two spheres: the non-conscription of *yeshiva* students and Haredi women[22] and a marked increase in budgeting for Haredi institutions. However, what may have been even more important was the change in political atmosphere and especially political 'language'. Begin was a prime minister whom the Haredim could appreciate. He spoke their language, rather than that of the native-born Israelis and the Zionist left: he replaced the secular-Zionist term 'State of Israel' with the more traditional 'Jewish' term 'Land of Israel'; he often used phrases like 'Blessed be the Lord' and 'With the help of the Lord', speaking authentically as if he himself were a Haredi Jew. Although Begin did not lead an Orthodox life, he was perceived by the Haredim as 'one of us'. For the first time, Haredim felt at home in the corridors of government, and not like stepchildren or total strangers. This atmosphere extended to other spheres as well. More and more ministers and other political personalities in the Likud and other right-wing parties began expressing their admiration and appreciation of the Haredi society of scholars. It appears that the Haredim had become part of the country's political centre.

The Society of Scholars, Agudat Israel and Traditional Sephardi Judaism

The ostensible increase in Haredi prestige was nevertheless largely illusory. The growth of the society of scholars and Haredi participation in political life posed serious ideological and economic problems for the Haredim, ultimately intensifying hostility towards them in the more established strata of Israeli society. Haredi society finds it difficult to extend beyond its limited boundaries, nor does it seek to do so, at least in practice, if not in principle. The phenomenon of 'return to Judaism,' is of limited scope. For most Israelis, the Haredi ghetto is more an exotic object, whose social remoteness conceals its seamier sides, than a genuine alternative to the disappointments of modernity. The alienation and isolation of the Haredim, their eagerness to claim exemption from service in the Israeli army, their demands for increasing allocations for their society of scholars and sometimes unrestrained use of political power arouse resentment and even hatred among large sections of the Israeli public. As indicated below, such feelings were clearly reflected in the results of the 1992 elections to the thirteenth Knesset.

While opposition to the Haredim prevails in much of Israeli society, especially the better-established sector, it is less common among the poorer, less-developed strata, which are comprised mainly of Sephardim. The exposure of this sector of the population, more traditional than religious, to Haredi influence has clearly led to a turning point in Israeli politics, with significant influence on the electoral power of the Haredim and hence also on the Israeli political structure as a whole.

At the same time, however, it has divided the Haredi camp, led to the establishment of a Sephardi Haredi party (Shas) and has intensified the internal crisis within Haredi society.

The emergence of Shas originates in the mass immigration to Israel from Islamic countries (especially the wave of immigration from North Africa during the 1950s), in the absorption of masses of traditional Sephardi immigrants into secular-Zionist Israel and in the immigrants' powerful feelings of discrimination by a remote, secular establishment identified with the 'Ashkenazi elite'. The story of Shas thus embodies an ethnic conflict between Sephardim and Ashkenazim which remains a dominant component of Israeli politics to this day. However, it is also linked with the militant secularism of the ruling party at that time (Mapai), with relations between religious and non-religious elements and with the development of the Haredi society of scholars.

Traditional immigrants from Islamic countries who sought to identify with a religious party largely turned to the National Religious Party (NRP) for both economic and cultural reasons. On the one hand, the NRP (then called *Hapoel Hamizrachi*) was an integral part of the ruling Zionist establishment and consequently possessed the tools and institutions that were so vital for the absorption of destitute immigrants. But on the other, it represented a modern religious culture that was more closely linked with the Israeli experience than with the Eastern European Diaspora. Its religious culture was based on the Hebrew language as the language of prayer and sacred writings, but also on modern Israeli clothing and appearance. The Haredi alternative was not even considered at the time by these immigrants. The Haredim represented an Ashkenazi traditional-religious culture, suffused with an Eastern European atmosphere. Their synagogue epitomized the traditional Ashkenazi culture: their language was Yiddish, which was also the language of instruction at most *yeshivot*; their clothing and outward appearance was utterly alien to the Sephardim. Hence the national-religious culture of the NRP appeared less 'Ashkenazi' to the Sephardi newcomers and more a part of the majority culture with which they sought to identify. Indeed, the national religious educational institutions fulfilled a most important role in the acculturation of many young Sephardim into Israeli society.

But absorption of the Sephardim into Israel was never a simple matter. The wounds of this process are still painful to this day and have a marked effect on Israeli social and political life. Without examining the issue in detail, the absorption process had a unique and often paradoxical character within the framework of religious society in Israel. An analysis of several of its more prominent features will explain how Haredi Judaism ultimately succeeded in breaking through to the traditional Sephardi sectors, thereby changing the balance of political power among the Orthodox religious public in Israel in favour of the Haredi parties.

Rabbis and historians claim that the Orthodox version of the Jewish religion preserved the unity of the Jewish People despite the lack of sovereignty and common territory. Under conditions of dispersion among various territories and survival amid a hostile population, *Halacha* (religious law) was undoubtedly an unparalleled uniting factor. Despite the differences that developed among the various Diaspora Jewish communities, consciousness of a common past, affinity for religious and Halachic literature and social dissociation from the inimical surrounding society nourished a unique national consciousness and sense of unity. However, somewhat paradoxically, when those same ethnic Jewish groups arrived in Israel, each with its own unique customs, liturgy and lore, the common denominator became a separating factor. In Israel, religion and tradition distinguished between Jews of Ashkenazi and Sephardi origin. For example, unlike any other official body in Israel, the chief rabbinates are divided: there are both an Ashkenazi and a Sephardi chief rabbi of Israel and also twin chief rabbis for the larger cities.

To surmount this wall of separation, a religious culture had to be developed that would obscure affinity for Diaspora traditions and create as broad a cultural-religious common denominator as possible for immigrants from various ethnic groups. The modern religious culture that developed during the second generation of religious Zionism purported to represent such a common religious culture and succeeded in doing so to a large extent. It enabled young people of varying ethnic backgrounds to enjoy a common community and religious life, with educational institutions – *yeshivot* for boys and *ulpanot* for girls – for students from families of differing ethnic backgrounds and traditions. However, the ecumenical Israeli nature of this religious culture also had a negative side, sometimes manifested in a lack of tolerance for essentially particularistic traditional religious culture. Many traditional religious Jews, especially Sephardim, began to feel that their prayers, liturgical melodies and customs were totally alien to the young modern religious generation. Moreover, the differences between the traditional Sephardi and modern ways of life were of major significance within the framework of the National Religious Party, in which political activity was combined with religious life and where the synagogue also functioned as a party branch to a large extent. Furthermore, the social and economic success of the children of modern religious Ashkenazi immigrants widened the already broad cultural, social and economic gap between them and the traditional religious Sephardim. Alienation and estrangement were mutual.

Another paradox was the affinity that traditional Sephardi Judaism felt for Haredi Judaism, albeit that the latter was an Ashkenazi phenomenon. Major components of traditional Sephardi Judaism were also part of the Haredi religious culture: tomb rites, faith in charms and amulets, belief that the righteous can cure the sick and perform miracles, etc. Haredi Judaism, with its prominent particularistic-local aspects, was more tolerant of traditional Sephardi culture. Moreover, Haredim, like traditional Sephardim, considered their past, prior to their migration to the Land of Israel as a positive frame of reference, reflecting religious-social integrity before the crisis of immigration and absorption in secular Israeli society. The entire essence of Israeli reality was characterized by a rift that needed to be healed through the 'return' to a romantic past, thus restoring 'the crown to its former glory'.

Several processes developed that accorded political significance to the common denominator between Haredi and traditional Sephardi Judaism. At the outset it was within Ashkenazi Haredi society that the society of scholars developed. However, even in the early 1950s, it had begun to reach out to the new Sephardi immigrants. In the course of the struggle for immigrants' souls between the leftist Israeli establishment and the religious parties, *Yeshiva* students organized Torah Camp Activists (*P'eylim*), whose main function was to convince the new arrivals to send their children to religious schools and *yeshivot* where, free of economic and family concerns, they could devote themselves to the social-religious struggle. P'eylim activists also visited towns inhabited by these new immigrants, in order to enroll children at Haredi schools. They established special institutions for young people to serve as substitutes for households disintegrating under the pressure of the absorption process. Although the number of participating children was minimal compared with those who attended regular state schools, and even though many of those who did attend Haredi schools left them after a brief period of time, the ones who remained and became integrated in Haredi culture later became the hard core of Shas, the Sephardi Haredi party, which was established in the early 1980s.

But the contribution of the society of scholars to Haredi penetration of traditional Sephardi population sectors did not stop there. Once the society of scholars began to include the vast majority of Haredi young people, it faced two serious financial problems: employment for *kollel* students and their wives and how to find relatively inexpensive housing. In the mid-1970s, families of *kollel* students began migrating to development regions in the Negev and Galilee, largely populated by traditional Sephardi Jews. Housing in these areas was cheap, almost free. The students' wives were hired by schools desperate for teachers, and the *kollel* students themselves found work at schools and also in conducting Torah classes for adults. In many localities, the *kollel* students and their wives established Haredi educational centres: *yeshivot, kollels,* seminars for women and the like. Thus the basic problems of the society of scholars – housing and employment – were transformed into a social and political advantage. Within a decade, most development towns had young Haredi residents who began to exert an influence on their surroundings.

Secondly, the standard of living rose and the social and political status of most Sephardim in Israeli society began to change. Even if there was still an economic and educational gap between Ashkenazi and Sephardim, the political status of the latter began to improve markedly from the second half of the 1960s. But this change worsened the situation of those traditional Sephardim who found it difficult to adjust to economic and social realities. The more that their fellow Sephardim succeeded in integrating into the Israeli economy and public service, the more they felt abandoned and weak. This reinforced for many of them their affinity for tradition and their pre-Israel past, now perceived in a romantic light. They considered that modern secular Israeli realities were characterized by severance with the past and by a social and moral deterioration. Similarity between this and the standard Haredi conception was not coincidental. Furthermore, along with the shift in the political status of the Sephardim, there was a change in public attitudes towards the traditional religious culture they brought with them from their countries of origin. The legitimization, however partial, accorded to Sephardi traditional religious culture was a necessary condition for the reinforcement of the status of their religious leadership and of the new religious Haredi elite that had been nurtured in Haredi institutions.

Thirdly, the development of modern religious educational institutions with an overtly modern, status-seeking character widened the gap between the more traditionalist Sephardim and the modern religious population of Ashkenazi origin. In contrast, the Haredi educational system was less achievement-oriented and also enabled and even encouraged the establishment of separate educational institutions for the Sephardi population, giving full expression to its unique cultural traditions.

By the mid-1970s, the curious onlooker could already discern an increase in the number of *yeshiva* and *kollel* students of Sephardi origin. The vast majority attended special *yeshivot* established for Sephardim, while a minority studied at Ashkenazi-Lithuanian institutions. Likewise, the number of Sephardi girls attending *Beit Yaakov* seminaries and other specially established schools also grew. They formed an elite that internalized the norms and values of Haredi society, while maintaining the prayers and other special ritual features of Sephardi communities. From a political point of view, its members identified with Agudat Israel and worked for the party in Knesset and municipal election campaigns. After the 1977 upheaval, when Agudat Israel joined Menachem Begin's coalition, the Haredim were promised additional allocations ('special budgets'), enabling the society of scholars to consolidate and expand its ranks, partly among the traditional Sephardim.

However, this prosperity had a political and social price. Internal crisis within the heterogeneous Agudat Israel Party was accelerated by the party's changing nature and its role as the representative of the society of scholars whose aim was primarily to ensure its own continuity through the attainment of government allocations. The distribution of these allocations sparked a sharp internal struggle among the the various elements of Eastern European Jewry that comprised the party. Agudat Israel's Knesset members functioned more as representatives of the different particularistic-traditional groups vying for their share of the special budgets than as representatives of the Haredi public as a whole. Even the Torah Sages, the *Roshei yeshiva* and Hasidic Rebbes belonging to Agudat Israel's Council of Torah Sages, who had only recently represented the unity of the Haredi camp, began serving as representatives of the groups they headed, causing crises and paralysis within the Council. This intensified the consciousness of particularistic characteristics at the expense of an overall Haredi identity. Historical rivalries among the various groups, such as the 200-year-old struggle between Hasidim and *Mitnagdim* (Lithuanians), now acquired a renewed significance.

Against this background, one may discern frustration and disappointment among the young Sephardi Haredi elite. The Sephardim found that in the struggle over distribution of special budgets, they and their institutions were last in line, compounding feelings of discrimination with humiliation. The Sephardi *yeshiva* and *kollel* students found that this society was not prepared to consider them as equals. This was reflected, for example, in the reluctance of Ashkenazi Haredim to marry Sephardim – a clear case of prejudice in a society in which marriage is the result of matchmaking on social and rational grounds. When mixed marriages occurred, the Ashkenazi partner generally had some kind of flaw or blemish that precluded finding a spouse or his or her own ethnic group. Sephardim also noted that at Haredi schools, especially seminars for women, there was a tendency to separate Ashkenazim and Sephardim, assigning the latter to the less prestigious vocational classes.

These tensions came to ahead in the Jerusalem municipal election campaign of 1982. Three Haredi lists competed for the Haredi vote: Agudat Israel, representing the old party establishment; a party associated with the Lithuanian *yeshivot* and *kollels* that sought the backing of Rabbi Schach, the venerable head of the Ponevezh Yeshiva; and a Sephardi Haredi list whose outstanding personalities were *kollel* students from the Porat Yosef Yeshiva and who were supported by the *Roshei Yeshiva* and by Rabbi Ovadia Yosef, the former Sephardi chief rabbi. As some of these *Roshei Yeshiva* were disciples of Rabbi Schach, they too felt obliged to seek his approval and backing. Schach faced conflicting pressures. Although he dissociated himself publicly from Agudat Israel, Schach did not want to be held personally responsible for the breaking up of a party founded under the auspices of Torah sages of a previous generation and enveloped in an aura of sanctity. Eventually, he instructed the Lithuanian *kollel* students to withdraw their candidacy, while encouraging their Sephardi counterparts. His motivation may be easily surmised: Schach, like other Agudat Israel leaders, realized that the Sephardim had suffered discrimination and were not accorded appropriate representation in Agudat Israel. The secession of a group that many Haredim did not accept as an integral part of the Haredi community was therefore not perceived at that time as an affront to the dignity of the Torah sages who supported Agudat Israel. One may also assume that no one imagined that a

Sephardi Haredi list would gain significant representation and threaten the parent Agudat Israel Party, but that is precisely what happened.

Shas succeeded in transcending the boundaries of Haredi society: by attracting a following among traditional Orthodox Sephardi Jews who felt that the new movement bore an old-new message, seeking to rehabilitate their past and accord them legitimacy within Israeli society. Its success in Jersualem led to the decision to run for election to the Knesset in 1984. The party repeated its success, this time on the national level: 63,605 votes gave Shas four Knesset seats, the same number as the NRP and twice as many as Agudat Israel. In the twelfth Knesset elections (1988), the number of Shas supporters increased by more than 60 per cent to 107,709 and Shas became the country's largest religious party. An analysis of the election returns indicates that its supporters were drawn from regions with concentrations of traditional Sephardi Jews, from Israel's lower socio-economic strata. Shas is responding to a personal and social need rather than a religious one. Its leaders and activists are Haredim, but most of its voters are traditional Jews who maintain a lifestyle conforming with accepted norms in Orthodox rather than ultra-Orthodox circles. Moreover, while Shas leaders follow a Haredi way of life, they do not consider themselves committed to the anti-Zionist ideology of the Haredi parties. Thus, for example, Shas political figures accepted positions as ministers in Israeli cabinets, while leaders of the Ashkenazi Haredi parties were not prepared to do so, partly because it might oblige them to participate in official ceremonies at which the national anthem is played and Zionist symbols are displayed. Furthermore Ovadia Yosef, the spiritual leader of Shas, served as the Sephardi chief rabbi of Israel in the state rabbinate, an office whose legitimacy is denied by the Haredim.

These features accord Shas an advantage over the other Haredi parties, which limit themselves to specific sectors of the Haredi population. However, they also constitute a drawback: while the other Haredi parties (Agudat Israel and Degel Hatorah) can rely on the regular and nearly unconditional support of the society of scholars that is almost totally dependent on them, Shas is in constant struggle with the larger parties (primarily the Likud) for the same constituency. From this point of view, the charismatic personality of Ovadia Yosef is the party's more valuable asset. Now, Shas must guarantee its own future and nurture its next generation of supporters.

To cope with this challenge, over the past few years, Shas has concentrated on establishing its own educational system, *El Hamaayan*. Its ultimate objective is to establish a society of scholars paralleling that of the Ashkenazim, but the process is an extended one whose success cannot be guaranteed. In the short run, however, Shas has acquired a relatively stable position in Israeli politics and a firm grasp on a permanent and apparently stable constituency. The rapid rise of Shas apparently came as a surprise not only to the Israeli polity but also to its leaders. Shas was compelled to consolidate its institutions rapidly and institutionalize its spiritual leadership. As the party's founders were graduates of Haredi *kollels*, it is hardly surprising that they sought to establish a leadership similar to the Council of Torah Sages.[23] This idea proved difficult to put into practice. For reasons still unclear, senior Sephardi *Roshei Yeshivot* and Torah sages – Rabbis Abba Shaul, Yehuda Yitzhak, Yaakov Adas and the like – did not join Shas's Council of Torah Scholars. The Council comprises four members, headed by Ovadia Yosef. The other three members, who pale in comparison, studied at Ashkenazi *yeshivot* and consider themselves part of the Haredi 'Torah world', committed not only to its values but also to its leader, Rabbi Schach. Shas thus emerged with a two-headed leadership: Rabbi Yosef, who attracted the traditional Sephardi masses, and Rabbi Schach, whom the party's Haredi elite perceived as its Rosh Yeshiva.

The first manifestation of this complex situation was the episode already described when, during the Cabinet crisis of winter 1990, Schach dealt a harsh and humiliating blow to Ovadia Yosef by asserting to a mass rally and in Yosef's presence his unambiguous opposition to a government headed by the Labour Party. Schach had not discussed the matter previously with Yosef, who had been involved in the plans of Shimon Peres, then the Labour leader. He just presented him with a *fait accompli* to be accepted as divine word. It is difficult to imagine a greater affront to a Sephardi leader like Yosef, who had to accept it in silence, realizing that if he did not toe the line his rabbinic colleagues and some Shas Knesset Members would abandon him and the party would disintegrate. Indeed, the head of the Shas Knesset list, Rabbi Yitzhak Peretz, did decide to leave the movement following this incident.

The rivalry between Rabbis Yosef and Schach is not personal. It expresses the contrast between the traditional Sephardi rabbinic leadership, of whom Yosef is the typical representative, and the leadership of the Haredi society of scholars, of whom Schach is the most outstanding example. Those who expected these differences to disappear over time were keenly disappointed. Ovadia Yosef is not the kind of person to forgive and forget, nor would Schach make it easy for him to do so. Matters rose to a crisis level as the thirteenth Knesset elections approached. Fearing that Shas would repeat the 1990 manoeuvre and join a Labour-led coalition, and also seeking to reward Rabbi Peretz for his loyalty during that crisis, Schach initiated a move that led to the establishment of a joint Haredi list *Yahadut Hatorah* (United Torah Judaism) consisting of the two Ashkenazi Haredi parties (Degel Hatorah and Agudat Israel), with Peretz at its head in the hope that he would attract some of the traditional supporters of Shas. This was a serious error. Peretz's drawing power cannot compare with the charismatic personality of Rabbi Ovadia Yosef.

Subsequently, Schach only worsened matters: just before the elections, he declared that the Sephardim were not yet ready for positions of leadership. This unfortunate declaration, that aroused the injured Sephardi masses, delivered the *coup de grace* to Peretz's chances of success among Shas supporters. However, the significance of this incident extends beyond the election campaign. When Shas increased its vote to 129,347, this success was attributed to Rabbi Yosef. The party was now his and his alone. No longer would he have to fear the disciples and supporters of Schach on its Council of Torah Scholars and among the Haredi elite of Shas. Shas was now free from the hold of Rabbi Schach and the Haredi-Ashkenazi 'Torah World'.

The Price and Future of the Society of Scholars

The Haredi society of scholars appears, *prima facie*, to have enjoyed success, with unprecedented achievements in halting the move away from traditional Judaism, in shaping a Sephardi Haredi elite and in formulating a Haredi culture as an alternative to permissive modern secular culture. However, it is precisely this list of impressive successes that has led to an existential crisis. A society of scholars that does not limit the number of its members is simply too costly to the State of Israel, to affluent patrons from the Diaspora and to Haredi society itself.

The cessation of the decline of its numbers is partly the result of a recent development: marriage in Haredi society has now become a substantive and inseparable part of the socialization process. Only after a few years of marriage, when the young Haredi family generally may have as many as six children, do *kollel* students seek appropriate employment. But the average young Haredi man's lack of an academic or vocational education necessarily limits him in his choice of occupations. In most cases, he turns to religious leadership (the rabbinate or rabbinic courts), teaching Jewish studies or service as a religious functionary (ritual slaughterer, supervisor of *kashrut* (Jewish dietary laws), scribe, etc). The constant and rapid growth in the number of *kollel* graduates thus puts heavy pressure on their limited sources of available employment.

Parents of *kollel* families are obliged to supply young Haredi couples with housing and furniture. Under present Israeli economic conditions, this has become too great a financial burden to bear, especially for large families. Furthermore, the second generation of the Haredi society of scholars, those *yeshiva* students whose fathers are either still enrolled in *kollel*s or have spent several years in such institutions after marriage (which at present applies to the vast majority of *yeshiva* students), are in a far harder position financially than the first. All this demands constant additions to the number of *yeshivot* and *kollel*s, entailing significant claims on the national budget for Haredi institutions. Thus the higher the birth rate and the more students accepted by the society of scholars, the greater the price of this social experiment and the clearer its latent internal conflicts become.

The increase in number of *yeshiva* and *kollel* students, the expansion of Haredi institutions and the pressure that Haredi politicians have applied to increase state allocations for the society of scholars has intensified the hostility felt towards Haredim by the Israeli polity in general. Demands that Israeli politics free itself from the influence of the Haredi parties are voiced with increasing frequency. The exemption of most Haredi young men from military service – the result of an agreement since the establishment of the State of Israel, in which Torah students are exempt from service so long as they are attending *yeshivot* or *kollel*s – accords legitimacy and emotional validity to the growing antagonism towards Haredim.

The unique socialization process and high birth rate in Haredi society threatens its ability to persevere as a society of scholars.

Elections to the Thirteenth Knesset and Their Significance
The results of the thirteenth Knesset elections in 1992, unlike those of the twelfth Knesset – and perhaps in reaction to them – signified a decline in the status of the Haredi parties. The Labour Party again

became the dominant party, without which no government could be formed. Furthermore, opposition to the involvement of Haredim in Israeli politics appeared to have had a considerable effect in recruiting support for Labour, Meretz and Tzomet. Some Shas voters, too, cast their ballots in protest against Rabbi Schach's attacks on the party. More importantly, this time, the Haredim were not the only group that could tip the balance of power in the Knesset. To protect its own vital interests and free itself from Schach's influence, Shas alone of the Haredi parties joined the coalition at the time of its formation, although, had it not been for the appointment of Meretz Party leader Shulamit Aloni, known for her provocative anti-Haredi stand as minister of education, Agudat Israel might also have done so. Rabbi Schach remains the only implacable Haredi opponent, but his influence has declined considerably.

The thirteenth Knesset election results placed the Haredi parties in a far more difficult situation than they had ever experienced previously. The question of whether the society of scholars can continue to exist is one that cannot be avoided. The economic difficulties now being faced by its patrons in the Diaspora have a direct influence on the already shaky economic status of the society of scholars. Apparently, the worse the crisis becomes, the more tensions will rise among Haredi parties.

Shas leaders are aware of this existential crisis. Despite heavy opposition from other Haredi parties and the outrage of the Haredi public at their participation in a coalition with Meretz, they are unlikely to succumb to this pressure and withdraw from the Labour-led government. Such a move would put Shas and its recently established institutions at the mercy of Ashkenazi Haredi leaders once again, a prospect that holds little appeal. Indeed, the need to sustain the society of scholars may well lead the other Haredi parties to tread the same path and join Shas in the government.

11. THE PLACE OF WOMEN IN ISRAELI SOCIETY

Juliet J. Pope

The prominence of Golda Meir, from her role in the founding of the state to her retirement as prime minister in 1974, created the illusion worldwide that women play a vital part in Israeli politics. This image is perpetuated today by the fact that one of the most highly respected public offices in Israel, that of state comptroller, is currently held by a woman, Miriam Ben-Porat. In spite of these individual achievements, however, the general level of female participation in political institutions remains very low. Yet it would be misleading to suggest that women are either uninterested or disinterested in politics.

Israeli Women in Formal Political Institutions

Although women constitute 51 per cent of Israel's population and 48 per cent of the electorate, they are severely under-represented in all formal political institutions. A recent report shows that of a total of 554 Members of Knesset elected since Israel's independence, only 41 (6.8 per cent) are women. Indeed, the proportion of female MKs in any single Knesset has never reached 10 per cent. The first three Knessets which convened between 1949 and 1959 each included 11 women (9.1 per cent of the total membership); following the elections of 1988 the proportion declined to a record low of seven female MKs (5.8 per cent of the Knesset membership).[1] Despite the persistent efforts of lobbying organizations such as the Israel Women's Network (IWN) to raise the profile of female candidates within their respective parties only 11 women were elected in 1992 to the present Knesset: four belong to the Labour Party; two to the Likud; three, including the party leader, belong to Meretz; one to the Democratic Front for Peace and Equality; and one to Tzomet.

Female representation in the cabinet has been similarly low. Indeed, between 1948 and 1992, only four women were appointed cabinet ministers (and no more that one at a time): Golda Meir, who served as minister of labour and minister of foreign affairs; Shoshana Arbeli-Almozilino, who was minister of health; and Shulamit Aloni and Sara Doron, both ministers without portfolio. In 1992 Shamir's outgoing cabinet of 33 ministers was entirely male but the present cabinet includes a record number of two women, namely Shulamit Aloni, who headed the Ministry of Education until May 1993 and then, concurrently, the Ministries of Communications and of Science and Technology; and Ora Namir, who held Environment until December 1992 and Labour and Social Affairs after that.

As in Britain, it has been suggested that stereotyped images of 'women's interests' have restricted the careers of female politicians; they are often considered more suitable to deal with issues such as health, education and welfare than with the weightier, and more prestigious, issues of defence and financial affairs. This is reflected in the distribution of posts among Knesset committees. It was not until 1984 that a woman was appointed to either the Foreign Affairs and Security Committee or the Finance Committee, the two most powerful Knesset committees.

In local government women have also been under-represented with the percentage of women in local councils remaining under 9 per cent. There are signs of gradual progress in this sphere; the percentage of female councillors doubled from 4.2 per cent in 1950 to 8.6 per cent in 1989 but more than one-third of the local councils remain all-male.[2] It is interesting to note that the first female mayor in Israel, elected in 1972 in the village of Kfar Yassif, was a Christian Arab woman named Violet Khoury. As head of the Arab Women's Department of *Moetzet Hapoalot* (the Council of Working Women) which constituted the women's section of the Histadrut, Khoury had developed an important powerbase within the labour movement.

The 1978 local government reforms which introduced the direct election of mayors were welcomed by those who believed that candidates would no longer need to rely so heavily on the political machinery of parties. It was suggested, for example, that women would find it easier to organize on a local rather than national level and would identify more closely with community issues. These hopes have yet to be fulfilled. In the local elections of 1989, of the 29 women candidates for mayoralties, only one was successful.

Women have also sought to influence the implementation of political, economic and social policies through the civil service. Within Israel, 40 per cent of all civil servants are women; indeed, the national and local civil service is the largest employer of women in Israel. The number in key positions, however, remains low. Figures from 1991 show that in the two lowest ranks of the civil service, women constituted 70 per cent of employees; in the two highest ranks, they constituted only 3 per cent. (In 1986 the figure was as low a 1.7 per cent.)[3] The position appears to vary within ministries; the Welfare Ministry, the Ministry of Health, and the Office of the Prime Minister for example, have a relatively high number of women in senior positions. Once more, this distribution of posts reflects the stereotyped notion that women are more concerned with health and welfare than other issues.

Among the most significant positions held by a woman within the Office of the Prime Minister is that of the prime minister's Adviser on the Status of Women. This was established in 1975 at the end of International Women's Year, when the government also appointed an ad hoc Commission on the Status of Women headed by MK Ora Namir. The 92 men and women serving on the commission were all personally appointed by Prime Minister Rabin to investigate 'the means – social, cultural and educational, economic and legal – by which equality and partnership between men and women in all spheres of life in Israel are promoted.'[4] The report, published in 1978, made over 240 wide-ranging recommendations. They included proposals for eliminating sex discrimination in the fields of employment, education and health and for improving the representation of women in political office and the civil service. A decade later, more than 170 of them had not been even partially implemented.[5]

Some of the reasons for the under-representation of Israeli women in formal political institutions reflect similarities in other western democracies; others relate to more specific conditions within Israel. Politicians aspiring to a parliamentary career are usually required to serve a long apprenticeship in party politics, establishing and strengthening a power base and gaining necessary skills. This period of networking and training often occurs between the ages of the mid-twenties and late thirties, a time when women are more likely to be preoccupied with family responsibilities in addition, perhaps, to a career. This is particularly true in a society such as Israel where family life is venerated even within secular circles. Political meetings are usually held in the evening and, while women are still regarded as primarily responsible for childcare, those who cannot afford babysitters are further prohibited from participating in public life.

Israeli women are frequently denied access to the specific power bases which for their male counterparts serve as a springboard into political life. For example, university students in Israel, as in other countries, have opportunities to gain political experience within party-affiliated campus organizations. Throughout Israeli universities, however, female students are noticeably absent from leadership positions in such political organizations. This may be due, in part, to the fact that most (Jewish) students do not start tertiary education until they have completed military service. Given that a high proportion of female students in their mid-twenties are married, possibly with children, as well as working at least part-time, it is not surprising that they have less time to devote to extra-curricular activities such as politics.

In the light of current debates over electoral reform, it is worth questioning whether the representation of women in these institutions is helped or hindered by the Israeli system of proportional representation. In fact, despite the disproportionately low number of women in the Knesset, most women's rights campaigners have not favoured proposals for abolishing proportional representation. There have, however, been calls for modifying the current electoral system; it has been suggested that the introduction of multi-member constituencies, for example, would provide more opportunities for female candidates. Tacit support for the existing system which concentrates so much power in the hands of central party bosses is difficult to comprehend. On the other hand, the nomination of party lists might offer a potential solution to the problem of under-representation since it could facilitate positive discrimination. An alternative system which introduced smaller constituencies has been opposed by those who believe the competition faced by women for local nominations would be intensified.

The Israel Women's Network (IWN), which was created in 1984 to lobby for legislative reforms, and other feminist organizations have called on political parties to address the issue of parliamentary representation of women by introducing a limited system of quotas. As early as 1978 the Namir Commission recommended that political parties should allocate to female candidates a minimum of 25 per cent of the 'realistic' places on their Knesset lists. The commission acknowledged that quota systems raise problems about democracy because they contradict the principle of equality. It concluded, however, that quotas were a necessary evil until there was 'a change in the attitudes of political parties and the public and in women's abilities to run as equals for adequate representation.'[6] Ten years later, a follow-up report on the effects of the Namir Commission showed that only the Labour Party and its left-wing ally Mapam, had partially complied by promising in their manifestos to ensure women received 20 per cent of the places on their Knesset lists.

Prior to the elections of 1988 and again in 1992, the IWN issued a further demand that all parliamentary parties allocate 40 per cent of their seats to women. They also suggested that male and female candidates should be given alternative positions on the party list, the so-called 'zipper' principle. This principle has only been adopted by one party to date, namely the Tikvah Party led by Charlie Biton and Leah Shakdiel which however, failed to gain a seat in the 1992 elections.

There is no evidence in Israel of a 'gender gap' in terms of electoral behaviour; as a result, women are not regarded by the parties as a separate constituency of voters whose support must be wooed through guaranteed representation. Since women are regarded as just one of several minority interest groups, political parties are tempted to promote female candidates representing a combination of other interest groups too. Such was the case of Nelly Karkaby, a Christian Arab who was allocated 42nd place on the Labour Knesset list for the 1988 elections. As head of the Arab Women's section of Na'amat, her inclusion was designed to make the party slate more appealing to members of the women's section of the Histadrut and to Arab voters.

As in other countries, the majority of those women who do succeed in politics do little to promote other women. When Golda Meir became prime minister in 1969 she was criticized by feminists for failing to appoint any women to her Cabinet. Until recently it was also noticeable that neither of the two political parties which were founded by women promoted other women to leadership positions. Geula Cohen of Tehiya (which belonged to the Likud coalition) did not include any other women on the party list in 1988 and the only other woman on the Tehiya list in 1992 was allocated eighth place. Shulamit Aloni, leader of the Civil Rights Movement (Ratz) which has campaigned vigorously for women's rights since its inception in 1973, has also opposed the notion of positive discrimination. The Ratz list for

1992 included one other woman in a realistic position, namely Naomi Chazan, at fifth place. When the Meretz coalition was formed between Ratz, Mapam and Shinui, the tenth and twelfth places on the list were allocated to female candidates, Naomi Chazan and Anat Maor, respectively, both of whom were elected.

This syndrome has been criticized by feminist scholars such as Galia Golan, founder of the women's studies programme at the Hebrew University of Jerusalem: 'We've had the experience of queen bees in politics in this country, of women who make it and feel no responsibility to help other women. Golda was a perfect example.'[7] This syndrome can be likened perhaps to the experience of Thatcherism in Britain; when prime minister, Margaret Thatcher made no attempt to increase the number of women in public office.

It has become clear to women's lobbies that increased representation for women will not guarantee an improvement in their status as long as this remains tokenistic. During the electoral campaign of 1992 the Israel Women's Network urged women to vote for parties that promote women. In an attempt to form a joint lobby, somewhat akin to Britain's 300 Group, members of eight different parties have established a Cross-Party Forum. This organization has led a voter registration drive for women in eight major cities and towns; it has also sponsored courses on political empowerment and leadership to promote the civic involvement of Arab and Jewish women on local and national levels, and has provided professional training in public speaking, organizational methods and strategic planning. Two of its members were among the female MKs elected in 1992.

The practical viability of a separate Women's Party has been debated since the mid-1970s when a small but significant feminist movement emerged in Israel. Undoubtedly influenced by the feminist movements emerging in North America and western Europe, the Israeli movement was highly decentralized; it grew out of a small number of consciousness-raising groups and educational seminars in the cities of Haifa, Tel Aviv and Jerusalem. Among the various campaigns launched during this period were protests against the attempt to restrict the availability of abortion. Feminist groups also demonstrated against beauty contests, published newsletters and called for legislative reforms to improve the status of women in the fields of health, education and work, etc.[8]

A strategic alliance was formed between the Israeli feminist movement and the newly-formed Civil Rights Movement prior to the 1973 election when Shulamit Aloni, founder of the Civil Rights Movement, invited Marcia Freedman, a leading feminist activist, to join her party list. Freedman was subsequently elected to the Knesset where she initiated discussion of the abortion issue and drew attention to the problem of domestic violence. Personal and political differences between Aloni and Freedman led to considerable tension, resulting in Freedman's decision in 1976 to launch a separate Women's Party. Despite widespread publicity, the party's failure to gain representation in the 1977 election – it won just 6,000 votes – led to its political demise. It had served an important function by raising awareness of feminist demands such as remuneration for housework and the liberalization of the abortion law. Many of the women who had been active within the Women's Party, including Marcia Freedman, renewed their commitment to working with feminist organizations at grassroots level. Among the campaigns the Israeli feminist movement spearheaded during the mid-1970s was the establishment of a network of shelters for battered women, rape crisis centres and feminist resource centres.

The issue of a separate Women's Party resurfaced in the early 1990s; it evidently reflected a sense of frustration with existing parties and a renewed interest in promoting political representation for women which may be partly attributed to the mobilization of female activists within the peace movement. Prior to the 1992 elections, a new Women's Party was launched by women who claimed it would raise awareness of issues affecting women's status and compel other parties to confront these issues. The supporters of this Women's Party promised that it would back any coalition that furthered the peace process, even if that involved territorial concessions.

This strategy for increasing female representation was challenged by other feminists who doubted whether an adequate consensus could be reached. As one opponent of the scheme asserted: 'Women are unlikely to vote on women's issues while ignoring existential issues that affect every one of us, irrespective of sex.'[9] Due to changes in the electoral procedures, almost 40,000 votes were required to gain a single seat in the 1992 elections; thus smaller parties faced an even tougher challenge. Feminists opposed to the separate Women's Party suggested that the inevitable humiliation of electoral defeat could severely harm the cause of women's rights. According to these critics, failure to secure representation could legitimize the further marginalization of 'women's issues'. In the event, the Women's Party won fewer than 3000 votes, failing by a considerable margin to pass the threshold. The appointment of two female ministers suggests, however, that Rabin's government does not intend to ignore completely the demands of the feminist lobby.

Traditional Women's Organizations

Given their under-representation in formal political institutions, how have Israeli women sought to effect political, social and economic change? One channel has been separate women's organizations, termed 'traditional' in order to distinguish them from the more feminist-oriented women's groups described above, which emerged from the early 1970s onwards. Many of the traditional women's organizations developed in the Yishuv, the Jewish community in Palestine during the period of the British mandate. Set up as the women's branch of a political party, each mirrored its respective political platforms. By mobilizing female support within these organizations, they subsequently contributed to the development of the many political movements, each distinguished by its own separate ideology. For example, *Moetzet Hapoalot* (the Council for Working Women), linked to the Histadrut was the women's section of the Labour Zionist movement. Other women's organizations linked to political parties include: the Organization of Herut Women in Israel; the Liberal Women's Organization; *Emunah*, the National Religious Women's Organization; and the Movement of Democratic Women, which supported the Israeli Communist Party. The exception to these party-affiliated women's organizations was the Women's International Zionist Organization (WIZO), which predated the establishment of the state.

Despite their different partisan affiliations, members of these organizations engaged in activities which were regarded as primarily social, educational, cultural and philanthropic; the political significance of their work has been largely ignored. Given Israel's need to absorb vast waves of immigrants from different ethnic, linguistic and cultural backgrounds, these organizations played a key role in their education and political socialization. Literacy classes and Hebrew language instruction, for example, could be interpreted as political acts which contributed to the formation of a civic Israeli identity. Before Israel's independence and during the early years of statehood these organizations helped to create the network of services such as schools and clinics which formed the backbone of the welfare state.

Today they continue to provide a range of important services such as vocational training and subsidized day-care centres which encourage women to join the paid labour force. Many traditional women's organizations such as Na'amat also provide important links between Jewish and Arab women within Israel by running educational and social activities in Arab villages and towns in addition to the 'mixed' neighbourhoods of Haifa and Jaffa.

Members of these organizations constitute a vast body of part-time, local volunteers whose low-budget activities attract little attention beyond their own locality and are rewarded with little prestige. It is noticeable, too, that they provide a necessary power base from which a few female leaders enter the fray of mainstream party politics. For example, almost all the women elected to the Knesset on the Labour Party lists, including Golda Meir and current MKs Ora Namir and Masha Lubelsky, gained vital experience of organizing through Moetzet Hapoalot/Na'amat. As noted above, Moetzet Hapoalot/ Na'amat also furthered the political career of Violet Khoury, the first Arab woman mayor, and Nelly Karkaby, the first Arab woman elected to the Knesset.

The involvement of women in these organizations has inadvertently helped to marginalize women's demands and may have prevented women from advancing to leadership positions within mainstream political parties. (These criticisms mirror the concerns of those opposed to 'women's sections', for example, in the British Labour Party.) The traditional women's organizations have often been criticized for a lack of feminist consciousness because for many years they expressed uncritical support for the policies of male-dominated parties. The emphasis on social and educational work also reinforces traditional female stereotypes of women as carers. For example, a significant proportion of their resources is spent on providing childcare facilities for women working outside the home; until recently, these organizations did not question the notion that mothers should be primarily responsible for childcare rather than sharing these tasks with their male partners.

It should be noted, however, that since the late 1970s, these women's organizations have begun to show greater awareness of the specific problems facing women in Israeli society and have begun to lobby more for the advancement of women's status. This is manifest in their support for shelters for battered women and rape crisis centres, and their greater willingness to demand more representation within their respective parties.[10] Na'amat, for example, has challenged conventions with a campaign to encourage men to 'help' with domestic chores and has successfully lobbied for the introduction of paternity leave. This ideological shift may be the result of pressure from the growing number of feminist organizations within Israel; it may also reflect the influence of a younger, more radical and dynamic leadership.

The Socialization of Israeli Women

In order to explain the political behaviour of Israeli women it is necessary to explore three particular aspects of Israeli society: the role of the military; the primacy of the family; and the effect of religious legislation.

Women in the Israeli Defence Forces

The active participation of women in military organizations such as the *Haganah* and the *Palmach* before and during the War of Independence in 1948, together with the general liability of women in Israel for military service, gives the impression of sexual equality; yet the role of women in the Israeli Defence Forces (IDF) is severely circumscribed by both law and convention. The 1949 Defence Law asserts that, in principle, all Jewish Israeli women over the age of 18 are obliged to serve two years in the IDF. Under this law, however, exemption is available to Orthodox women whose religious lifestyle would preclude their service and to women who are already married, pregnant or have children. Recent figures show that the criteria allow for a greater proportion of exemptions among women than men: 25 per cent of women eligible for call-up are granted exemption on religious grounds, whereas only 2 per cent of men meet the much more stringent requirements of full-time religious study.

The majority of women in the IDF serve in separate units called *Chen* (Hebrew for 'charm') which mostly provide clerical and administrative support. Since the Yom Kippur War in 1973, when labour shortages became more apparent, women have also served as instructors to male soldiers; indeed, most basic training for male recruits is now provided by female instructors. Despite this change in policy, the Namir Commission found that, in 1976, women in the IDF were performing only 30 per cent of the jobs available to men. A decade later, this figure was doubled as many more technical and mechanical positions were opened to women. In 1988, however, more than 40 per cent of female conscripts were still providing clerical services to the IDF.[12]

This pattern of discrimination has been justified by the military on two grounds: first, since women serve only two years instead of three and are rarely called on to do reserve duty beyond the age of 24, it is not considered cost-effective to offer them highly skilled positions which require lengthy and costly training. For similar reasons, the IDF offers special education opportunities for illiterate or educationally subnormal men but not for women. The Namir Commission revealed that, of those women reaching draft age in 1976, 19 per cent were exempted because of substandard education or ability.[13] Thus the IDF deprives women from under-privileged backgrounds or those with learning difficulties of a second chance of an education.

Secondly, although women are trained as instructors in tanks and artillery, for example, they are excluded from all combat units because of fears concerning the mistreatment of female prisoners of war. This protective attitude is based on speculation about how an enemy (Arab) army would behave; it is often informed by racist portrayals of Arabs as particularly brutal. The paternalistic concern for the welfare of female soldiers is also regarded by many feminists as overtly hypocritical; if Israeli men were genuinely concerned about women's safety, one could argue, male policy-makers would pay more attention to problems such as rape and domestic violence within Israeli society.

The debate over opening up positions within the armed forces is similar to that occurring within the United States today. Those who identify with the 'right-to-fight' strand of feminism assert that women will be granted equal rights only when they assume equal duties in society. This argument seems particularly relevant to Israel, where security is a major preoccupation. Perhaps if women were seen to be playing more prominent and prestigious roles in the IDF, their status would be improved in other areas of public life. Higher status and broader experience within the IDF would certainly improve the credibility of female parliamentarians dealing with issues relating to security and defence.

Women themselves are partly responsible for perpetuating the patterns of inequality within the IDF. General Amira Dotan, the current commander of the Women's Corps, for example, regrets that many young women entering the IDF seem reluctant to opt for less conventional jobs, such as those involving modern technology. She blames this situation on stereotypical views of femininity which deter young women in particular from attempting 'male' jobs. There are relatively few women in senior positions in the military to serve as female role models. Until 1988 the highest-serving woman in the IDF, the commander of the Women's Corps, was a colonel; that position was elevated to the rank first of brigadier-general and, more recently, of general. Even the small proportion of women who have remained in the IDF as professional military personnel hesitate to press for complete equality of opportunities. General Dotan, for example, invokes traditional and religious arguments to explain why she rejects the notion of women serving in combat positions: 'We cannot ignore our heritage. There is a special role for the Jewish woman as a mother and the centre of the family. I fight for equal opportunities for male and female soldiers, but we must recognize that there are certain differences.'[14]

What are the political implications of this role differentiation within the IDF? One of the first Israeli sociologists to examine how socialization determines ideology about roles in Israel, Rifkah Bar Yosef, described the army as the most important influence outside the family for late adolescent boys and girls: 'Service in the army can be looked upon as a rite of passage into adulthood, a categorical end of parental authority and the institutionally defined expectation of individual responsibility not only for self, but for a collective goal.'[15] Thus the limited role of women in the IDF certainly affects the self-image and career expectations of young women. (Conversely, it must also influence how young men perceive the role of women.) More directly, the IDF is very important because it provides the basis for the 'old boy network' which determines who runs the country. It is significant that many senior politicians benefit from lateral career moves, from responsible military posts to high-status civilian positions, often in industry or political institutions.

The Primacy of the Family

The centrality of family life and the pressure on young women to bear children also have significant effects on the socialization of women. There is little doubt that strong family ties produce pressure on women to marry early and have children, not only for the sake of the individual but also for the community as a whole. Hence motherhood may be seen at times as less of a personal choice than a national duty. The cult of motherhood can be viewed as a kind of perpetual 'baby boom', necessitated by the series of wars and military attacks suffered by Israel. It also reflects concern over the euphemistically termed 'demographic problem' which highlights the difference between the birthrates of Jewish and Arab communities within Israel.

The pressure on women to reproduce is compounded within some communities by religious values; within ultra-Orthodox Jewish communities, rabbis interpret Jewish law as prohibiting the use of birth control and the birth of a child is regarded as a divine blessing. It is usual, therefore, for ultra-Orthodox women to have very large families. It should be noted that these communities constitute only a minority of Israeli society. Even within the most secular communities of Israel, young women are not encouraged to delay marriage and child-rearing. Among Jews the median age for first marriage is 22.8 for women and 25.9 for men. Among Muslims the figures are lower: 20 for women and 23.9 for men.[16]

Throughout the welfare system, certain assumptions are made about women and family life – a special birth allowance is paid by the National Insurance Institute to all mothers, generous provisions are made for maternity leave, and until recently it was only female employees in the public sector who were granted paid leave to look after sick children. These allowances clearly reflect the notion that children are best cared for by their own mothers. There are recent signs of more progressive thinking concerning the roles of male and female parents. The 1988 Employment Opportunities Law, for example, grants the right to sick leave to either parent to care for a sick child. As noted above, since 1990, Israel has joined a small number of countries offering paternity leave but it remains to be seen how many fathers will take advantage of this.

Another issue reflecting the primacy of the family which severely affects female employment patterns is the length of the school day. Despite the availability of public and private childcare facilities, the school day finishes at 3.30 pm, making it very difficult for many mothers to work a full day. This helps to explain the concentration of women in part-time, low-paid work, where they are also particularly vulnerable to redundancy. A recent report showed that 42 per cent of women in the Israeli workforce are part-time workers and the average wage gap between men and women is 30 per cent.[17] In order to improve opportunities for women, both traditional and feminist organizations have set as a campaign priority the extension of the school day and the improvement of day-care facilities for working women.

The centrality of family life in Israeli society also contributes to the relatively low level of female participation in public life. While many women in their twenties and thirties are preoccupied with the tasks of juggling work and family responsibilities, there is little time available for attending meetings and political engagements. It is noticeable that those women who do enter the political arena are single, childless or from privileged backgrounds, capable of affording private childcare.

The Impact of Religious Legislation

The peculiar relationship between religion and state in Israel has affected the political participation of women and helped to shape their political concerns. A series of recent controversies concerning the right of women to elect and be elected to certain public offices has highlighted particular conflicts between religious and secular institutions. Among the most publicized cases was that of Leah Shakdiel, an Orthodox woman from Yeruham who was elected in 1986 as the Labour Party representative on the local religious services council. A coalition of religious parties on the nine-member council attempted to prevent her taking office by petitioning the minister of religious affairs, Yosef Burg, who subsequently refused to endorse her position on the council on the grounds that she was a woman. It should be noted that the religious services councils are publicly funded bodies under the jurisdiction of the Ministry of Religious Affairs which function alongside local councils; their role is to cater for the ritual needs of the local community by maintaining synagogues, cemeteries and ritual baths (*mikvaot*), paying local officials, issuing licences to kosher restaurants and hotels, etc. The religious services councils are therefore administrative bodies which have no judicial authority and cannot issue rulings on the interpretation of religious law.

Shakdiel's supporters claimed that the orthodox parties controlling the Ministry of Religious Affairs were infringing the democratic rights of women to participate in municipal agencies funded by public money. They also pointed out that, according to the regulations governing these procedures, the ministry was entitled to express an opinion on nominations to religious councils but candidates were to be judged solely by their suitability for the position. There were also a significant number of religious women who challenged the particular interpretation of Jewish law which was invoked to prohibit female representation. The matter remained unresolved for over two years while a committee of representatives from the Ministry of Religious Affairs, the Ministry of the Interior and the Prime Minister's office deliberated over the objections to Shakdiel's appointment. Meanwhile Shakdiel turned to the Supreme Court which upheld her right to sit on the council. In October 1988 she took office and the following year another three women were elected to the religious services council in Tel Aviv.[18]

The Supreme Court was also instrumental in securing female representation on the municipal boards which elect local rabbis. Like religious services councils, the committees which select local rabbis were made up of (male) representatives of the municipality and the Ministry of Religious Affairs and the local rabbi. In 1987 the Labour Party faction on the Tel Aviv city council nominated two women, Haviva Avigai and Lily Menahem, to the board to elect the city's next Ashkenazi chief rabbi, whereupon the prime candidate threatened to withdraw from the election. Arguing that their democratic rights were in jeopardy, Avigai and Menahem also appealed to the Supreme Court which ruled in their favour.[19]

An important precedent had been established by the two cases cited above; the democratic right of women in Israel to vote and be voted into public office was upheld by the law. The women involved in these cases received widespread support: both of the campaigns were backed by an extra-parliamentary pressure group, the Civil Rights Movement while Avigai and Menahem were supported by the women's organiz-ation Na'amat. In fact legal history was made because in both cases an organization, and not only an individual, was involved in petitioning the Supreme Court in order to secure women's rights. It was also significant that for the first time, the Supreme Court recognized equality in the public sphere as a fundamental right.[20]

Women are also profoundly affected by the fact that there is no civil marriage or divorce in Israel: matters of personal status such as these are governed entirely by the relevant religious authorities. (All citizens are registered as members of religious communities, regardless of their level of religious observance.) Among Jews, these matters are ruled by the rabbinical courts which not only prohibit women from serving as judges but even ban the appearance of women as witnesses. According to Jewish law, a woman cannot receive a divorce without the consent of her husband. Even in extremely difficult cases where a wife is physically abused or where the husband is missing or insane, the civil courts cannot grant her a divorce. Theoretically, rabbinical courts can pressure a husband to co-operate in divorce proceedings by threatening him with excommunication, but in practice, they will rarely intervene.

A recent report suggested that in Israel there are currently as many as 7000 women, termed *agunot*, who have been refused divorce, many of them subjected to blackmail and extortion.[21] Pressure groups such as *Mitzvah*, formerly known as the League for Women's Rights in Israel, address the issue from a religious perspective, by providing couples with trained mediators and counsellors to negotiate an amicable divorce. Women's organizations such as Na'amat also seek modern solutions which are compatible with religious law; Na'amat recently published a report which advocated the introduction of prenuptial agreements. Many feminists, among others, have demanded a more radical, political solution – the complete separation of religion and state. Shulamit Aloni and Ratz, for example, argue that civil marriage and divorce ceremonies are needed to prevent religious authorities from circumscribing women's rights.

The Political Effects of the Intifada and the Gulf War on Israeli Women

The advent of the *intifada*, the Palestinian uprising in the West Bank and Gaza Strip which began in December 1987, polarized public opinion within Israel. At one end of the political spectrum, it strengthened support for the Greater Israel movement which demands the consolidation of control and increased Jewish settlement in the occupied territories. Among the secular advocates of this position is one of the most prominent female politicians, Geula Cohen of the Tehiya. At the other end of the spectrum are supporters of the so-called 'peace camp', who are not, on the whole, pacifists; their views are based on opposition to government policies in the occupied territories and some degree of support for the idea of territorial compromise with the Palestinians. It is interesting to note that among the best-known spokespersons for the peace movement is another female MK, Shulamit Aloni, now minister of communications, science and technology. The peace movement has been reinforced by the political mobilization at grassroots level of thousands of Israeli women, many of whom had little or no previous experience of demonstrations or political organizations. The identification of feminist groups with the peace camp and the resulting linkage of ideas has given rise to a separate women's peace movement.

Following the outbreak of the *intifada*, thousands of women participated with men in a range of protest activities and mass rallies organized by Peace Now, the best-known group within the peace movement. Under the slogan 'There is Someone to Talk To', Peace Now supporters called on the government to end the use of violence in the occupied territories and enter into negotiations with the PLO. In addition to these public demonstrations, women played an important role in the planning and administration, fund-raising and publicity work of local branches. The contribution of these female activists was afforded little public recognition; at public meetings and rallies, for example, women were rarely invited to make speeches.

Women were similarly well-represented in dozens of other organizations within the movement which came to be known as the 'peace camp'. Some of these were identified with the interests of particular groups such as: *Oz Ve'Shalom* (Strength and Peace), a peace group made up of religious Jews; and *Olim Neged Ha'kibbush* (Immigrants Against the Occupation). Others developed campaigns around specific issues such as *Yesh Gvul* (There's a Border) originally founded as a support group for Israeli soldiers jailed for refusing to serve in Lebanon. From the beginning of 1988, Yesh Gvul was reactivated to provide legal, political and moral support for the small but significant number of Israeli soldiers, mainly reservists, refusing to serve in the occupied territories. Another peace group with a specific purpose was *Shnat Esrim Ve'Ehad* (Twenty-first Year) which marked the twenty-first anniversary of the occupation by organizing a boycott of goods manufactured by Jewish settlers in the West Bank and Gaza.

As increasing numbers of female activists became disenchanted with what they perceived as the male-dominated ethos of these peace groups, many chose to initiate or participate in separate women's actions. The best-known all-female protest group was undoubtedly that of the Women in Black, a weekly vigil which began in Tel Aviv and grew into an identifiable movement with groups in over 30 locations nationwide. Dressed in black to symbolize mourning for the victims of violence, women demonstrated together under the slogan 'End the Occupation'. In Haifa, Acre and Nazareth it was noticeable that Israeli Arab women also joined the protests. The organization of Women in Black, which was clearly influenced by certain feminist traditions, was designed to maximize democracy: the network of groups was decentralized; there was no form of hierarchical leadership; membership was spontaneous and informal; and decision-making was by consensus.

In addition to the Women in Black, other autonomous ventures were initiated by women to protest against the occupation. The Peace Quilt, for example, was a creative project launched by a small group of women in Tel Aviv to which over five thousand Jewish and Arab women in Israel contributed. The Quilt, made up of small squares of fabric which were painted, embroidered and decorated with peace slogans, was subsequently used as the centrepiece for a number of peace demonstrations. Women were also mobilized within groups which organized practical campaigns, rather than demonstrations, around specific issues: Women for Political Prisoners was established by Jewish women in Tel Aviv and Jerusalem to provide material and moral support to Palestinian women who had been detained or arrested on political grounds; SHANI (Israeli Women Against the Occupation) organized a variety of activities to provide information about the *intifada* and campaigned, in particular, against the closure of schools and kindergartens in the West Bank.

Attempts to promote co-ordination and communication between these different groups, many with overlapping membership, led to a series of meetings which publicly acknowledged the existence of a separate women's peace movement. In December 1988, a year after the *intifada* began, a conference entitled 'A Call to Peace: Feminist Responses to the Occupation' was held in Jerusalem to discuss the linkage between women's liberation, nationalism or national liberation and peace activism. Representatives of various peace groups were also invited to an international conference of Jewish and Palestinian women entitled 'Give Peace a Chance: Women Speak Out' which was sponsored in Brussels by the Centre for Secular Humanistic Judaism. As a result of this meeting, a co-ordinating committee called *Reshet* (Network) was set up in Jerusalem to promote further contacts between Israeli and Palestinian women.[22]

The development of the women's peace movement raised a number of questions concerning the relationship between feminism and political activism within Israel. Some feminists have suggested that women are naturally more inclined than men to support peace and compromise. This socio-biological argument is difficult to prove; there is no evidence in Israel, for example, that women as a whole tend to favour those parties that are identified as 'dovish'. The reasons for women opting to participate in autonomous groups have also been debated, especially since many in the women's peace movement continued to resist the term 'feminist'. Some claimed to prefer the non-hierarchical structure and supportive atmosphere of the women's groups in which they were involved: others simply recognized the advantage of women's protests in attracting publicity.

These debates have also contributed to broader discussion of the effects of militarism and prolonged conflict on women and families. One of the issues which has received widespread public attention within Israel, largely as a result of female lobbyists, is the growth of domestic violence such as wife battering and child abuse. The advent of the *intifada* led to speculation that the legitimization of violence against Palestinian youths by Israeli soldiers and reservists could increase the level of violence against women and children within Israel. These anxieties were heightened after the Gulf War; numerous cases of rape and incest were reported to rape crisis centres during and immediately after the war. It has been suggested that the enforced passivity of men and the long periods spent at close proximity in sealed rooms produced high levels of tension and frustration, resulting in violence against women and children. Following the revelation by the Knesset Committee on Labour and Social Welfare that during the first year after the Gulf War there had been 34 cases of wife-murder, the IWN drafted the Domestic Violence–Urgent Remedy Law which is currently being implemented. This legislation allows for the removal of a violent husband from the family home pending a full court discussion within seven days.

A recent 'Conference on Feminist Lessons of the Gulf War' publicized two other areas of concern for women. During the war when schools were closed, it was invariably women who chose to stay at home to look after their children. When schools and day-care centres re-opened one parent was required to remain at hand in case of day-time missile attacks. Since the government did not offer compensation, it usually made economic sense for women to fulfil these duties. These moves compounded the problems of working mothers. The conference also criticized the fact that female broadcasters were excluded from the media during the war on the grounds that 'women's voices sound less authoritative'. Awareness has increased the need to accompany political representation and legislative change with efforts to challenge popular perceptions of gender stereotypes.[23]

Conclusion

While the quest for Israel's peace and security continues to dominate the national agenda, campaigns for sexual equality and social justice are regarded as of secondary importance. The centrality of defence and foreign policy issues in Israel has undoubtedly helped to keep women's rights to the margins of the political agenda. As one pamphlet recently published by the IWN suggests: 'The urgency of Israel's security and chronic economic problems has consistently shifted national priorities away from social issues, leaving women to continue their struggle against erosion of their status in Israeli society.'[24] Since part of the problem has been the identification of women with social issues to the exclusion of other political matters, it is ironic that one of the most influential women's lobbies perpetuates this notion.

The failure of the Israeli feminist movement to establish a broad-based network of support attests to the relatively low level of consciousness among Israeli women (and men) of how political issues affect women. This situation appears, however, to be changing, albeit gradually. This is not due to a revival of interest in feminism per se, but rather to the increasing numbers of women participating in protest groups which challenge government policies in the occupied territories. The political repercussions of the *intifada*, have therefore contributed to renewed discussion of women's status in Israeli society.

The most important task facing the Israeli feminist movement today is the need to convince the general public that it is in the interests of the whole nation to address their concerns. In other words, it is vital to proclaim that matters regarded as 'women's issues' are actually political issues with much broader implications. It has been suggested by Naomi Chazan, for example, that the under-representation of women in political institutions undermines the democratic workings of the state because an enormous wealth of female talent remains untapped. As a result, it is society as a whole which suffers, not just women. Similarly an increase in educational and professional opportunities for women, accompanied by an improvement in childcare arrangements, could benefit the entire economy.

During the recent round of Middle East peace talks, the leading Palestinian spokesperson, Hanan Ashrawi, captured the attention of the world media, challenging many stereotyped images of Arab women. Women, however, were notably absent from the Israeli delegation during the initial talks; a token woman was admitted to the negotiating team, almost as an afterthought, but did not play a prominent role in the discussions. Until considerable numbers of Israeli women are admitted to the centres of political power and are seen to be promoting constructive reforms, it seems unlikely their demands will be met. One of the political lessons learnt by feminist movements worldwide is that token representation cannot improve the status of women. The experience of Golda Meir's premiership has confirmed that Israeli women must continue to seek full integration into political organizations at all levels in order to attain substantial and lasting change.

12. CIVIL–MILITARY RELATIONS IN ISRAEL

Yehuda Ben-Meir

Israel enjoys a special position as far as the study of civil–military relations is concerned, as its unique character and situation make it an ideal research laboratory. The uniqueness of the Israeli case is a result of a number of factors. First, Israel is the only country in the world, with the possible exceptions of India and Turkey, that lies at the crossroads of the developing and the advanced nations, at the meeting point of the Third World and the western world. Geographically and, to a large degree, historically, Israel is part of the Third World. Situated in the Middle East, Israel was created in 1948 as a result of a bitter struggle against British colonial rule. Economically it is better off than the underdeveloped nations and most of the developing nations, but it is still far from having an economy and maintaining a standard of living commensurate with that of the most advanced nations of the western world (the United States, Japan, the EC, etc). Politically, Israel is a western-style modern liberal democracy, an island of democracy and individual liberty in the Middle East.

Israel's position as an ideal laboratory for the study of civil–military relations stems not only from its being at the same time part of the Third World and part of the western world, but even more from the centrality of security issues to Israel's very existence and from the central and dominant role played by the Israel Defence Force (IDF or *Zahal*) in the life of the country. Israel shares with western nations both a commitment to democratic government, and a highly developed military force and organization. Furthermore, Israel does indeed, enjoy a deeply rooted tradition of, and commitment to, democratic government, and the constitutional principle of civilian supremacy over the armed forces is firmly and clearly grounded both in law and

223

in custom. At the same time Israel has developed a highly efficient, effective, and modern military organization as well as highly respected intelligence and security services. Yet it stands out, all by itself, as the only western democracy to be in a continuous and perpetual state of war during its entire lifetime. Israel, born in war, has always faced a direct military threat to its national existence. Even today, though Israel has fought six wars in 45 years of independence, many of its Arab neighbours still refuse to recognize its right to exist. Forged by dire necessity and embodying the instinct for survival, the Israeli army has become both a symbol of national unity and a highly involved and dominant force in Israeli life – to a degree without parallel elsewhere in the western world.

Scholars and students of civil–military relations have not been unaware of the important lessons which can be learned from the Israeli experience. Samuel Finer writes that Israelis should be proud of the fact that Israel is not mentioned even once in his book *The Man on Horseback* – a book devoted primarily to the dynamics of military usurpation. He adds that the fact that the Israeli army does not pose a threat to civilian government is, in and of itself, 'a fascinating story'. The question arises as to why, despite the fact that the IDF occupies a far more central place in Israeli public life than does the military in any other democracy, it nevertheless does not pose any real threat to the democratic institutions of the state.[1] Finer suggests that the answer is, 'because [the IDF] is itself a civilian institution.'[2] Yoram Peri also makes the point that Israel's image in the eyes of many students of civil–military relations has been one of an abnormal and unique case.[3] But Peri claims that attempts, mainly by scholars outside Israel, to explain Israeli civil–military relations have resulted in an image of the IDF and its relationship with the civil system that is unrealistic and oversimplified. In his opinion, there is a need for a re-evaluation of the prevailing image of the IDF and a revision of previously accepted theories of civil–military relations in Israel.[4]

A key variable of civil–military relations, as Samuel Huntingdon among others recognizes, is 'civilian control'.[5] Amos Perlmutter and William Le Grande have noted that, 'historically, the issue of civilian control has attracted the most attention among scholars of civil–military relations: how do civilian political actors manage (or fail to manage) to subordinate the military to their authority?'[6] As Yehoshafat Harkabi points out in his monumental work *War and Strategy*, the basic differences in mentality, background, approach, aims and needs between civilians and soldiers, between the political and military elites, will inevitably lead to friction and misunderstanding and thus pose a major challenge to civilian control. Civilian control, however, is seen as an essential ingredient of civil–military relations in a democratic society.[7]

What does civilian control really mean? It is clear that a narrow definition, namely one which puts the entire emphasis on the exercise of ultimate formal authority by the elected representatives of the people, is insufficient. This definition has been characterized as civilian control 'in the old sense'. According to a more modern view, the essential problem of civilian control is the proper combination of military advice and opinions with political advice and popular opinion. The whole issue of the 'military–industrial complex' clearly indicates the need for a broader definition. President Eisenhower's warning, in his farewell speech, of its growing influence was not intended to imply that there existed a danger that military officers and industrialists would conspire to take over the government of the United States, or that the generals would refuse to obey the president. Rather, it was meant to suggest that the growing size and economic power of the defence establishment, that is, the growing involvement of the military in domestic affairs, posed a potential threat to the ability of the civilians to control the military genuinely and effectively.

The view that the over-involvement of the military in a given area, even if it does not threaten ultimate formal civilian authority, runs contrary to civilian control is not limited to the area of domestic affairs, but applies as well, if not more so, to the area of national security. Since the Second World War, and especially during the Cold War, many decisions relating to diplomacy and economics, areas usually reserved for civilian involvement, were heavily influenced, and, in many instances, actually made, by the military. This was seen by many as a threat to civilian control.

Evaluation of civilian control in Israel is particularly complex because of the unique Israeli security milieu and social environment. A number of key questions immediately come to mind. Can a society experiencing protracted war in which security is such a salient factor preserve an instrumentalist army, i.e., one that does not penetrate into civil institutional spheres? Has there been an erosion or increase in civilian control during the past 40 years? How healthy is the current system and what changes are necessary?

The scholars who have studied Israeli civil–military relations have not reached any consensus on these questions, and have offered different evaluations of civilian control in the Israeli context. Thus Perlmutter argues, 'The rapid turnover of officers . . . the economic and social integration of Zahal's veterans, the nation's dependence upon the reserve system, the identity of political goals, and the army's professionalism preclude Zahal's actual intervention in politics. In addition, the institutionalized legitimacy of the independent civilian political structures furnish an effective guarantee of civilian control.'[8] At the same time, he emphasizes that: 'The military in Israel – as a pressure group similar to those in other non-praetorian states where the civilian is formally and informally supreme – will nevertheless continue to challenge the civilian, especially in the realm of defence and foreign affairs.'[9] Luttwak and Horowitz cite Israel's extensive reserve system as a major factor causing military life to be pervaded by civilian influences, i.e., the civilianization of the military.[10] Peri, on the other hand, takes a dimmer view of the status of civilian control in Israel. He speaks of nominal civilian control, but of only weak instrumental control, and describes Israeli civil–military relations as being characterized by a political–military partnership.[11] In his opinion, while one can legitimately speak of the civilianization of the military in Israel, there is a definite process of militarization of civil society as well.[12]

These conclusions suffer from oversimplification and fail to do justice to the unique intricacies and subtleties of the relationship. The overall picture of Israeli civil–military relations so far is a positive one. Israel's short history is replete with examples of actual, not nominal, civilian control. Indeed, the record on this issue is quite impressive. If there has ever been a case of a democracy being ripe for the development of Lasswell's 'garrison state', it is Israel; nevertheless Israel shows no sign of becoming such a garrison state. At the same time, there are certain areas where civilian involvement is barely present, and where military over-involvement and domination are the rule. This is found at both the decision-making and the organizational levels. Although a positive assessment of Israeli civil–military relations holds true for the present, the future is fraught with uncertainties and with potential sources of tension and crisis for these relations. Social, cultural, and demographic changes as well as polarization and political instability might, at some point in the future, seriously threaten the principle of civilian control.

Using a narrow definition of civilian control, namely the noninvolvement of the military in political affairs, we may rightly argue that Israel manifests a high degree of civilian control. There is no instance in Israel's history of military intervention or even of a veiled threat of military intervention in the electoral process or in the political institutions of the state. This holds true not only for blatant interference, but for minimal involvement – such as influence on political appointments or interference in the decision-making process – as well. As Perlmutter so aptly points out: 'General Dayan was appointed defence minister in the crisis of June 1967, not because he had great influence with the Zahal, but because it was the will of the Israeli electorate.'[13]

But this issue is not as simple or as clear-cut as it may seem on the surface. The issue of military involvement in the political process is related to the expanding role of retired senior military officers in government, and the entrance of ex-generals into politics. There are those who consider this phenomenon, which is now quite widespread in Israel, a case of indirect military intervention in the political and electoral process. In their opinion, it is a dangerous convergence of the military and civilian sectors of society and thus poses a definite threat to civilian control. It should be noted that this practice can be found in other western countries, especially in the United States, which has a long history of military heroes running for and being elected to the presidency. Huntington tends to play this down, claiming that it does not constitute a threat to civilian control. Israel, however, is a special case and this phenomenon, in the Israeli context, may give rise to a greater degree of concern. This is primarily for two reasons: the large number of former senior IDF officers in government and politics, and the informal nature of Israeli society.

At first glance, the extensive role played by retired IDF officers in government and politics does not seem to have contributed to increased military involvement or influence in political affairs. There is little, if any, evidence that, upon entering civilian life, former generals tend to serve military interests or even to advocate specific positions supported by the IDF. On the contrary, it was Ezer Weizman, Ariel Sharon and Yitzhak Rabin, all ex-generals, who instituted, or attempted to institute, the most far-reaching cuts in defence spending and in the IDF budget. Similarly, some of the strongest and loudest critics of the IDF in the Knesset and in the Foreign Affairs and Defence Committee have been ex-generals.

More careful examination, however, points to at least two subtle, yet significant, effects of this phenomenon on civil–military relations. Firstly, the expectations of senior IDF officers as to their future role in civilian life may influence their decisions and behaviour while they are still in uniform. The fact that almost all of Israel's generals leave the army in their late forties or early fifties is a significant contributory factor to such a situation. The desire of most chiefs of staff, as well as most of the officers of the general staff, to attain upon leaving the service key positions in politics, government, industry or business results in an unhealthy dependence of these senior officers on the politicians and may compromise their professional integrity. This is a subtle case of politicization of the military. Secondly, the integration of so many senior IDF officers, after 20 to 30 years in the army, into the higher echelons of civilian activity and decision-making, results in a massive transfer of manners, work habits, nomenclature, norms and values from the military to civilian society. Both effects are hard, if not impossible, to quantify and are not easily visible, yet both can be quite impressive.

A somewhat wider definition of civilian control puts the emphasis on the question of who exercises ultimate control, that is on the readiness of the military to comply with civilian authority. There is no question regarding nominal civilian control in Israel. There may be a difference of opinion as to the degree of instrumental civilian control, but few would argue that from the formal point of view the IDF has always complied with civilian authority and the principle of civilian supremacy. Even Peri writes that, 'Never since the establishment of the state was there any expression of the army's desire to question the roles the political national institution allotted to it, to take part in the process of power transition or to usurp political power.'[14]

However, current thinking in the field tends to dismiss these definitions, claiming that they reflect civilian control 'in the old sense'. The more recent position is that the litmus test of civilian control should disclose who in fact, not theory, establishes national security policy and determines the allocation of finite resources to fulfil security needs. The degree of civilian control is, in effect, a function of the relative involvement of the military and civilian echelons in the various areas of social endeavour and national decision-making. Civilian control means the maintenance of an appropriate balance between civilian and military involvement in each of the various areas. Careful examination of civil–military interaction in the area of national security, and, more specifically, of the relative involvement of the civilian political leadership as against the IDF general staff, shows a mixed picture: over certain activities there is a high degree of civilian control, whereas over others military involvement is paramount. Samuel Huntington has differentiated two areas within which governments have to take decisions on defence: strategy and structure. The former is concerned with strategic doctrine, contingency plans, disposition and deployment of forces and resources, and defence policy and priorities; the latter addresses more practical and detailed questions of weapons acquisition, defence budgetary matters, and armed services' morale, organization, equipment, resources and training.[15] Martin Edmonds points out that this analytical distinction is satisfactory only in peace time; in war, an additional area has to be included, namely, the overall conduct, control, and command of fighting units involved in combat. He adds that the complex character of nuclear warfare 'has made this area, once a responsibility that devolved largely on to the armed services, one that political leadership has increasingly assumed the authority to control.'[16]

The interaction and inter-relationship between civilian and military involvement in national security affairs has therefore to be examined under three headings: the operational dimension, strategic planning, and force development. The operational dimension shows a high degree of civilian involvement. The responsibility and authority to conduct military operations is firmly and securely in civilian hands. In this area, the degree of civilian control found in Israel is comparable to that of any other advanced western country. On the other hand, the dimensions of strategic planning show a totally different picture. Civilian involvement in the actual formulation of national security policy is minimal, and this is the most serious threat to civilian control in Israel. The dimension of force development, involving the allocation of resources, lies somewhere in the middle. Here, there has been a definite increase in civilian involvement over the past decade.

The principle that military operations can be undertaken only under the direction of the civilian authority and within the parameters determined by the civilian authority has never been questioned in Israel. In our opinion this is not a case of nominal control, but of genuine instrumental control. Time and again, throughout Israel's short history, the military has complied with the operational directives of its civilian superiors, even when these directives were diametrically opposed to the recommendations, desires, and judgment of the military leadership. The twin cases of the waiting period prior to the

Six Day War and the refusal to sanction a pre-emptive air strike on the morning of the Yom Kippur War are prime examples of instrumental civilian control. Very few civilian governments have ever faced such heavy pressure from the military to go to war as did Eshkol and his colleagues during the two-week period preceding the Six Day War. Nevertheless Eshkol and the Israeli government held their own. The eventual decision to go to war was genuinely that of the Cabinet, influenced by public opinion and by certain political and diplomatic developments, and was not dictated by the army.

The central problem and the most serious flaw in Israeli civil–military relations can be summed up in the words of Samuel Huntington; 'In many countries strategic planning is effectively dominated, if not totally monopolized, by the military acting through a central military staff. What is often lacking is an effective civilian counterweight to the strategic advice the military provides the government'.[17] This dimension is clearly characterized by heavy over-involvement by the military and under-involvement by civilians. Strategic planning is almost completely monopolized by the planning branch of the IDF general staff. Nowhere is this more evident than in the crucially important area of war aims and objectives. In the tradition of Clausewitz's famous dictum that 'war is a continuation of politics by other means', it is universally accepted that the prime responsibility of the civil authority is to determine the goals and objectives of war, leaving it largely to the military to decide on how they are to be achieved. The Israeli paradox is that while, as was shown above, the civilian echelon intervenes quite actively in deciding on the 'how', it fails dismally to meet its primary responsibility to determine the 'what'.

In the absence of clearly defined war aims or national security goals, the military has no choice but to produce these aims and goals on its own. As a result, it has been the IDF, more than the government, which has determined the strategic outcome of Israel's wars. Thus, it was the IDF General Staff and Chief of Staff Yitzhak Rabin, who, during the Six Day War, convinced Defence Minister Moshe Dayan – against his better instincts and against his initial directive and orders – to permit the IDF to reach the Suez Canal and to establish its forward positions on its eastern bank. Here we can discern a pattern of nominal though definitely not instrumental, civilian control. Israel's extensive reserve system (whereby every able-bodied male till the age of 50 serves 30 days a year reserve duty in the IDF) gives the planning branch of the IDF almost unlimited access to Israel's academic brainpower in the areas of strategic studies, international relations and political science. This is a major, and uniquely Israeli, factor contributing to the military's dominance of this area.

Unlike the operational dimension which has manifested a high degree of civilian control since the early days of the state, and unlike the strategic dimension which to date has been characterized by a highly limited civilian involvement, the dimension of force development has been undergoing an evolutionary process of change, moving from almost total military involvement and control to a much more balanced civil–military interaction. During the early years of the state, the structure and organization of the IDF as well as priorities in the allocation of resources within the armed forces were almost the private domain of the military; civilian involvement – to the degree that it was present – was limited to the defence minister (or to the prime minister and defence minister when both posts were combined) and was primarily nominal. As time passed, and especially during the 1980s, the role of the defence minister became much more prominent and decisive, and there was a slow but perceptible increase in the involvement of the Cabinet. For the first time in Israel's history, questions regarding procurement or development of key weapons systems were debated and decided in the full Cabinet, or in the Ministerial Committee on Defence. Such was the case regarding the Lavie project and the acquisition of new submarines.

In vivid contrast to the strategic dimension – where the defence minister usually encounters a monolithic military approach – the existence of quasi-independent services means that, in the area of force development, the defence minister is often presented with alternative proposals and different options. The fierce competition between the air force (and, to a lesser degree, the navy) and the ground forces over the priorities and the allocation of resources leads to a great deal of controversy and to sharp disagreement within the general staff. These disagreements are too severe to be resolved within the confines of the IDF, and are invariably brought to the attention of the defence minister – as well as the prime minister and even to the entire Cabinet. A second factor working in favour of increased civilian involvement is the progressive tendency of the Israeli media to discuss these issues. Until the Yom Kippur War, this entire question was considered beyond the bounds of public debate. The media co-operated fully in this 'conspiracy of silence'. The Yom Kippur War, however, led to the defence establishment losing its aura of invisibility.

The Israeli public, as well as the media, started to question the wisdom of decisions made by the IDF general staff. Politicians began to feel heavy pressure to deal more effectively with these issues, lest they be accused of squandering and wasting public funds.

A final factor which is crucial for civilian control is the firm and unwavering ideological commitment of the military to democratic government coupled with a deep and unshakeable belief in the principle of civilian supremacy. This factor is consistently and strongly present in the Israeli context, and would seem to be one of the most effective forces guaranteeing civilian control.

There are a number of important circumstances which enhance the firm ideological commitment of the Israeli military to democratic government. First is the high degree of internal democracy within the IDF itself. This is a direct result of the popular character of the army. This manifests itself not only in the fact that three-quarters of the IDF's order-of-battle are reservists, but also in the rapid rotation system, the early retirement programme, the universal draft, the lack of a military academy, as well as in the existence of a young, inquisitive, and intelligent officer corps. Second is the deep-rooted democratic nature of the Jewish people. Israel may be a young country, but its society reflects the age-old traditions and mentality of the Jewish people. Many scholars credit Ben-Gurion's leadership and vision for the fact that in Israel, unlike many other new nations, the IDF did not become predominant and never showed any praetorian tendencies. The commitment of the IDF's officer corps to a free, pluralistic and democratic society reflects the cultural heritage of the people and society of which they are part.

Looking toward the future, however, there is room for some concern regarding the continued effectiveness of this key factor. There are two major reasons for such concern. First, the changing composition of the Israeli officer corps. In the past, the cadre of IDF commanders was strongly inbued and indoctrinated from childhood with Zionist, democratic, and liberal values, that is, with the revolutionary ideology of the Jewish national liberation movement. It is for this reason that one finds it so inconceivable that Moshe Dayan, Yigal Allon, Yitzhak Rabin, Motta Gur, Rafael Eitan, Moshe Levy, Dan Shomron or any chief of the general staff would ever seriously challenge civilian supremacy. This picture is, however, slowly but surely changing. The IDF officer corps will, inevitably, reflect the demographic and cultural changes within Israeli society. Officership in the IDF is seen today by many young soldiers as a key to socio-economic mobility. It is seen less and less as a calling, and more and more as a career; the IDF itself is, thus, becoming a more corporate body. There is room for doubt whether a future chief of staff, in ten or twenty years' time, will possess the same deep commitment to the principle of civilian control as has been characteristic of chiefs of staff to date.

The second factor is connected to the deeper and far-reaching changes in Israeli society and in its political system. The past two decades have seen a growing polarization within Israeli society. Israeli public opinion is split down the middle on many issues and is characterized by a basic lack of consensus, or what is technically known as a 'state of desensus'. The most troublesome and even dangerous feature of this polarization is that many of these divisions seem to go together. This has led to the country being divided into two hostile camps: the right or so-called 'national camp', composed mostly of religious and traditional Jews, of Oriental origin, hawkish and anti-Arab and Likud supporters on the one hand; and the left or so-called 'peace camp', composed of secular Jews of western origin, dovish and Labour supporters on the other. The debate over the future of the occupied territories is becoming more and more bitter, even bordering on the violent, and may be quickly approaching the state of 'a house divided against itself'.

At the same time, the Israeli political system is showing signs of a deep malaise and seems to be suffering from stress and from a basic structural weakness. Many observers characterize the Israeli political system as sick, and some even see it as on the verge of paralysis. As a result of Israel's perfectionist system of proportional representation, parliamentary system of government and an electorate split between right and left, effective government is becoming more and more difficult. The result has been that a number of small parties or even individual members of the Knesset acquire totally disproportionate power and influence. Coalition negotiations have been characterized by what amounts to open blackmail, causing revulsion among the Israeli public and bringing the entire political-electoral process into disrepute. The political parties are at their lowest ebb ever and the public seems to have lost confidence in them.

The combination of a lack of common purpose and ideological consolidation, and a weak and ineffective political system are high among the conditions which give rise to praetorianism, to a breakdown in civilian control and to direct military involvement in the governing of the country. Perlmutter emphasizes that a professional army has a corporate orientation and is motivated to 'protect a stable regime' – which is characteristic of professional states. However, this same army will be motivated to 'challenge an unstable [regime]'.[18]

Given the changing nature of the IDF, and especially of its officer corps – from a professional revolutionary army to a professional-corporate one – one may ask how such an army would react in the face of severe social and economic instability coupled with near political paralysis of the civilian government. Most Israelis are certain that even in a situation where the civilian government is hardly functioning and the country is facing national paralysis, the IDF would not take over power unless it was given some sort of civilian legitimacy, such as a call by the Knesset, to do so. Nevertheless, there is still room for doubt and for concern. One can only hope that Israel will never have to face such a situation.

Whatever the future may hold for Israel, and the aforementioned discussion is in the realm of conjecture, the principle of civilian control is, for the time being, firmly rooted in Israeli society. The essential and intriguing paradox of Israeli civil–military relations is that while the IDF is, indeed, a symbol of national unity and a highly influential and dominant force in almost all areas of Israeli life, its actual impact on the core value system of Israeli society is minimal. Israel has not become a 'garrison state', and Israeli society does not manifest any significant signs of militarism. Civilian control remains firmly entrenched, and actual instrumental civilian control is increasing with the passage of time. While researchers from outside Israel tend to stress the influence of the IDF on Israeli values and norms, Israeli scholars emphasize the fact that, in the final analysis, the IDF does not mould Israeli society, but rather reflects it. This is probably due both to the fundamentally democratic and civilian nature of the Jewish people, as well as the basic strength of Israeli civilian institutions.

13. QUESTIONS FOR THE FUTURE

Keith Kyle[1]

On 17 May 1954 the second Knesset expressly censured a senior American State Department official, Assistant Secretary of State Henry Byroade, on account of a series of speeches in which he had argued that Israel's Law of Return (allowing Jews anywhere in the world the right to migrate to Israel and receive automatic citizenship) was a cause for legitimate concern to its Arab neighbours, especially in view of the huge overhang of up to two million Jews living in and currently prevented from leaving the Soviet Union. 'The ingathering of the exiles is the supreme ideal of Israel,' the Knesset proclaimed and, speaking in the debate, Israel's first foreign minister, Moshe Sharett, accused Byroade of being willing 'to aim an arrow, as it were, at the very pupil of its eye, at the most precious and sacred aspect of Israel'.[2] Thirty-eight years later, the then prime minister, Yitzhak Shamir, was to tell the French newspaper *Le Figaro* (1–2 February 1992), 'From the start our national liberation movement was different from any other. In all other countries there was an aspiration to independence. In our case, we had to bring the population here and then give them independence.'

It was because Israel was 'unique and *sui generis*,' Sharett said in the 1954 speech, that 'it is idle to call its peculiarities into question. It is such and it can be no different. All quests for precedents and analogies would be in vain. There is no state exactly like it in the present international world because there is no parallel to Jewish history in the annals of mankind.' This large claim (with the strange and terrible history of the Jewish people behind it) was understandably, as Henry Byroade had implied, an exceptionally difficult proposition for the entire region to stomach. It was to be 41 years after the 1947 UN resolution on partition before the Palestine National Council declared itself ready to acknowledge that Palestine had been permanently divided into predominantly Jewish and predominantly Arab states.

The peace process has not been the theme of this book – though as Mordechai Bar-On has pointed out in Chapter 2, one of the presumptions, stated or implied, of the Zionist project has always been the eventual achievement of peace and mutual recognition between the 'Old-New Land' (to use Theodor Herzl's expression for a Jewish state) and its neighbours. But whereas the amount of territory to be included within Israel's permanent boundaries is a subject that bitterly divides one type of Zionist from another, the need to accept, and indeed to foster, all Jewish immigration, irrespective of political convenience or (as Pinchas Landau illustrates in Chapter 4) of economic rationality, remains the undiminished core of all types of Zionist conviction. Loyalty to this ideology was perhaps most dramatically illustrated when, in the middle of the most strained period of the Russian immigration, Israel took immediate advantage of the fall of the marxist regime in Ethiopia to airlift in the remaining 14,500 'black Jews' although everyone knew from previous experience they would prove far more difficult to assimilate than the Russians.[3]

Two things were soon known of the wave of Russian immigrants that started arriving in 1989: that they were in the main of high educational quality and that they were not, unlike *refuseniks* who had come earlier after a long and painful struggle for the right to emigrate, as a whole motivated by Zionist ideology. There was less 'ascending up to Zion', more quitting Russia or the other republics while the going was still good for any country that would open its doors. Some native Israelis were unperturbed by this. Indeed, in 1990 one could hear it said in Israel by senior Jewish Agency officials that it was in some ways easier to deal with newcomers who did not see themselves as idealists and heroes, that they expected less.[4] One could also hear Israelis promising themselves, in tones of satisfaction and awe, that 'We are dealing with the cream and elite of Soviet society.' While there may have been some exaggeration in this, it was indeed the case that, in terms of academic and professional qualifications the newcomers were, on average, much better equipped than the veteran population. Over half of them had at least one university degree; over a fifth had more than one.

The glowing prospect of a quantum leap had thus, it seemed, been held out to Israel's economy, but only provided that within a short space of time the society would show itself capable of the quite exceptional imagination and effort required to grasp the unique chance offered. Many Israelis would say that they had done it once, in the first decade of the state when the population more than doubled in four years, and they could do it again. But here the second factor, that most of these immigrants are not strongly Zionist by conviction, asserts itself. Their occupational profile does not fit that of the absorbing community. Of the immigrants who could expect to join the labour force, 25 per cent were engineers and architects (compared to 2 per cent among Israelis), 15 per cent were technicians and 12 per cent were in the medical profession. A high proportion were academics.[5] A witness before a subcommittee of the United States House of Representatives put it in February 1992, 'There is nothing that is going to happen in the next year that will make it possible to absorb in any system musicians and talented mathematicians on the scale in which they are arriving.'[6] As someone in Israel said, 'When you've formed the third new orchestra, how do you go on to form the fourth and fifth?' Also, for musicians as for every other category of immigrant, not all could be of the highest class, and some are finding it harder than others to adapt themselves to life outside Russia.

Most of the new immigrants are pragmatic: that is, they understood before they arrived that they could not all get the jobs for which they were best qualified at once, but, on the other hand, those that have internationally recognized qualifications might be expected, if nothing seemed in prospect within a year or two that remotely matched their talents, to take the first opportunity to depart. Men with PhDs would not sweep the streets for ever. Israel did not have long in which to demonstrate that it had not lost the capacity to work miracles.

The challenge provided by the Russian *Aliyah*, urgent as it is, has served to make more urgent still the accumulation of social and political issues outlined in the preceding chapters. Many of them have been apparent for some considerable time and some have become more acute in recent years for reasons other than the arrival of the Russians – until 1990 the economy had not grown at sufficient speed (and in most years had grown hardly at all) since the Yom Kippur war in 1973 brought to an abrupt halt Israel's hitherto dazzling performance as an economic 'tiger'; the political system of proportional representation within one national constituency, which had been troubling some people (including David Ben-Gurion, the first prime minister) since the founding of the state, was the object of mounting

criticism from 1983 onwards, reaching a crescendo in 1990; the
unresolved frontiers between religion and state were, it seemed to the
secular majority, repeatedly being pushed back in a regressive direction; and the long-term consequences of earlier imperfections both in
the methods used to absorb Jews from the Middle East (in 'development towns' and agricultural settlements near the country's extremi-
ties) and in evading basic questions about Israel's Arab minority had
left nagging ethnic problems. The Russian immigration has drama-
tized not only itself but also the need to confront these other issues.

The Russian *Aliyah*

The Russian immigration, as it is called for short (although many of
the immigrants come from other ex-Soviet republics) is a very
noticeable phenomenon. Russian is now one of the most frequently
heard languages spoken in Israel. There are many Russian newspapers
and magazines. And, perhaps most decisively, the Russians, mainly on
account of their disillusionment with the Likud government's performance over absorption, played a significant part in the defeat of
that government and the victory of Labour in the election to the
Knesset on 23 June 1992.

In fairness to Yitzhak Shamir and his colleagues in the defeated
government, it must be said that it has been impossible to forecast the
incoming rate with any accuracy. The state budget for 1990 assumed
40,000 Russian immigrants; more than 200,000 arrived. The 1991
budget consequently forecast 300,000; 150,000 came. Whereas at the
peak period 25,000 a month were arriving, the monthly figure in 1992
was at times down to 3,500. Pinchas Landau has examined in Chapter
4 the 'push' and 'pull' factors, operating in Russia and in Israel, whose
complex relationship determined at any one time the rate of flow.
Certainly by 1991 the 'pull' of Israel had much diminished. A poll
taken among Soviet immigrants in July 1991 disclosed that 37 per
cent were advising relatives still in the Soviet Union to delay *Aliyah*
because of adverse conditions in Israel as against only 32 per cent
who were telling them to come at once. Most significantly 30 per cent
of all Soviet Jews who had arrived since September 1989 said they
would leave Israel if there were openings elsewhere.[7] In early 1992 a
witness to the Obey Subcommittee of the House of Representatives
expressed it dramatically, 'The *raison d'être* of Israel's Zionism was
failing the test for Soviet Jews.'[8]

It is difficult to believe that any government of a country of only five million people could have handled with complete smoothness such a massive implant as occurred in 1990. The rate of immigration in 1990 was, Landau writes, 'beyond any reasonable expectation of absorptive capacity.' Nevertheless the feelings of vexation and comparative failure were palpable and were undoubtedly reflected in the way the newcomers voted in the 1992 election. The president of the Russian Jewry Zionist Forum, Natan Sharansky, had spoken of 'the tremendous gap between the nature of the historic moment we are facing and the ineptitude of the government in dealing with the task.' It did not help that Prime Minister Yitzhak Shamir, despite being ideologically committed to the full demographic as well as geographical achievement of Eretz Yisrael, was reputed to have taken little interest in social and economic policy.[9] In practice, two versions of Zionist priority were brought into collision, the one which gave pride of place to spreading Jewish settlement throughout the whole of Eretz Yisrael, including the West Bank and Gaza, and the other which put above all else the effective absorption and continued large inflow of Russian immigrants.

The Likud Party headed by Shamir had at first been expected to attract the newcomers' vote, since it represented the government that had brought them to Israel and stood at the opposite pole to Soviet communism. Many in 1990 agreed with a leading political scientist, the late Dan Horowitz, who said that the Russians would go with Likud for the first one or two elections but that, after they had had time to settle in, they would, as Ashkenazi people of above-average qualifications, gravitate towards the party that traditionally attracted their socio-economic group, which in Israel was the Labour Party. It had, after all, long been remarked that the highest Labour score usually came from the ward containing the highest incomes. This was for historical reasons to do with the early days of the state, just as the assignment of poor Sephardi immigrants to remote 'development towns' was an essential feature of the Likud's success.

But in June 1992 the immigrants' rejection of the Likud happened at the first test. Throughout the campaign the Labour leader, Yitzhak Rabin, had pounded away against the diversion of current budgetary resources to finance housing and infrastructure in the occupied territories that might otherwise have been devoted to the absorption of the refugees (and in a manner too, according to a series of quite withering reports from State Comptroller Miriam Ben-Porat, that was hugely wasteful and quite probably corrupt). More graphically, by persisting with the rapid expansion of the settlements – a policy which the Bush administration could not abide – the Shamir government had brought on confrontation with the United States at the very moment when a very special favour of crucial importance to the immigrants was needed from Washington. This was the granting of $10 billion of loan guarantees over a five-year period, to enable the stalled Israeli economy to lift off and thereby provide high-quality jobs for the newly available talent.

According to Alvin Rabushka's submission to the Obey congressional subcommittee, 'The distinguishing characteristic of the Israeli economy and its singular failing is the absence of direct foreign investment.'[10] It was thought that this deficiency could be made good on a dramatic scale, provided Israel could demonstrate by way of the loan guarantees that it 'enjoys the Americans' faith', thus opening the way to a flow of real money acquired exceptionally cheaply on a scale necessary to bring about a massive upgrading of Israel's infrastructure to equip it for export-led growth. A north–south arterial road, plus extensive development of the metropolitan road systems in the three large cities, Tel Aviv, Haifa and Jerusalem, would aim to eliminate the economic significance of precise location inside a small country. Israel's rudimentary railway system would be radically upgraded. At the same time Israel is supposed to complete a thorough programme of privatization and deregulation, so that its economy can be exposed to world markets.[11] With its great influx of talent, it could perhaps, metaphorically, turn itself into one big science park and then, as one Israeli economist put it, say to the world, 'If you want to find a highly qualified chemist *cheap*, Israel is the place.' But a part of the sub-text, admitted more readily by some than by others, was that this happy outcome of the latest *Aliyah* would be far more realistic if Israel were able to obtain real peace.

The newcomers, who with very few exceptions had no interest in the settlement of the West Bank, drew their own conclusions from Shamir's inability to obtain the support of President Bush for the guarantees. Within weeks of Rabin's taking office and halting new housing starts (though not the 10,000 houses that were already under construction nor any projects within 'Greater Jerusalem') and most road-building in the occupied territories, Bush received him cordially and backed him over the guarantees; Congress speedily complied.

Forty-seven per cent of the Russian vote, which had been counted on by the Likud to save the Shamir government in 1992, went instead to Labour and a further 11 per cent to Labour's left-wing ally

Meretz,[12] which campaigned against the tight hold of the religious parties on important aspects of Israeli life. This cause was quite attractive to the mainly secular Russians, who were disconcerted at encountering religious ministers and their staffs, allies of the Likud, in the ministries with which they were most concerned, Immigration and Absorption, Education, Labour and Social Affairs.[13] The rest of the immigrant vote was scattered, a little of it (11,697 votes) going to DA (Democracy and Aliyah), an ethnic Russian party, which did not succeed in winning any seats; only 18 per cent went to the Likud, in contrast to the 85 per cent support indicated by an opinion poll at the end of 1990. It was interesting (and a little puzzling) that none of the parties placed a Russian immigrant candidate in a winnable place on its list.

Rabin's campaign had been carefully targeted at a few particular segments of society – the Russians, first-time voters, and the 10 to 20 per cent of former Likud voters, who were thought to be wavering – and each sector contributed, though unevenly, to the result. To each the appeals were carefully tailored, none more so than to the immigrants. The Red Flag, whose presence in Labour Party offices in 1990 had been a culture shock to men and women who thought they had left socialism behind for ever, had quite disappeared, party posters were not in the usual red colours and, in the campaign advertisements inserted in the Russian-language press, the words 'privatization' and 'encouragement of private initiative' cropped up as frequently as did the name of Rabin, which, in a campaign in which even the party's name was changed to that of 'Rabin-led Labour', was often indeed.

But the immigrants' vote was lent, not given; within six months of the election victory of Labour, there was ample evidence in the Israeli press of grumbles that little had changed on the economic front and that a business-as-usual budget was being proposed. 'It is a shame that the days of grace are being wasted and that a change is nowhere to be seen,' wrote *Davar*, the Histadrut paper, after the government had been in office less than three months. And a columnist in the liberal *Ha'aretz* was saying, 'There is no feeling that the country is moving towards a free economy. There is no real privatization . . . There is no revision of the laws on investment and capital, no clear monetary policy. Given this grim and unimaginative picture how and why should big investors come here?'[14] This was rather unfair on so new a government but it indicated both the hopes that had been aroused by the change and the frustrated sense of time rushing by.

Natan Sharansky was calling the attention of Rabin's ministers to what was now being written about them in the immigrant press. 'The same journalists and cartoonists who were so quick to criticize the previous government,' he wrote, 'now sarcastically refer to the current leadership as "the last communist government in the world."'[15] And ten months after the election, on 4 May 1993, a large crowd of immigrants were doing what the Russians had until then been reluctant to do: taking part in a large march and demonstration to confront the government with their demands.

Israeli voluntarism, the outpouring of neighbourly support for newcomers, is unquestionably an admirable and even a formidable force; there has been no absence of response to the present challenge. But, with Israelis today more conscious of mistakes that were made 40 years ago with lasting social results, there is to be found in the press evidence of alarm at some of the social consequences of the new waves of immigration. According to a report in the *Jerusalem Post* on 31 July 1992, professionals involved in the absorption of Russian immigrants were seeing frightening parallels between the handling of immigration in the 1990s and the way in which mass immigration from Arab countries was handled in the 1950s. The consequences of that earlier experience has been discussed by Sammy Smooha in Chapter 9. Of course, many of the circumstances are different. The Russians are Ashkenazim, ending for a time at least the majority status of the Sephardim, and they have not been directed to live, as the Oriental immigrants were, on the periphery. Some, though, have been obliged for financial reasons to seek cheaper housing in the 'development towns', where they have often found the schools academically weaker and existing pupils less welcoming, and in huge, bleak caravan sites, remote from any possible employment.

The journalist Yossi Klein Halevi wrote for the fortnightly magazine *The Jerusalem Report* a feature on 'life in little boxes', describing 247 mobile home parks populated by 12,000 families of whom 7000 were Russian, 3500 Ethiopian and the remainder homeless Israelis. 'Homeless Israelis resent immigrants for getting government subsidies,' he said. 'Russians despise Ethiopians as primitives. Ethiopians suspect Russians of being less than real Jews. And both Ethiopians and Russians fear the homeless Israelis.'[16] In Sephardi neighbourhoods, too, the feeling is liable to be expressed that today's newcomers have already been given far more allowances and privileges than the old immigrants ever had. There is the living allowance during the six to eight months that the immigrant spends at a Hebrew language school (*ulpan*), the rent allowance, and the 'basket of services', which was initially quite generous but got nibbled away during successive economy drives. New jobs are subsidized by the state for the first year or two. Funds raised abroad enable universities to offer extra posts to qualified academics for two years, though this creates a problem of what to do with the extra staff after that. Unlike Sephardi *olim* (immigrants), these newcomers suffer as a rule from having too many qualifications rather than too few.

Although there are these substantial differences from the 1950s, some symptoms already suggest that comparisons might not be altogther misplaced. There are worrying reports in the Israeli press about the difficulties encountered by some of the 80,000 new immigrants in Israeli schools. Faults are no doubt on both sides, producing at times barriers of non-communication. In some schools it is reported that Russian newcomers have not been well accepted by Israeli children; some of the younger immigrants in turn are said not to show much eagerness to overcome the barriers by, for example, acquiring competence in Hebrew, while some of them (in striking contrast to the, in other respects, more difficult Ethiopians) display 'a severe lack of motivation to serve in the army.' Extra tuition which the immigrants were promised was afterwards cut back; and 2000 immigrant teachers, selected for retraining, were then not employed. Hundreds of Russian pupils have dropped out of schools, sometimes as the result of violence, and bands of such Russian-speaking dropouts are said to be highly visible. One alarmist has claimed that, 'Children are fleeing from the education system and the authorities are ignoring it.'[17]

Not all faults in these circumstances can be avoided, and it may in any case be questionable how much Israeli society should have to submit itself to be judged by newcomers. Yet it is because Israel has made such a *raison d'être* of being the rightful homeland of all Jews that Israelis know in their hearts that they will be judged and will judge themselves by how well they will perform the task of absorption. Anyone else would have welcomed the dwindling of the numbers involved during 1991 and 1992, giving time for Israel to catch up with itself. The Zionist ideology is still strong enough in this context for most Israelis to wish that the large influx should resume. The biggest question for the future is whether Israel will prove willing to draw all the logical consequences of that choice in sufficient time.

The Socio-economic Structure

There might appear to be a paradox about the result of the 1992 Israeli election. Israeli opinion, alert to the need for rapid market-oriented reforms to the structure of the Israeli economy, nevertheless voted out a right-wing government and voted in the party most clearly identified with the old socialist system and whose own institutions still to some degree symbolize it. These grew out of the previously existing institutions of the Yishuv, the pre-state Jewish community in Mandatory Palestine, which were overwhelmingly socialist and secular in inspiration and nature. Political parties and especially the Labour Party are, indeed, still structured as if membership of a party was the most important defining principle of life, although this is increasingly becoming less of a reality.

As has been remarked by more than one contributor to this volume, the most prominent example of an institution associated with labour is the Histadrut, this unique combination of trade union, employer (after the government, the largest in the country), welfare organization, and cultural impresario. In addition, the manifestations of idealistic socialism – the kibbutzim, the completely communal farms with equal pay for all and common ownership of everything, and the moshavim, the more conventional rural co-operatives, are mainly (though not all) Labour-oriented.[18] Mordechai Bar-On in Chapter 2 has rightly cited these as world-renowned social innovations in which the Jews of Palestine used to take much pride. Unfortunately, almost all these socialist experiments have for some time been running up huge losses and have required frequent subsidies to survive. The confusion of purposes and cross-subsidization of activities of the Histadrut combined with its powerful political clout were not friendly to the operation of market forces. This is an organization that even in its salad days had never seen profit maximization as its goal; it was tacitly understood that, because it was 'undertaking national goals,' the government would underwrite or otherwise assist its activities, which indeed at the beginning would not otherwise have been undertaken at all. When the policy changed, the Histadrut's behaviour did not. It carried on as before, hoping that the previous policy would come back. Those advocating radical economic reform are now zeroing in on targets especially close to the heart of the government, which, however, came to power on a cry of reform.

The Likud is classed as a right-wing party (and, insofar as 'right' and 'left' are habitually used in Israel in relation to the peace issue, quite rightly so) but its record in office was less than dynamically pro-market. Yitzhak Klein and Pinchas Landau (in Chapters 3 and 4) have indicated that something was achieved at the time of the Likud and national unity governments in moving Israel towards a free market position but are in no doubt that at the start of 1993 the bulk of necessary reform remains to be done.[19] Many Israelis who had given up on the Likud's capacity to initiate reform on an adequate scale and who were excited by Rabin's slogan about making a fundamental change in priorities were willing to give Labour's newly proclaimed enthusiasm for private enterprise a chance. All the same, there was an element of misgiving shared by many reformers about the return to power of a party carrying so much seemingly inappropriate baggage from the past. It was partly for this reason that so much attention was directed to the handling of the bankrupt condition of one of the Histadrut's key affiliates, the *Kupat Holim Clalit*, which is by far the largest element in the Israeli health service and therefore the Histadrut's most effective recruiting agent.[20] The Likud government had been trying unsuccessfully to put a successor health service in place; when the election handed that hot potato to Labour, sceptics were from the outset ready to pounce on any evidence of a tendency to prop up the trade union connection.

The market reformers are now very much in the ascendancy in the media. However, there is another side to this question, a feeling that what is most characteristic of the Israeli is 'the combination of a talent for accomplishing the unusual with an instinct for working together' and that this quality ought not to be sacrificed to 'the passion for Americanizing the country.' It is not forgotten that, for instance, the socialist ethos of the kibbutzim has always produced more than proportionate numbers of volunteers for the IDF's various special forces, with their exceptionally tough training and maximum exposure to danger. If, it is argued in some quarters, the only principle of the Israel of the future is to be 'anything for a fast buck', it will always be apparent that 'bucks' will be larger and faster in the United States, so why should people want to stay in Israel? Thus some Israelis call for a new ideology, putting stress upon national goals and the importance of the community, which could serve to integrate the newcomers into Israeli society.[21]

This, then, is a major question for the future: whether the drive for the supremacy of market forces, which has so much intellectual steam behind it, is going to prevail and, if it does, will it deprive Israel of the specific qualities that the state drew from the circumstances of its conception and birth?

Coalition Politics

All Israeli politics are coalition politics. That has been true both when, as with the early governments headed by Ben-Gurion, the object was to incorporate within the Cabinet as wide a spread of opinion as was thought prudent and when, as has proved to be the case with the Rabin government of 1992, it has been possible to rally only a little more than the bare minimum required for a majority. Elaborate pacts are negotiated between potential partners, often stipulating just where and when one partner is to be allowed off the reservation of agreed coalition guidelines. The voting figures in the Cabinet for important decisions are regularly disclosed immediately after a meeting and often the way each minister voted.

As explained by Klein and Galnoor in Chapters 3 and 5 there is only one nationwide constituency, which elects the 120 members of the Knesset by proportional representation. A large number of parties (ten after the 1992 election) pass the modest threshold (1.5 per cent or a little under 40,000 votes) for entry into the Knesset. The election result is therefore followed by an intense period of bargaining, in which special attention is liable to be drawn, because of their swing position, to the religious parties, both Zionist and non-Zionist, who use their advantage to fortify rabbinical views in a majority secular state and, in the case of the ultra-Orthodox parties, to take hold of and wherever possible expand privileges, subsidies and exemptions that have enabled a segment of the population outside the normal economic system and enjoying deferment (*recte* exemption) from the military draft to flourish and grow. It must be added that there have also been notorious instances of what the press routinely labels as 'blackmail' on the part of secular politicians. It is this bargaining whose blatancy after the 1988 election and during the mid-term crisis of 1990 alienated the majority of the public from the existing political system and prompted the mobilization of a mass demand for change. Significantly many of the Russian immigrants, who did not feel qualified to express themselves about many domestic issues, nevertheless grasped the importance to them of political reform as a means of improving the capacity for making decisions.

Yitzhak Klein outlined in Chapter 3 the alternative which seems to be favoured by most reformers: a directly elected prime minister and a Knesset half of whose members should be elected in 20 three-member constituencies and the remaining 60 as at present. The first half of the reform – the directly elected prime minister – was provided for in somewhat truncated form in the final days of the twelfth Knesset, but is only to take effect to coincide with the election to the fourteenth Knesset. Rabin, who is a strong supporter of reform, made statements immediately after he won the 1992 election which suggested that he intended to proceed with the formation of his Cabinet with the same freedom as if he had been directly elected. 'I will decide who will be ministers. There will be no horse-trading. The ministers will be appointed according to their capabilities and not their factional obligations.' However, afterwards he made the fact of having had to reach the premiership under the old system the excuse for the defects which he rather ungraciously acknowledged in his actual Cabinet-making. 'Wherever there is a coalition,' he remarked, 'there inevitably are some disgusting phenomena.'[22] It will be up to the thirteenth Knesset to decide whether to split Israel into constituencies and if the new presidential prime minister is to have complete freedom of choice over his ministers or be obliged to seek for them a vote of confidence in the Knesset.

The election on 23 June 1992 saw a sensational setback for the Likud (and the elimination of Tehiya, one of the radical right parties discussed by Ehud Sprinzak in Chapter 7) but, as Emanuel Gutmann convincingly argues in Chapter 6, there was no comparable landslide in favour of the left party bloc as a whole. The Likud vote in the Knesset went down from 40 seats to 32; Labour went up from 39 seats to 44, but 61 votes are needed for a majority. Gutmann has even demonstrated how, on certain assumptions, it is possible to show that more popular votes were cast for parties committed before the election to the right-wing bloc than for those committed to the left. In terms of seats, the left could have just made it on its own if, in addition to Labour's 44 and the 12 seats won by its left-wing Zionist ally Meretz (a gain of two seats), it had allowed itself to count the two Arab parties, Hadash (communists and allies) with three seats (one of them occupied by a communist Jew) and the Arab Democratic Party (2 seats) as part of the coalition. The Arab parties were willing but in the election campaign Rabin had foresworn relying on them.

When the Labour Party had achieved a political 'first' by holding party primaries to select its leader and list of candidates, two features of the results were prominent. The 'dovish' wing among the candidates usually won and the 'dovish' candidate for leader, the incumbent Shimon Peres, lost. Before casting their votes for leader, Labour Party members had clearly reflected on the opinion polls, which were showing, at the time of the primaries, that Labour would start out nine points behind Likud with Peres as leader but only one point behind with Rabin. The whole campaign for 'Rabin-led Labour' revolved around the absolute reliability and impeccable record of the new party leader on matters of military security and how he personally would provide the closest supervision of those negotiations with the Palestinians which, he solemnly undertook, would get a powerful new impulse from his presence at the helm. In other words, he seemed to offer peace without any risk; a bargain that, as Sprinzak has pointed out, many Israelis had once thought they might get from Yitzhak Shamir but not any longer. So, whereas in 1990, during the frantic coalition-building competition from March to June of that year, Peres had held out to Abdel-Wahab Darawshe (of the Arab Democratic Party) the prospect of his being treated for once as a full potential partner, there was now no way in which Rabin would leave himself open to the charge of being prepared to let decisions on security depend, however contingently, upon Arab support.

Joel Peters explained in Chapter 1 how Rabin at first thought he could get an overwhelming Jewish majority by signing on four of the parties that had pledged themselves before the poll to support the right – the National Religious Party, the two ultra-Orthodox parties, United Torah Judaism and Shas, and the anti-clerical Tzomet of General 'Raful' Eitan, a fellow ex-chief of staff, whose ballooning upwards from two seats to eight was one of the most remarkable phenomena of the election. Tzomet was classed on the right because of its total opposition to any territorial concession to the Arabs but it also stood for some things that would seem to place it with the left, such as the shaking up of the educational system, clean government, political reform and vigorous opposition to the privileges won by the religious parties, including, especially, draft exemption. It was not so eccentric to learn that many young first-time voters had been hesitating whether to vote for Meretz or Tzomet; whether Tzomet, with only one figure of some political experience and seven 'political virgins', will have the staying power to make a lasting impact on the political scene is one of the major unknowns.

In the event, although negotiations for the new coalition were unusually brisk[23] – the new list of ministers was announced a mere 20 days after the election – it lacked many of the ingredients for which the prime minister had hoped. Instead of having what he wanted, as he later reflected in public, 'Labour in the centre, Tzomet to its right, Meretz to the left and the ultra-Orthodox'[24] – which was exactly what Labour's traditional posture, described in Gutmann's chapter, might have led one to expect – he got instead a vehicle which to his way of thinking was weighted down heavily on the left. Joel Peters has described how negotiations with Eitan actually broke down but, judging by Eitan's subsequent eagerness to press the 'vote of no confidence' button quicker than anyone else in the Knesset, if they had not broken down over the education portfolio they would surely have done so over the peace process. Nevertheless the very fact that Shulamit Aloni, the Meretz leader, ended up with the education portfolio itself helps explain why Rabin had to make do with only one extra ally – the party of the Sephardi ultra-Orthodox, Shas (six seats), described by Menachem Friedman in Chapter 10. The other religious parties, however anxious for patronage, were not willing to abide Mrs Aloni as education minister and she wasted no time in making statements that set their teeth on edge.

The result was that Rabin's first year in office was punctuated by a succession of polemical explosions until May 1993, when Shas precipitated the crisis described in Chapter 1. It did so after months during which the other religious parties' ample reserves of vitriol had been employed not only against the verbal provocations of the 'anti-religious' education minister but, even more pointedly, against the one ultra-Orthodox party that had dared to serve alongside her.

At the expense of his clearly expressed wish to concentrate on the peace issue, Rabin was then forced to take time off between Aryeh Deri's resignation of the Ministry of the Interior on 9 May and the Cabinet reshuffle of 30 May to cobble together a barely acceptable compromise in which Deri returned to the Ministry of the Interior and Shulamit Aloni was levered into another one.[25] The episode threw light on the narrowness of Rabin's political base and also on the extreme difficulty of trying to govern Israel at a time of great demographic and structural change as a part-secular, part-religious state. Because the divisions in Israeli society – over such issues as peace, or religion and the state – do not coincide, prime ministers are forced to make do with governments that barely cohere. Because, for instance, secularists are divided between hawks and doves on the peace issue, it is seldom possible to mobilize their full strength in order to modify the rabbis' stranglehold on subjects like marriage, divorce and regulation of the Sabbath under the religious 'status quo'. In such circumstances, colleagues in the same Cabinet exchange remarks that raise eyebrows among foreigners and, indeed, among many Israelis.

There is no doubt that the direct election of the prime minister will give a big jolt to political behaviour, but the net effect is less certain. Rabin's remarks have sometimes given the impression that he would expect, if directly elected, at one bound to be free of all the tiresome constraints of the present system. This would partly depend on whether the prime minister would still need a vote of confidence in his Cabinet. If not, there could well be two opposite dangers, the first being that decision-making in Israel would be paralysed by the sort of gridlock between executive and legislature seen in the United States under President Bush and in Russia under President Yeltsin. Conversely, many supporters of change in principle feel that, in Israeli circumstances, direct election without checks and balances would give the prime minister too much unrestrained power unless and until an Israeli written constitution were fully in force.

The attempt to draft such a constitution immediately after independence was soon abandoned and segments of an eventual constitution, known as Basic Laws, are from time to time wheeled into place. But this piecemeal process is far from complete. Specifically, provisions for the protection of civil rights and for enabling the courts to override the Knesset on constitutional points have still to be made. Any attempt to entrench a full list of freedoms is certain to invite collision with the religious and ultra-Orthodox parties.

The will to break free from an existing system that was intended from the outset (at least by Ben-Gurion) to be only temporary seems to be present in sufficient force to ensure some changes in the near future. But a change of machinery will not be enough to alter the basic political facts about Israel which are that the right bloc remains, even after the 1992 election, very evenly balanced against the left bloc and that the religious parties (which under a different electoral system which penalized small parties could conceivably combine forces) hold the balance between them. In any case, no one has seriously suggested the total abandonment of proportional representation in favour of the distortions of the British first-past-the-post system.

Three types of question remain outstanding. The first is one of machinery, whether a much greater separation of powers really will result in more decisive government; the second is one of law, whether a fully written constitution can provide adequate safeguards against abuse of power; and the third is one of substance about Israeli society, whether fresh lines should now be drawn defining the place of the rabbis in Israeli society and, in the case of the ultra-Orthodox community, the extent of immunity and subsidy that can reasonably be devoted to the special world of the ultra-Orthodox.

The Israeli Arabs

In addition to the impact of the Russian immigrants on the 1992 election result another identifiable factor in favour of 'Rabin-led Labour' and Meretz was the Arab vote. The Israeli Arab population now numbers 740,000 out of a total Israeli population of five million. Before every election the argument has been put that if only the Arabs could work together politically in one party or electoral bloc they should be able to return at least 14 and perhaps more members to the Knesset (instead of the eight Arab MKs including two Druze, divided between the Arab Democratic Party, Hadash, Labour and Meretz, returned in 1992); and when one sees what an ultra-Orthodox party can do with four, five or six members it can be readily visualized what a much larger political wedge could achieve under the prevailing system of bargaining.

Majid Al-Haj has shown in Chapter 8 the various reasons why this has still not happened. In 1992 the party that had been urging the merits of this course most strongly, the Arab Democratic Party of Abdel Wahab Darawshe, doubled its representation but only from one seat to two. Votes were wasted because one Arab group that was represented in the twelfth Knesset, the Progressive List for Peace, which favoured Israeli Arab self-reliance for such services as education and health, did not this time clear the threshold and, since it had failed to form a pre-electoral alliance with Darawshe, its votes could not be used to help elect an extra Arab member. The Islamic groups, which as Al-Haj explains are steadily gaining in strength and have recently been taking an active part in municipal politics, had been expected to abandon their previous boycott of national elections and thereby increase the Arab vote. But, although one of their leaders did advocate participation, they did not all do so and those that did failed to give decisive electoral advice. Perhaps for this reason, but mainly because the failure to produce a united Arab list put people off, Arab participation in this election actually went down (70 per cent compared with 75 per cent in 1988).

There was, therefore, no decisive move towards Arab political mobilization. On the contrary, the most striking result was that the degree of support given by Arabs to the 'Zionist' parties (principally Labour and Meretz), which had hitherto shown a consistently down-ward trend from election to election, this time went up. It was the Labour Party, which proved to be the second largest (20.4 per cent) beneficiary of this constituency, the largest (23.1 per cent) being still the communists (Hadash), who though down were clearly not yet out. 'The myth of a single Arab list has exploded,' declared the mass circulation daily *Yediot Aharonot*.[26]

Hadash's three seats and Darawshe's two had a vital role in giving the left-wing bloc the 'blocking vote' of 61, which told Likud immediately that, however hard it bargained, mathematically it could not form a government. But as neither was allowed to count positively as part of the coalition, none of these Arabs obtained office. However Rabin did reward the Arab votes cast for Zionist parties by making available posts as deputy ministers for Health and Agriculture to Arab MKs elected on the Labour and Meretz list respectively. But the Arab sector had to show its teeth before more material dividends were forthcoming. An 11-day strike by Arab local authorities and the appearance of a tent encampment outside the prime minister's office were required before the Arab council heads received a promise of 70 million shekels for development (the first substantial sum for that purpose since the state began), together with 10 million shekels extra for school classrooms. On 9 September 1992 Nawaf Massalha, the new deputy minister of health, threatened that all Arab MKs would vote against the budget unless the allocations to the Arab sector were substantially increased across the board. An alarmed *Jerusalem Post* wrote in its editorial two days later, 'The fact that a credible threat against the government can be made by an Arab Knesset member is as sobering as it is unprecedented.'

The same *Jerusalem Post* leader, however, went on to acknowledge that, 'the state of the infrastructure in many Arab towns is nothing short of shameful. Almost throughout the sector, the classroom shortage is critical, the water supply poor, garbage disposal mediaeval and public lighting non-existent. The town of Taibe, for instance, has no modern roads and sewage.' It is said in mitigation of these conditions that Arabs pay very little in local taxation, whereas Jewish communities contribute financially to their own development and that Arabs have a tendency to ignore master plans when putting up buildings, so that hooking them up to facilities is neither cheap nor easy. But even worse than the problems of the Arab councils is the plight of the 'unrecognized villages', where thousands of Arabs have for decades lived in limbo without proper services and with no security of tenure.[27]

Sixty per cent of Israeli Arab children live below the poverty line, nearly three times the percentage for Jewish children; their parents, not having served in the Israeli Defence Forces, get child allowances two or three times smaller than those available to most Jews with children. The state comptroller's report for 1992 referred to the major imbalance in standards and facilities in Arab schools as compared to Jewish schools, with the Education Ministry spending nearly double the amount per Jewish pupil as per Arab, with 35 per cent of Arab classrooms rated as 'unsuitable' and the drop-out rate in Arab schools reaching a very high 20 per cent.

The figures for unemployment tell a similar tale. In Nazareth, the largest Arab town, it is about 20 per cent, compared with a national average of 11. Even where, as in Nazareth, it is possible to find well-equipped schools with highly motivated children, there remains the problem of what professional outlets are open to them. Skill in computer-programming, however advanced, would seem to lead nowhere so long as such a high percentage of Israeli industry is, even tangentially, linked up with security. There is considerable reluctance among these young people to consider careers abroad, and a firm insistence that Israel is and will remain their country. But of the 800 Arab high-school graduates accepted each year by Israeli universities, half drop out in the first year, mainly because of problems of integration into institutions that are culturally Jewish.[28] Nevertheless in the last decade the emergence of a distinct Arab intellectual elite has become much more noticeable. There are now over 14,000 Arab graduates of Israeli universities, but of some 5000 academic posts only 20 are held by Arabs.

One finds among Israeli Arabs (or Palestinian Israelis or just Arab citizens as they often prefer to call themselves) a reluctance to be impaled on such formulaic horns as 'dual loyalty' or 'dual identity'. They have, Ahmed Tibi wrote in *New Outlook*, 'managed with great skill to manoeuvre between these two components in any given situation.'[29] Yet there is a problem. Israel is everywhere and all the time described as the Jewish state and they are not Jews. In addition, they are and feel Palestinian. Across the 'Green Line' their fellow-Palestinians in the occupied territories have been engaged for years in the bitter struggle of the *intifada* and in the frustrations of the peace process. During the course of 1992 the Israeli Arabs began to take some distinct initiatives. In the Gaza Strip they were active in mediating between the PLO and Hamas (the Islamic fundamentalists) at a time when violence had broken out between them; they sought to promote contacts between the PLO and the Israeli public; and in December 1992, when 413 prominent figures in Hamas and Islamic Jihad were thrust over the Lebanese frontier they rallied strongly and noticeably to their support. Arab countries and Palestinian organizations for the first time have begun to acknowledge the positive involvement of Israeli Arabs in Arab affairs.[30]

So long as Israel is even nominally at war with Arab states, the Arabs of Israel will be divided from the vast majority of their fellow-citizens by not serving in the Israel Defence Forces. That carries with it direct financial and career consequences; Arabs do not qualify (not as Arabs but as non-reservists) for many grants, preferences, jobs and incentives. They find themselves pushed down the queue behind each new intake of Jewish immigrants, who in turn qualify for assistance of various kinds for which Arabs are not eligible.

There is increasing awareness of these discrepancies among Jews in Israel, not unmixed in some quarters with alarm. The alarm is occasioned by nightmares about a possible consequence of a successful outcome of the peace process. 'Full autonomy' for Palestinians on the West Bank, still more the launch of a Palestine state might, some Israelis think, have a deeply unsettling effect on the Israeli Arabs in that substantial area of Galilee in which they are in a local majority. The sight of Palestinians in political power just across what is now the Green Line will, they fear, cause them to question their own Israeli allegiance. Is the next *intifada* to be inside the Green Line? they ask.[31] When these apprehensions are put to Israeli Arabs, they maintain that they are unreal. But, unless Jewish responsiveness to the call of their Arab minority for equal treatment evolves at a much greater pace than hitherto, this could well be a problem for the fairly near future.

There have, in this respect, been some recent signs of grace: the award of Israel's main literary prize to an Arab author; the drawing up under the Shamir government of a five-year comprehensive programme to bring the quality of services to Arabs up to the level elsewhere, which was however never funded; and the promise in the Rabin government's 'basic guidelines' to 'close gaps between the Jewish and Arab sectors' in every field, to 'make allocations to Arab, Druze and Bedouin authorities on a par with those of Jewish authorities,' and to make 'special efforts' to 'induct Arabs and Druze, particularly university graduates, into the civil service . . . in order to integrate them into Israeli public life.' A striking remark of Rabin's to an overseas congress was that Israel's treatment of its own minorities should help to set a standard of how Jews expect to be treated abroad.[32] But there is a good deal of ground to make up and not too much time.

The Right-Wing Opposition
The 1992 election left the Likud Party in a very battered and bruised condition. Although it could be argued that the right as a whole had not been badly beaten, the principal ruling party of the Shamir coalition ended up with only 32 seats out of 120, heavily in debt, without leadership following the 76-year-old Shamir's announcement that he was going to retire, without a party constitution and, because the law courts had already had to intervene in the party's domestic affairs, without even a legal existence after 28 February, 1993. It was not strictly true that the figure of 32 had not been predicted – it had been in one or two of the public opinion polls – but no one in the Likud took this at all seriously, and indeed past elections had lent weight to the notion that the party could always pull out the stops with remarkable effect on election day. This miscalculation had serious financial implications, because under Israeli law state funds to help meet election expenses are distributed after the election according to the number of seats won. Likud had incurred expenditure on the basis of winning at least 38.

Likud's very existence under Shamir, a man who though tactically astute enough at derailing developments to which he was opposed was not otherwise over-endowed with the arts of political leadership, had been put into question by its failure to complete the process of building one party out of two main components, Herut and the Liberals. Since the long-heralded merger had been finally proclaimed in 1988 no united governing body had been elected and seats on the 3,500-strong central committee were perforce filled by co-opted persons. No party convention had been held since the Herut convention of 1986. A district court judge having ruled that enough was enough, the time-expired, co-opted central committee ceased to exist at the end of February 1993. 'There will,' the judge said, 'be no further extension of this date for any possible reason.'[33]

From this low point the Likud had nowhere to go but up and, in the nine months after the election defeat, steps were taken to emulate and even overtake Labour by creating a larger mass membership – 220,000 as compared with Labour's 160,000 – and staging party primaries on 24 March 1993 to elect a leader and a fresh central committee.[34] The leader chosen, Binyamin ('Bibi') Netanyahu, could not have been a greater contrast to his predecessor. Of an entirely different generation – he was 46, Yitzhak Shamir was 76 – he owed his success to a slick, glamorous, well-financed, American-style campaign and to an established reputation as an extremely effective purveyor of right-wing policies on television, particularly to the United States. Netanyahu had never been in the Cabinet; his background was that of an ambassador to the UN and a deputy foreign minister. Party members had therefore taken a big gamble in investing all their hopes in a comparatively untried man. There was also the immediate danger that in going for Netanyahu so decisively – he gained a two-to-one margin over the next candidate, David Levy – the Likud could have bought itself an ugly split. Levy, one Sephardi politician who has no hesitation in invoking the ethnic issue, sometimes in the crudest terms, had attacked Netanyahu bitterly during the campaign, did not take his defeat at all well, and did not attend the Likud convention on the Golan Heights held in May. At the convention – the first that the fully merged Likud had ever been able to hold – a new constitution was adopted, giving Netanyahu as leader sweeping powers of a kind that Yitzhak Shamir could only dream of.

The right assumes that on the peace issue either Rabin will be obliged, in order to obtain results, to concede more than he intended in which case the country can be roused against him or, true to his pledges about security, he will not yield more than he set out to do, which will be insufficient to secure agreement, thereby leaving his claim to possess a method of obtaining peace without risking security to appear hollow. In the latter circumstance and if Rabin is sufficiently fed up by then with Meretz, the opportunity might even occur for another national unity government. The main task of the Likud is to ensure that if there is a swing back to the right it benefits them rather than someone else, say Tzomet. Further out on the right, the radical, extra-parliamentary forces to which Ehud Sprinzak made reference in

Chapter 6 are only likely to become a serious threat to public order if
Rabin seems to be going far beyond, in terms of concessions to the
Arabs, what he had led Israelis to expect. Nevertheless some potential
Jewish terrorists are known to exist; the possibility in some circumstances of a Jewish civil war, much discussed in the 1980s only to be
generally dismissed, came out into the open again in the spring of
1993. It was alleged on Israel Television that some settlers in the
occupied territories were training to establish an illegal 'Judean Police
Force', prepared to oppose by force of arms any Palestinian police
force that came into existence as the result of Palestinian autonomy.
One spokesman for the Jewish local councils in the territories publicly
warned that settlers would treat any Palestinian policemen carrying
guns as armed terrorists and would open fire on them. After this it
was made known that the General Security Services had stepped up
their intelligence operations among Jewish settlers, to prevent the
formation of an underground organization, and that the army had
confiscated a number of weapons. There was talk of resistance by
settlers on the Golan Heights should Rabin agree to surrender any
part of it to Syria, and a Gallup poll gave the impression that there
would be majority support for the use of force in that eventuality. 'The
government is pushing us towards civil war,' said the Knesset member
responsible for drawing up the Likud's new centralized constitution.
And a Labour MK, taking up this remark, warned of the danger of
the rhetoric of violence spreading from 'a few crazies' to Knesset
members. 'If we don't nip it in the bud,' he said, 'we could really find
ourselves locked in civil war.'[34]

Apart from Tzomet (with its eight seats) and the extremist Moledet
(with three) the remaining opposition to Rabin is provided by the
religious parties. The National Religious Party with six seats, headed
by Zevulun Hammer, has always been a party of government, accus-
tomed until 1992 to run the ministries of Education and Religious
Affairs, with the immense control over patronage (through nomination
to the network of religious councils and the Chief Rabbinate) and the
more subtle influence over ideology that this has implied. Unlike the
Haredi parties, the NRP is a political party in the western sense, with
members and elected leaders. Whereas it was rather 'dovish' during
the years when it worked in partnership with Labour, it has taken on
since 1977, when it moved into the right camp, much of the political
colouration of its Likud allies. In the 1992 election it deviated even
more markedly to the right and pitched its appeal strongly to the

settler vote, so that the unexpected eclipse of the Tehiya party was largely caused by defections to the NRP of religious-minded settlers. While it was hitherto been a principle of the NRP to arrange whenever possible to be in the government so as to defend the religious status quo, this time it had placed itself so vitriolically at odds with Rabin's policies that this was scarcely thinkable.[35]

While the NRP is Zionist and is organized like a western political party, the ultra-Orthodox parties are not. Menachem Friedman has traced in Chapter 10 the background of the special world of the Haredim. Another scholar answers the question 'Who is a Haredi?' by saying, 'Whoever views and experiences life in the Jewish state in Eretz Yisrael as exile – the Exile of Israel in the Holy Land,' since, according to Rabbi Schach, 'The Jewish people is still in exile until the arrival of the Redeemer, even while it is in Eretz Yisrael.' The phrase ultra-Orthodox (or Haredi) covers a wide spectrum of less than total acceptance of the Zionist state – from total rejection, as with the *Neturei Karta* (the Guardians of the City), who boycott the institutions of the state completely, through practical accommodation with those institutions, as with the Agudat Yisrael until June 1992, whose scruples against serving in a Zionist Cabinet did not apply to serving as deputy (and de facto) minister of a department (Labour and Social Services) which was in a position to enforce and extend the application of sabbath laws, and applied still less to the long-term occupancy of the chairmanship of the Knesset Finance Committee (which carried with it the stranglehold over fixing the agenda for handling vital items that afforded infinite opportunities for the making of deals), to virtual acceptance, as with Shas which gained an impressive purchase on the Ministry of the Interior in Likud and Labour Cabinets alike.[37] The United Torah Judaism Party, which was intended to bring most of the squabbling Haredim together under one political roof, in fact links (very imperfectly) the three MKs from Agudat Yisrael with the one elected from Rabbi Schach's Degel Hatorah. Rabbi Schach's instructions to Shas that it should also line up with the new alliance failed miserably. That party, having kept its six seats (and missed a seventh only by a whisker), felt quite free to join the government, despite the nonagenarian rabbi's virulent rejection of Labour. The Agudat members are clearly uneasy at being out of office, partly on account of the lost patronage but also because they would rather fight from inside the major cultural battle that they see coming.

Conclusion

As this book has attempted to illustrate, the coming years in Israel will be crucial not only for the question of whether there is to be a peace settlement with the Arabs but also for a whole agenda of other domestic issues of central importance for the character of the future Israeli state. Israel appears to be heading for a written constitution and a separation of powers. If it accomplishes this change, will it succeed in escaping from those features of multi-party politics which most repel the critics of the present system? Or will the new system generate defects of its own, every bit as frustrating in their turn as those of the old, including a demonstration that changes of machinery do not resolve the existence of real contradictions? Will Israel be able to derive the full advantages of an economic system in harmony with the international market while at the same time not forfeiting the special Israeli edge that is attributed to the circumstances in which the state was created and grew up? If a written constitution must contain a full set of human and civil rights, can this be done without the major showdown with the religious authorities and parties that has been avoided (not without periodic strains) since the birth of the state? Above all, will Israel be able to find the capacity to transform its own society and mobilize outside support from the Diaspora and elsewhere on the quite exceptional scale needed to make the absorption of the latest *Aliyah* from Russia a success? And can this be done fairly not only from the point of view of the Russian immigrants themselves but in the estimation of those sections of the Israeli community, such as the Sephardi Jews and the Israeli Arabs, who might be expected to fear that any apparent success for the Russians would be at their expense? What will be the judgment on Israel of the Jews still in Russia and are there to be other large waves of immigrants from Russia and the other former Soviet Republics? But finally one must end with the question that is the subject of much discussion, though not in this book; can anything on the scale required be achieved so long as no peace is concluded between Israel and the Palestinians and between Israel and the Arab states?

APPENDIX A

PARTY	SEATS 1992	SEATS 1988	VOTES 1992	VOTES 1988
Labour	44	39	906,126	685,363
Likud	32	40	651,219	709,305
Meretz (Ratz, Shinui, Mapam)	12	10	250,206	193,396
Tzomet	8	2	166,247	45,489
National Religious Party	6	5	129,601	89,720
Shas	6	6	129,310	107,709
United Torah Jewry (Agudat Yisrael, Degel Hatorah, Moriah)	4	7	86,138	136,933
Moledet	3	2	62,247	44,174
Democratic Front (Hadash)	3	4	62,138	84,032
Arab Democratic Party	2	1	40,799	27,012
BELOW THE THRESHOLD*				
Tehiyah		3	31,928	70,730
Progressive List		1	24,069	33,695
New Liberal Party			16,753	
Geulat Yisrael			12,844	
DA			11,681	

* *KNESSET THRESHOLD 1.5 percent of total votes cast (39,227)*
TOTAL VOTES CAST 1992: 2,657,327 (1988: 2,283, 123)
TURNOUT 1992: 77.3% (1988: 78.8%)

Source: *The Jerusalem Report*, 16 July 1992.

APPENDIX B

Government formed in July 1992 by Yitzhak Rabin
(as reshuffled, December 1992 and May 1993)

Prime Minister and Minister of Defence	Yitzhak Rabin (Lab)
Foreign Minister	Shimon Peres (Lab)
Finance	Avraham Shochat (Lab)
Housing and Construction	Binyamin Ben-Eliezer (Lab)
Interior	Rabbi Aryeh Deri (Shas)
Education and Culture	Amnon Rubinstein (Meretz)
Transport	Yisrael Kessar (Lab)
Justice	David Libai (Lab)
Immigration and Absorption	Yair Tsaban (Meretz)
Industry and Trade	Micha Harish (Lab)
Police and Energy	Moshe Shahal (Lab)
Health	Haim Ramon (Lab)
Agriculture	Ya'acov Tsur (Lab)
Communications, Science and Technology	Shulamit Aloni (Meretz)
Religious Affairs (acting)	Yitzhak Rabin (Lab)[1]
Labour and Social Affairs	Ora Namir (Lab)
Environment	Yossi Sarid (Meretz)
Economics	Shimon Shetreet (Lab)
Tourism	Uzi Baram (Lab)

[1] Rafael Pinhasi (Shas) was appointed deputy minister for religious affairs on 21 December 1992.

FURTHER READING

Arian, Asher, *Politics in Israel: The Second Generation* (Chatham, NJ: Chatham House, 1985)

Avineri, Shlomo, *The Making of Modern Zionism* (London: Weidenfeld & Nicolson, 1981)

Avishai, Bernard, *A New Israel: Democracy in Crisis 1973–1988* (New York: Ticknor and Fields, 1990)

Beilin, Yossi, *Israel: A Concise Political History* (London: Weidenfeld & Nicolson, 1992)

Eisenstadt, Shmuel, *The Transformation of Israeli Society* (Boulder, CO: Westview Press, 1985)

Horowitz, Dan & Lissak, Moshe, *Trouble in Utopia: The Overburdened Polity of Israel* (Albany: SUNY Press, 1989)

Lacqueur, Walter, *A History of Zionism* (London: Weidenfeld & Nicolson, 1972)

Liebman, Charles and Don Yehiya, Eliezer, *Religion and Politics in Israel* (Bloomington: Indiana University Press, 1984).

Lustick, Ian, *Arabs in a Jewish State* (Austin: University of Texas Press, 1980)

Moskovich, Wolf, *Rising to the Challenge: Israel and the Absorption of Soviet Jews* (London: Institute of Jewish Affairs, 1991)

Peri, Yoram, *Between Battles and Ballots: Israeli Military and Politics* (Cambridge: Cambridge University Press, 1983)

Sharkansky, Ira, *The Political Economy of Israel* (New Brunswick: Transaction Books, 1987)

Shipler, David, *Arab and Jew: Wounded Spirits in a Promised Land* (New York: Times Books, 1986)

Sprinzak, Ehud, *The Ascendance of Israel's Radical Right* (Oxford: Oxford University Press, 1991)

Swirski, Barbara and Safir, Marilyn, *Calling the Equality Bluff: Women in Israel* (Oxford: Pergamon Press, 1991)

NOTES

Chapter 1

1. The school week has currently shrunk to 26 hours. The former education minister, Shulamit Aloni, proposed a three-year programme which would expand the school week to 39 or 40 hours, build 4000 more classrooms and employ 15,000 more people, besides rescuing schools in 30 'neglected' communities and paying teachers higher salaries. But the price will be high and for that reason the programme's prospects are uncertain. Sasha Sadan, *Jerusalem Post International Edition*, 6 March 1993, p 20.

2. It is interesting to note that Shulamit Aloni made a point of stressing that she was minister for education and culture, the full and correct title of her ministry. For a feel of the intensity of the controversy surrounding Aloni's appointment see *The Jerusalem Report*, 30 July 1992, pp 18–19.

3. Excerpts of this speech, in which Rabin outlined the new government's policy, were published in the *Jerusalem Post*, 14 July 1992.

4. For an excellent overview of the issues involved see Wolf Moskovich, *Rising to the Challenge: Israel and the Absorption of Soviet Jews*, (London, Institute of Jewish Affairs, 1991)

5. Shas was given a deputy minister for religious affairs, Rafael Pinhasi, in the minor reshuffle of December 31, 1992.

Chapter 2

1. I use here the term 'ideology', not in the sense sociologists and anthropologists have used it in recent years to describe the ubiquitous spiritual and intellectual expressions of all human societies, but in the more traditional sense of a contrived, comprehensive, well-argued and organized analysis of certain human conditions and a set of prognostic proposals for their correction and improvement. For the sociological approach see Clifford Geertz, 'Ideology as a Cultural System' in Daniel

265

Apter, *Ideology and Discontent* (New York, The Free Press, 1964). For a good general survey of the development of the concept see J. S. Roucek, 'A History of the Concept of Ideology', *The Journal of the History of Ideas*, vol IV, no 2, October 1944, pp. 479–88.

2. For more on this subject see Mordechai Bar-On, *Israel's Political Culture and the Middle East Conflict* (New York, Michael Harrington Occasional Papers, City University of New York Press, 1991).

3. The following derogatory definition of the terms 'Zionism' can be found, among more positive designations, in a colloquial Hebrew dictionary: '*Zionut*; Nonsense, lofty but empty talk, a moralizing speech, user of exaggerations.' Dan Ben Amotz and Netiva Ben Yehuda, *Milon le Ivrit Meduberet*, Vol. I (Tel Aviv, Levin Epstein Publication, 1972).

4. The *stetl* was a small Jewish town in Eastern Europe.

5. *Aliya* means in Hebrew literally 'Ascending'. This ideologically loaded word is the common term used for the act of Jewish immigration to Israel. Conversely, *Yerida* ('Descending') refers to hundreds of thousands of Israelis who have emigrated and now live everywhere around the globe.

6. This may well explain why the pathetic plea of the Israeli writer A. B. Yehoshua failed to impress Jews in the Diaspora. See A. B. Yehoshua, *Between Right and Right* (New York, Doubleday, 1981).

7. Geula Cohen was a leading figure in the Tehiya (Resurrection) Party, which represented the settlers' interests in the last Knesset. It did not qualify for any seats in the election of 23 June 1992 for the thirteenth Knesset.

8. 'Brit Shalom' was a group of intellectuals (including Martin Buber) who advocated in the 1930s a compromise with the Palestinians, based on limitation of Jewish immigration to Palestine. The Revisionists, led by Ze'ev Jabotinsky, demanded, as early as the 1920s, a Jewish state on both sides of the Jordan.

9. Zionists have always used the term 'exile' to signify the condition in which Jews lived outside Israel. The term 'Diaspora' came to be used only in the 1950s as a result of the demand of the American Zionist women's organization Hadassa, presented to the twenty-third Zionist Congress in 1951.

10. The classical work which predicted that Jews would not be able to survive modernity in exile was *Autoemancipation* by Leo Pinsker. Jabotinsky warned the Jews that 'if they will not put an end to exile, exile will put an end to them'. The main proponents of the theme of 'soft negation of exile' were Yehezkiel Kaufman in his book *Exile and Alienation* and Jacob Klatzkin in his book *Thumin* ('Spheres').

11. An important proponent of this line of thought is the philosopher Nathan Rotenstreich. See his many contributions to the five volumes of *Hagut* (in Hebrew) (Jerusalem, The Zionist Library, 1953–61). A good summary and update of his opinions on the state of Zionism and Judaism can be found in his 'Reflections on the Contemporary Jewish Condition' (A. Philip Klutznick International Lecture, Institute of Contemporary Jewry of the Hebrew University of Jerusalem, 1975).

12. *Gegenwartsarbeit* is the German term used at the time. It meant literally

'work of the present'. This was an action programme that the Russian Zionist Movement adopted in a special conference in Helsinki in 1906. It included measures to defend Jewish interests in Diaspora communities and educational and cultural work needed to foster Jewish life everywhere. For good analyses of early Zionist history see: Walter Z. Laqueur, *A History of Zionism* (London, Weidenfeld & Nicolson, 1972), David Vital, *The Origins of Zionism* (Oxford, Oxford University Press, 1975), Howard Sacher, *A History of Israel from the Rise of Zionism to our Time* (New York, Knopf, 1976)

13. The full exchange of letters is reprinted in the appendix to the *American Jewish Yearbook, 1952*, Vol 53 (The American Jewish Committee, New York), pp 564–8.

14. *Der Judenstaat* ('The State of the Jews') was the name of the blueprint for the Zionist project written by Theodor Herzl shortly before he founded the World Zionist Organization in 1897. Most English translations use erroneously the name 'The Jewish State'. More on this see David Vital, *The Origins of Zionism*, pp 259–66.

15. See Mordechai Bar-On, 'Status Quo Before or After?', (Leonard Davies occasional paper 1992).

16. On the way those territories were 'emptied' see Benny Morris, *The Birth of the Palestine Refugee Problem, 1947–1949*, (Cambridge University Press, Cambridge, 1987).

17. Theodor Herzl, *Altneuland* (Haifa, Haifa Publishing Co, 1960).

18. Ben-Gurion expressed this opinion on numerous occasions. See for example his article 'Yichud ve Ye'ud' (Uniqueness and Destiny), originally given as a lecture to a meeting of the high command of the Israeli Defence forces in 1951. It was reprinted in David Ben-Gurion, *Yichud ve Ye'ud* (Tel Aviv, Ma'arachot, 1971).

19. See David Biale, *Power and Powerlessness in Jewish History* (New York Schocken Books, 1986).

20. *Divrei Ha Knesset* (Parliamentary Proceedings), Vol 102. 17 July 1985, pp 3572–6. *Historia* is the Hebrew word for 'History'.

21. The then prime minister, Yitzhak Shamir, exclaimed early in 1990: 'We need a large land for the large immigration.' This declaration caused an uproar since it established, to the detriment of Israeli interests, a link between the immigration and the occupation, and gave a false vindication of Arab propaganda against the new wave of Soviet immigration.

22. Article 21. Reprinted and annotated by Yehoshafat Harkabi, *Palestinians and Israel* (Keter Publications, Jerusalem, 1974), p 64.

23. Mordechai Bar-On, 'Jewish Marginality and the Problem of Identity' (in Hebrew), in *Gesher* (Jerusalem, 1987).

Chapter 3

1. Classic discussions of the problem of reform in democratic polities are Mancur Olson, *The Logic of Collective Action, Public Goods and the Theory of Groups* (Cambridge, MA Harvard University Press, 1965); Anne O. Krueger, 'The Political Economy of Rent Seeking,' in *American Economic*

Review, 64, June 1974, pp 291–303; James A Buchanan, 'Rent-Seeking and Profit Seeking', in James A. Buchanan, Robert D. Tollison and Gordon Tullock (eds), *Toward A Theory of the Rent-Seeking Society* (Texas, AGM University Press, 1980), pp. 3–15.

2. Arye L. Hillman, 'The Economy of Israel' (unpublished), Department of Economics, Bar-Ilan University, Israel (1992), pp 12–14.

3. Since 1989 the Israeli economy has exhibited trends of faster growth, rising investment, and a falling rate of inflation. The evidence for this is somewhat blurred by the unusual conditions of 1991, when the government of the day artificially pumped up the economy by building tens of thousands of flats for immigrants from the Commonwealth of Independent States. Government stimulus of the building sector appears to have drawn off investment resources from other sectors, though the magnitude of the diversion is not clear. See Bank of Israel, *Din Ve-Heshbon Lishnat 1991* (Report for 1991), Jerusalem, May 1992, Table B–3, p. 19. Investment in other sectors continued to grow, however. Leaving the artificial boom in housing construction to one side, the figures for 1990, combined with preliminary estimates for the first months of 1992, seem to confirm a secular trend of increased growth and investment. The end of the artificial boom will of course have a dampening effect on overall performance figures in 1993 and perhaps 1994.

4. See Bank of Israel Research Department, *Economic Policy in a period of Immigration* (Jerusalem, 1990) and *Tochnit Le-Hiddush Ha-Tsemikhah Ul-Heatat Ha-Inflatsiah* (Programme for Renewing Growth and Slowing Inflation) (Jerusalem, December 1988).

5. However, before the 1992 election the threshold had been even lower at 1 per cent, and Tehiya, which had enjoyed three seats in the twelfth Knesset, was eliminated altogether, although by the previous rules it would have still qualified for one seat.

6. *Changing the System of Government in Israel. Proposed Basic Law: The Government* by David Libai, Uriel Lynn, Amnon Rubinstein and Yoash Tsiddon (Jerusalem Centre for Public Affairs, 1990) [The authors were Knesset Members in the twelfth Knesset, 1988–92].

7. This is the literal translation of the Hebrew term, *rosh ha-memshalah*, which has been used since the founding of the State of Israel. It conventionally has been translated as 'prime minister,' an appropriate term given the complete dependence of the executive upon the confidence of the legislature, parallel to the British parliamentary model. The institution of direct election of the chief executive would seem to call for a different title, however; and the Israeli political system already has a president, who is the head of state and possesses no executive powers.

8. Bernard Susser, '"Parliadential" Politics: A Proposed Constitution for Israel', *Parliamentary Affairs*, vol 42, no 1, January 1989, pp 112–22.

9. The Likud refused to post bond, and though the deal was struck the Likud reneged prior to the 1992 elections. The electoral reform law passed on 18 March 1992 specifically voids any monetary or other guarantee of a coalition agreement.

10. The text of the amended law may be found in *Hatza'at Hok Yesod:*

Hamemshala ('Proposed Basic Law: The Government'; Knesset Proceedings, Fourth Session, 399th Convention of the twelfth Knesset), 18 March 1992, vol 24, Appendices, pp 3945–54.

11. For an interesting perspective on an expert's experience in working with politicians to implement a technically complex social programme, see Michael Bruno, 'From Sharp Stabilization to Growth: On the Political Economy of Israel's Transition', *European Economic Review*, no 36, 1992, pp 310–19; and Bruno, 'Economic Analysis and the Political Economy of Policy Formation', *European Economic Review*, no 34, 1990, pp 273–301.

Chapter 4

1. Even Professor Michael Bruno, the chief external academic adviser to the government in planning the ESP, and subsequently governor of the Bank of Israel from 1986 to 1991, admitted in various speeches and papers delivered in the late 1980s and early 1990s that far less had been achieved on the reform front than had been envisaged or than was desirable. Others, more independent, were also more outspoken in their criticism both as regards aspects of the ESP itself and, especially, the very tight monetary policy implemented in 1985–6, and as regards the slow pace of structural reform.

2. Ariel Sharon, the minister of defence during the Lebanon War, was appointed in the belief that he, with his reputation as a man of initiative, leadership and action, would solve the housing crisis. For details of Sharon's career see Uzi Benziman, *Sharon: An Israeli Caesar*, (London, Robson Books, 1987).

Chapter 5

1. I. Galnoor and Y. Peres, 'Those Who Vote Have Influence' (Hebrew), *Democracy*, summer 1992, p 31.

2. A high rate of participation is also evident in public demonstrations and protests. See G. Woldsfeld, *The Politics of Provocation*, (New York, State of New York Press, 1988).

3. A. Arian, *Consensus in Israel* (New York, General Learning Press, 1971); P. Y. Medding, *Mapai in Israel: Political Organization and Government in a New Society* (Cambridge, Cambridge University Press, 1972); Y. Shapira, *Israeli Democracy*, (Hebrew) (Ramat Gan, Masada, 1977); I. Galnoor, *Steering the Polity*, (Beverly Hills, Sage Publications, 1982).

4. We shall mainly discuss here the political parties, but in fact they were part of the broader ideological and social clusters, known as the 'political camps'. The main camps were: Labour, dominated by the Histadrut General Federation of Workers and the socialist parties; the 'civic' camp of the middle class, with the General Zionist Party and the Herut; and the religious camp, dominated by the National Religious Party (NRP).

5. A. Diskin and I. Galnoor, 'Political Distances between Knesset Members and Coalition Behaviour: The Peace Agreements with Egypt', *Political Studies*, 38, December, 1990, pp 710–17.

6. Of the ten parties elected to the Knesset in 1992, no fewer than six are new, having been established in the last decade. On the left, the new Meretz bloc; on the right, Tzomet and Moledet; in the Arab sector, the Arab Democratic Party; and in the ultra-Orthodox community, Shas and the United Torah Party Bloc.

7. See M. Negbi, *Above the Law*, (Tel Aviv, Am Oved, 1987) Hebrew.

8. Y. Yishai, *Interest Groups in Israel* (Tel Aviv, The Levi Eshkol Institute, 1987).

9. On the dominant party, see A. Arian and S. H. Barnes, 'The Dominant Party System in a Neglected Model of Democratic Stability', *Journal of Politics*, vol 36, no 3, 1974.

10. If another religious party joins the coalition, it will strengthen Labour's position as a pivotal party. If the right-wing Tzomet joins, it will establish a precedent in Israel's coalition history, because of the ideological distance (on the issue of the future of the territories) between the two extreme participants in such a coalition, Tzomet and Meretz.

Chapter 6

1. In Hebrew the term *Ma'hapach* is commonly used to refer to the election in 1977 when the Likud gained power for the first time. When the first exit polls were announced on Israeli television, the possibility of a Labour victory was described as a *Ma'hapach*.

2. The Labour Party was founded in 1930 under the name Mapai. In 1968 it merged with Ahdut Ha'avodah and Rafi to form Mifleget Ha'avoda (Israel Labour Party). In 1969 it formed Ha'Ma'arach (Alignment), an election bloc with Mapam. In 1992 election, it ran, under the name Ha'avoda Bereshut Rabin (Labour under the leadership of Rabin).

3. One example of these will have to suffice here: Rael Jean Isaac, *Party and Politics in Israel: Three Visions of a Jewish State* (New York and London, Longman, 1981).

4. Abraham Diskin, *Elections and Voters in Israel* (New York, Praeger, 1991)

5. Emanuel Gutmann, 'Parties and Camps: Stability and Change', in Moshe Lissak and Emanuel Gutmann (eds), *The Israeli Political System* (Tel Aviv, Am Oved, 1977) [in Hebrew]. What is termed here 'hegemony' has usually been called 'dominance' following Maurice Duverger in his book *Political Parties* (1951), and the Israeli Labour Party was first called 'dominant' in this sense in the article cited here. One of the latest discussions of dominance is Myron Aronoff, 'Israel under Labor and the Likud: The Role of Dominance Considered', in T. J. Pempel (ed), *Uncommon Democracies: The One-Party Dominant Regimes* (Ithaca, Cornell University Press, 1990), pp 260–81.

6. Asher Arian and Ilan Talmud, 'Electoral Politics and Economic Control in Israel', in Frances Fox Piven (ed), *Labour Parties in Postindustrial Societies* (New York, Oxford University Press, 1991), pp 169–89.

7. Ariel Levite and Sidney Tarrow, 'The Legitimation of Excluded Parties in Dominant Party Systems: A Comparison of Israel and Italy', *Comparative Politics*, vol 15, April 1983, pp 95–327.

8. Arian and Talmud, 'Electoral Politics and Economic Control in Israel'. For a somewhat different analysis see Michael Shalev, 'The Political Economy of Labor Party Dominance and Decline in Israel', in Pempel (ed), *Uncommon Democracies*, pp 83–127.

9. It has been quite common in the last 15 years to write about the decline and fall of the Labour Party. See, for example, Myron J. Arnoff, 'The Labor Party in Opposition', in Robert O. Freeman (ed), *Israel in the Begin Era* (New York, Praeger, 1982), pp 76–101.

10. Articles by Arian, Kieral and Reich, and Elazar in Bernard Reich and Gershon R. Kieval (eds), *Israeli Politics in the 1990s* (New York, Greenwood Press, 1991).

11. Charles S. Liebman and Eliezer Don-Yehiya, *Civil Religion in Israel*, (Berkeley, University of California Press, 1983).

12. This was achieved in the election to the fourth Knesset in 1959.

13. For a discussion of the Lavon Affair see Natan Yanai, *Split at the Top* (Tel Aviv, Lewis-Epstein, 1969) Hebrew.

14. For previous, partially successful internal reforms of Labour see Myron J. Aronoff, 'Better Late than Never: Democratization in the Labour Party', in Gregory S. Mahler (ed), *Israel after Begin*, (Albany, State University of New York Press, 1990), pp 257–72.

15. Under the method used in the 1992 Labour primaries, the 'realistic' positions on the Knesset list (i.e. numbers 2–45, the previously chosen leader being number 1) were filled by two electorates – all registered members of the party voting nationwide for (presumably) more widely known candidates and the same members this time grouped in voting districts, of which five were territorial, three urban, and three sectoral (kibbutzim, moshavim, minorities) and perhaps choosing figures with a more local following. The first 11 names were taken from the national list, then two from the districts and one from the national list up to the point where there was parity between the two lists. Thereafter the candidates were elected alternately from the two lists. The only reserved places were number 20 for an Arab and number 30 for a Druze.

Chapter 7

1. Yaacov Shavit, *Jabotinsky and the Revisionist Movement 1925–1948* (London, Frank Cass, 1988), pp 24–5.

2. Ehud Sprinzak, *The Ascendance of Israel's Radical Right* (New York, Oxford University Press, 1991), pp 23–5.

3. Joseph Heller, *Lehi: Ideology and Politics 1940–1948* (Jerusalem, Keter, 1989) Hebrew.

4. On Labour's historical hegemony see Dan Horowitz and Moshe Lissak, *The Origins of Israeli Polity* (Chicago, University of Chicago Press, 1978); Peter Medding, *Mapai in Israel: Political Organization and Government in a New Society* (Cambridge, Cambridge University Press, 1972).

5. Horowitz and Lissak, *The Origins of Israeli Polity*.

6. Michael J. Cohen, *Palestine and the Great Powers, 1945–1948*, (Princeton, Princeton University Press, 1982), Chapter 10.

7. Sasson Sofer, *Begin: An Anatomy of Leadership* (Oxford, Basil Blackwell, 1988), pp 80–93.
8. Ehud Sprinzak, *The Ascendance of Israel's Radical Right*, pp 33–4.
9. *Ibid*, pp 60–61.
10. Ehud Sprinzak, 'Extreme Politics in Israel', *The Jerusalem Quarterly*, 5, autumn 1977, pp 40–41.
11. On the 1977 political turnover in Israel see Dan Horowitz, 'Not Just A Political Change', *The Jerusalem Quarterly*, 5, autumn 1977.
12. On Gush Emunim, see Ehud Sprinzak, *The Ascendance of Israel's Radical Right*, Chapter 5.
13. On the Tehiya see *Ibid*, Chapter 6.
14. Gerald Cromer, 'The Debate About Kahanism in Israel Society, 1984–1988' (Occasional Paper, New York, The Harry Frank Guggenheim Foundation, 1988).
15. Ehud Sprinzak, *The Ascendance of Israel's Radical Right*, pp 245–50.
16. Ze'ev Schiff and Ehud Ya'ari, *Intifada: The Palestinian Uprising* (New York, Simon and Shuster, 1990).

Chapter 8

1. Majid Al-Haj, 'The Arab Internal Refugees in Israel: The Emergence of a Minority within the Minority', *Immigrants and Minorities*, vol 7, no 2, July 1988, pp 149–165.
2. David Shipler, *Arab and Jew: Wounded Spirits in a Promised Land* (Harmondsworth, Penguin, 1988).
3. Sammy Smooha, *Arab and Jews in Israel, Conflicting and Shared Attitudes in a Divided Society*, Vol 1 (Boulder, Westview Press, 1989)
4. Sammy Smooha, *The Orientation and Politicization of the Arab Minority in Israel*, (Haifa, The University of Haifa, Jewish–Arab Centre, 1984)
5. Majid Al-Haj, 'Elections in the Shadow of the Intifada', *Israeli Studies*, no 3, winter 1990, pp 9–14.
6. Henry Rosenfeld, 'The Class Situation of the Arab national Minority in Israel', *Comparative Studies in Society and History*, vol 20, no 3, July 1978.
7. Majid Al-Haj and Henry Rosenfeld, *Local Arab Government in Israel* (Boulder, Westview Press, 1990).
8. See Jacob Landau, *The Arabs in Israel: A Political Study* (Oxford, Oxford University Press, 1969); Ian Lustick, *Arabs in a Jewish State: Israel's Control of a National Minority* (Austin, University of Texas Press, 1980); Subhi Abu-Ghosh, 'The Elections Campaign in the Arab Sector', in Alan Arian (ed), *The Elections in Israel* (Jerusalem, Jerusalem Academic Press, 1972).
9. Subhi Abu-Ghosh, 'The Elections Campaign in the Arab Sector'; and Eli Rekhess, *Between Communism and Nationalism: Rakah and the Arab Minority in Israel (1965–1973)*, doctoral dissertation, Tel Aviv University, 1986 (Hebrew).
10. Eli Rekhess, 'The Arabs in Israel and the Territories: A Political Linkage and National Solidarity (1967–1988)', *Hamizrah Hehadash*, vols 125–8, 1989, pp 165–91.

11. Majid Al-Haj and Henry Rosenfeld, *Local Arab Government in Israel.*
12. Under the current electoral system, surplus votes over the percentage threshold required for a seat in the Knesset can be transferred to another party if such an agreement has been made before the election. If no agreement is made then these votes are distributed in proportion to all parties.
13. Majid Al-Haj and Henry Rosenfeld, *Local Arab Government in Israel.*
14. Ian Lustick, *Arabs in a Jewish State: Israel's Control of a National Minority.*
15. Itzhak Galnoor, 'The Israeli Elections: The Flight from Freedom and Responsibility', in *Tikkun*, vol 4, no 1, 1989, pp 38–40.
16. Majid Al-Haj and Avner Yaniv, 'Uniformity or Diversity: A Reappraisal of the Voting Behaviour of the Arab Minority in Israel', in A. Arian, *The Elections in Israel – 1981* (Tel Aviv, Ramot Publishing, Tel Aviv University, 1983), pp 139–64; and Eli Rekhess, 'The Arab Nationalist Challenge to the Israeli Communist Party (1970–1985)', *Studies in Comparative Communism*, vol 22, no 4, winter 1989, pp 337–50.
17. Asaad Ghanem, *The Arabs in Israel: Towards the 13th Knesset Elections* (Givaat Haviva, The Institute of Arab Studies, 1992).
18. Majid Al-Haj and Henry Rosenfeld, *Local Arab Government in Israel.*
19. See Jacob Landau, *The Arabs in Israel: A Political Study.*
20. Majid Al-Haj and Henry Rosenfeld, *Local Arab Government in Israel.*
21. Minutes of the National Committee of Heads of Arab Local Authorities, 8 February, 1984.
22. Majid Al-Haj and Henry Rosenfeld, *Local Arab Government in Israel, pp. 136–7.*

Chapter 9

1. 'Orientals' (*Mizrahi*) refers to Jews of Middle Eastern or North African descent. 'Sephardi' refers to Jews, primarily but not exclusively Orientals, who share a common religious liturgy and style, different from that of Ashkenazi Jews.
2. The research literature on Jewish ethnicity in Israel is enormous. For a review and a selected bibliography with abstracts, see Sammy Smooha, *Social Research on Jewish Ethnicity in Israel 1948–1986* (Haifa, Haifa University Press, 1987). For a comprehensive study of the available data on ethnic differences in socio-demographic characteristics, residential distribution, mixed marriages, educational attainment and voting behaviour, see U. O. Schmelz, S. Della Pergola and U. Avner, *Ethnic Differences among Israeli Jews: A New Look* (Jerusalem, The Institute of Contemporary Jewry and American Jewish Year Book, 1991). Documentation is here kept to a bare minimum. If not otherwise indicated, figures are quoted from the *Statistical Abstract of Israel 1991*, No. 42 Jerusalem, (Central Bureau of Statistics, 1991).
3. Among Jews born abroad, the ethnic gap in the proportion of persons without schooling was 0.9 per cent (among Ashkenazim) to 12.0 per cent (among Orientals), and the gap in the proportion of persons with post-

secondary or college education (13+ years) was 41.4 per cent to 16.5 per cent, respectively.

4. These figures are standardized by age. The unstandardized percentages are a bit smaller.

5. But this impressive quantitative gain is less significant than it appears on the surface because of the inflation and depreciation of education. To illustrate, the number of their graduates rose from 36,000 in 1961 to 205,658 in 1984. At the same time the proportion of Oriental university graduates increased from 6.6 per cent to 14.6 per cent, namely, only twofold.

6. The discrepancy ranges from a half to one standard deviation.

7. In the absence of vocational schooling in the Arab sector, Arabs go to academic high schools and then proceed to college. It is not necessary to discriminate against Arabs in academically oriented education in high schools and universities because it is possible to practise overt discrimination against them after graduation when they seek employment. For these findings and explanations, see Yossi Shavit, 'Tracking and the Educational Spiral: Arab and Jewish Patterns of Educational Expansion', *Comparative Education Review* vol 33, no 2, May 1989, pp 217–31; and Yossi Shavit, 'Segregation, Tracking, and the Educational Attainment of Minorities: Arabs and Oriental Jews in Israel', *American Sociological Review*, vol 55, no 1, February 1990, pp 115–26.

8. Yaacov Nahon, *Patterns of Education Expansion and the Structure of Occupational Opportunities: The Ethnic Dimension*, (Jerusalem, The Jerusalem Institute for Israel Studies, 1987) Hebrew.

9. The gaps at the bottom 10 per cent and the top 10 per cent of the income scale were much larger.

10. In 1990 the proportion of Jews born abroad living in households with a density of under one person per room was 58.7 per cent Ashkenazi to 34.3 per cent Oriental. It was 40.2 per cent to 21.8 per cent among those born in Israel.

11. Israel lacks affirmative action in the American sense that publicly funded universities and employers are required by the government to make special efforts to recruit members of disadvantaged groups. For a review of what programmes exist, see Natan Lerner, 'Affirmative Action in Israel', in *International Perspectives on Affirmative Action, A Conference Report* (New York, The Rockefeller Foundation, 1984), pp 110–53.

12. Elazar argues that contemporary ethnic cultural differences stem from the gulf between the classical and romantic cultures on which Sephardi and Ashkenazi Jews draw respectively; see Daniel Elazar, *The Other Jews: The Sephardim Today* (New York, Basic Books, 1989), pp 30–40.

13. *Ha'aretz*, 21 May 1978.

14. The Israeli anthropologist Gideon Kressel maintains that Oriental Jews are still imbued with 'Arabism', which is a serious impediment to their social mobility; see Kressel, 'Arabism (Urubah): a "Concealed" Cultural Factor in the Ethnic "Gap" in Israel', *Israel Social Science Review*, vol 2, no 1, 1984, pp 66–79.

15. In a representative survey of the adult Jewish population conducted in

1988, 37.8 per cent of the respondents favored a distinct western culture for Israel, 23.9 per cent a western culture in which Arab elements are incorporated, 20.1 per cent a mixed culture consisting of western and Arab elements, 5.6 per cent an Arab culture in which western elements are incorporated, 0.6 per cent a distinct Arab culture and 12 per cent rejected both cultures. Support of a mixed (Arab–Jewish) or predominantly Arab culture was 33.5 per cent among Orientals as compared to 17.9 per cent among Ashkenazim. In view of the stigmatization of Arab culture in Israel today, its relatively larger endorsement by Oriental Jews should be appreciated. However, peace may widen the ethnic cultural preferences further. For further findings from this survey, see Sammy Smooha, *Arabs and Jews in Israel*, vol 2 (Boulder, CO, Westview Press, 1992), pp 38–49.

16. For a discussion of Begin's version of Revisionism, see Ilan Peleg, *Begin's Foreign Policy, 1977–1983: Israel's Move to the Right* (New York, Greenwood Press, 1987).

17. Erik Cohen, 'The Changing Legitimations of the State of Israel', *Studies in Contemporary Jewry*, vol 5, 1989, pp 148–65.

18. Shlomo Avineri, 'Political Aspects', in Alouph Hareven (ed), *On the Difficulty of Being Israeli* (Jerusalem, Van Leer Foundation, 1983), pp 289–95, Hebrew.

19. Daniel Elazar presents another, equally unconvincing, view that the Sephardi-Oriental majority, organized in the Likud and embodying a new Sephardi Zionism that blends tradition with nationalism, is becoming Israel's dominant group; see Elazar, *Israel: Building a New Society* (Bloomington, Indiana University Press, 1986).

20. Since the proportions of Orientals and Ashkenazim in the population at large and among brides and grooms is more or less the same, the maximal intermarriage rate under random selection would be 50 per cent (that is to say, the probability of choosing a marital partner from the other ethnic group without any ethnic preference is 50 per cent). The actual 25 per cent intermarriage rate is equal to half of the maximum and hence quite impressive.

21. Smooha, *Arabs and Jews in Israel*, vol 2 p 77.

22. Riots broke out in July 1959 in Wadi Salib, a poor neighbourhood in Haifa inhabited largely by Jewish immigrants from North Africa, after rumours had circulated that a policeman had shot and killed one of the inhabitants. This was the first outbreak of the kind in Israel. The Black Panther movement was a radical ethnic protest movement in the 1970s of second generation Israelis of Oriental background. Aharon Abu-Hatzeira, of Moroccan origin, was minister of religious affairs in the first Begin government. In August 1980, while in office, he was charged with corruption and when forced to resign he founded a separate party, Tami, which won three seats in the election of 1981.

23. Levy accused Shamir, Arens and Sharon of joining in conspiracy against him and his faction during the internal election of the Likud candidates to the Knesset in February 1992. The Likud's central committee, the governing body of the party, was elected in the early 1980s; over 1000

members (a third of the total) were co-opted to the central committee, most of them supporters of the Shamir/Arens faction. Shamir was accused of resorting to this undemocratic procedure precisely to undermine Levy's power. See Rami Rosen, 'Forgive Me For Not Having My Grandmother Know Jabotinsky', *Ha'aretz*, 3 April 1992.

24. For some initial data from a post-election survey taken by Kalman Gayer, an adviser to the Labour Party, see Uzi Benzamin, 'A Week', *Ha'aretz*, 17 July 1992.

25. The economic distribution of the 55,904 Soviet Jews in the labour force who came to Israel from 1 November 1989 to 30 September 1990, showed 41 per cent in the top category of scientific and professional occupations and 39 per cent in the technical and semi-professional fields (compared with 27 per cent and 21 per cent respectively for the previous 1974–81 wave of Soviet immigrants). Displaced downward, these immigrants will successfully compete with upwardly mobile Israelis of Oriental origin. The figures were released by the Research and Planning Branch, Ministry of Immigrant Absorption, Jerusalem.

Chapter 10

1. The term is used to describe the non-Hasidic faction and does not necessarily attest to national origin but rather to identification with the Lithuanian Jewish tradition and studies at *yeshivot* that maintain the scholarly heritage of the *yeshivot* of Lithuania. It originated in the opposition to Hasidism (in the second half of the eighteenth century) prevailing among Lithuanian Jews and in the scholarly tradition of the *yeshiva* of Volozhin and similar institutions that developed in Lithuania and White Russia from the beginning of the nineteenth century; see *Encyclopaedia Judaica*, vol 16, pp 762–73.

2. The Hasidim are a mass mystical and revivalist movement originating in Eastern Europe in the eighteenth century. The best-known Hasidic sect is the Lubavitch/Chabad movement, whose spiritual leader, Rabbi Schneerson, is known as the 'Lubavitcher Rebbe'.

3. For a discussion of the phenomenon of return to Judaism, see J. Aviad, *Return to Judaism: Religious Renewal in Israel* (Chicago, University of Chicago Press, 1985); D. Glanz and M. Harrison, 'Varieties of Identity Transformation: The Case of Newly Orthodox Jews', *The Jewish Journal of Sociology*, vol 20, no 2, 1978, pp 121–41; W. Shaffir, 'The Recruitment of Baalei Tshuva in a Jerusalem Yeshiva', *The Jewish Journal of Sociology*, vol 25, no 1, 1983, pp 33–46; M. Singer, 'Chasidic Recruitment and the Local Context,' *Urban Anthropology*, 1978, pp 373–83.

4. See G. Aran, 'Jewish Zionist Fundamentalism: The Bloc of the Faithful in Israel (Gush Emunim)', in M. E. M. Marty and R. S. Appleby (eds), *Fundamentalisms Observed*, (Chicago and London, University of Chicago Press, 1991), pp 265–344; E. Don-Yehiya, 'Jewish Messianism, Religious Zionism, and Israeli Politics; Gush Emunim', *Middle Eastern Studies*, vol 23, no 2, 1987, pp 215–34.

5. The subject is discussed at length in G. Scholem, *The Messianic Idea In*

Judaism and Other Essays on Jewish Spirituality (New York, Schocken, 1972), pp 1–36.

6. See M. Friedman, *Society and Religion: The Non-Zionist Orthodoxy in Eretz-Israel, 1918–1936* (Jerusalem, Yad Ben-Zvi, first edition 1978; 2nd edition, 1982) Hebrew.

7. Hasidim, their various courts, Mitnagdim (opponents of Hasidism), the various shades of Hungarian Orthodoxy, etc.

8. For example, consider the contrast between German neo-Orthodoxy, that exposed itself to general education and a modern lifestyle, while scrupulously adhering to Halacha, and traditional Eastern European religious Jews, who radically opposed general education and any change in the traditional lifestyle. See M. Friedman, *The Haredi (Ultra-Orthodox) Society – Sources, Trends and Processes* (Jerusalem, The Jerusalem Institute for Israel Studies, 1991) Hebrew.

9. Yiddish (from Hebrew) for 'purpose'. Among Eastern European Jews, the word connoted general education enabling admission to institutes of higher education.

10. Rabbi Haim of Volozhin established a new type of *yeshiva* in 1803. In April 1858 it was closed down by the Russian authorities after the faculty refused to conduct classes in the Russian language. However, other *yeshivot* of the Volozhin type were founded at the same time in Lithuania and White Russia. See *Encyclopedia Judaica*; M. Friedman, 'Life Tradition and Book Tradition in the Development of Ultra-Orthodox Judaism', in H. E. Goldberg (ed), *Judaism Viewed From Within and From Without: Anthropological Studies* (Albany, State University of New York Press, 1986), pp 235–55.

11. See *Encyclopedia Judaica*.

12. See J. Katz, *Tradition in Crisis* (New York, Shocken, 1961).

13. See M. Friedman, 'The Chronicle of the Status Quo: Religion and State in Israel', in: V. Pilowsky (ed), *Transition from 'Yishuv' to State – 1947–1949: Continuity and Change* (Haifa, University of Haifa, Herzl Institute for Research in Zionism, 1990), pp 47–80, Hebrew; J. Shilhav and M. Friedman, *Growth and Segregation – The Ultra-Orthodox Community of Jerusalem*, (Jerusalem Institute for Israel Studies, 1986) Hebrew.

14. M. Friedman, *Growth and Segregation*, pp 115–61.

15. M. Friedman, 'The Haredim and the Holocaust', *The Jerusalem Quarterly* 53, winter 1990, pp 86–114.

16. A common expression in Israel after the Holocaust, referring to Jews who went to their death without resisting the German Nazis (cf. Jeremiah 3:12).

17. During the first five years after the establishment of the State of Israel (1949–53), the number of students at Agudat Israel schools increased from 6957 to 24,133.

18. 1878–1953. One of the most important Talmudic sages of the last few generations and a founding father of the Haredi society of scholars. The name is derived from the title of one of his books.

19. The earliest *kollels* were established in Lithuania at the end of the

nineteenth century. One of the first was the Kovno (Kaunas) *kollel*, founded in 1878.

20. At present the average stay in the *kollel* is ten to 15 years.
21. See M. Friedman, 'Haredim Confront the Modern City', in P. Medding (ed), *Studies in Contemporary Jewry*, vol 2, (Bloomington, The University of India Press, 1986), pp 74–96.
22. The exemption of *yeshiva* students and religious women from military service was guaranteed by David Ben-Gurion, the first prime minister of Israel, but with certain conditions: the number of *yeshiva* students so exempted was limited and all religious women seeking exemptions were to appear before a committee that examined their knowledge of Jewish tradition and *Halacha*. These restrictions were subsequently waived by the government headed by Menachem Begin.
23. Agudat Israel and its Knesset faction always defer to the right of its rabbinical leaders, sitting as the Council of Torah Sages (*Moetzet Gedolei HaTorah*), to determine the party's position on major issues. Shas's rabbinical leadership is the Council of Torah Scholars (*Moetzet Hachmei HaTorah*). The similarity in the names is no coincidence.

Chapter 11

1. See 'Women and Politics in Israel 1990', *Fact Sheet no 1*, (The Israel Women's Network, Jerusalem, 1990).
2. *Ibid*. Statistics reproduced from Sara Herzog, 'Involvement of Women in Local Politics', (Unpublished MA thesis, University of Tel Aviv, 1987).
3. Miriam Benson and Dorit Harverd (eds), *The Status of Women in Israel: The Implementation of the Recommendations of the Israel Government Commission of Investigation* (Jerusalem, Israel Women's Network, 1988), pp 112–13.
4. *Ibid*, p xv.
5. *Ibid*, p xiii.
6. See 'Recommendation 207', in Benson and Harverd (eds), *The Status of Women in Israel*, p 111.
7. Interview with Galia Golan quoted in Randi Jo Land, 'The Half-Won Battle', *The Jerusalem Post*, 8 January 1988.
8. The development of this movement is documented in Barbara Swirski, 'Israeli Feminism New and Old', in Barbara Swirski and Marilyn P. Safir (eds), *Calling the Equality Bluff: Women in Israel*, (Oxford, Pergamon Press, Athene Series, 1991) pp 285–302.
9. Naomi Nevo, 'A Women's Party Will Not Serve Our Needs', *Networking for Women*, vol 5, no 1, Israel Women's Network, Fall 1991, p 7.
10. See Juliet J. Pope, 'Conflict of Interests: A Case Study of Na'amat', in Swirski and Safir (eds), *Calling the Equality Bluff*, pp 225–34.
11. Anne F. Bloom, 'Women in the Defence Forces' in Swirski and Safir (eds), *Calling the Equality Bluff*, pp 128–39.
12. Benson Harverd (eds), *The Status of Women in Israel*, p 81.
13. *Ibid*, p 80.

14. 'Amira Dotan: Israel's First Female General', in Swirski and Safir (eds), *Calling the Equality Bluff*, pp 139–41.
15. Rifkah Bar Yosef, Anne Bloom and Tzena Levy, *The Role Ideology of Young Israeli Women* (Jerusalem, Work and Welfare Institute, Hebrew University, 1978), p 8.
16. Marilyn P. Safir, 'Religion, Tradition and Public Policy Give Family First Priority' Swirski and Safir (eds), *Calling the Equality Bluff*, pp 57–66.
17. *Jerusalem Report*, 26 March 1992, p 22.
18. These cases are analysed further in Juliet J. Pope, 'Waiting for Justice', *The Jerusalem Post*, 27 December 1987. The small but growing number of Orthodox Jewish women eager to redefine the role of women in ritual and public life have been largely inspired by the emergence of an Orthodox Jewish feminist movement in North America.
19. For further details, see 'Women, Rabbis and the Tel Aviv Municipal Council', *IWN Newsletter*, No 5, April 1988, pp 1–2.
20. Frances Raday, 'The Concept of Gender Equality in a Jewish State', in Swirski and Safir (eds), *Calling the Equality Bluff*, pp 18–29.
21. *The Israel Women's Network for Justice and Equality* (pamphlet, Jerusalem, Israel Women's Network, 1991), p 3.
22. For further details see Juliet J. Pope, 'Dialogue and Dissent: The Emergence of an Israeli-Palestinian Women's Peace Movement', in Haleh Afsher (ed), *Women in the Middle East* (Macmillan, forthcoming); and Naomi Chazan, 'Israeli Women and Peace Activism', in Swirski and Safir (eds), *Calling the Equality Bluff*, pp 152–65.
23. These debates are outlined in Lesley Sachs, 'The War, Violence against Women, and Political Representation', *Spectrum*, June 1991, pp 27–9.
24. *The Israel Women's Network for Justice and Equality*, (pamphlet, Jerusalem, Israel Women's Network, 1991), p 2.

Chapter 12

1. Samuel E. Finer, *The Man on Horseback* (Tel Aviv: Ma'arachot, 1982; Hebrew), p 22.
2. *Ibid.*
3. Yoram Peri, *Between Battles and Ballots: Israeli Military in Politics* (Cambridge, Cambridge University Press, 1983).
4. *Ibid*, p 5–8.
5. Samuel P. Huntington, *The Soldier and the State* (New York, Vintage Books–Random House, 1957), p 80.
6. Amos Perlmutter and William Le Grande, 'The Party in Uniform: Toward a Theory of Civil-Military Relations in Communist Political Systems', *American Political Science Review*, vol 76, no 4, December 1982, pp 779–80.
7. Yehoshafat Harkabi, *War and Strategy* (Tel Aviv, Ma'arachot, 1990; Hebrew).
8. Amos Perlmutter. *Military and Politics in Israel* (London, Frank Cass, 1969), p 126.
9. *Ibid.*

10. Edward Luttwak and Dan Horowitz, *The Israeli Army* (London, Allen Lane, 1975), p 203.
11. Peri, *Between Battles and Ballots*.
12. Yoram Peri, 'Patterns of the IDF's Relations with the Political Establishment in Israel', in Joseph Alpher (ed), *A War of Choice* (Tel Aviv, Hakibbutz Hamechuad, 1985; Hebrew).
13. Perlmutter, *Military and Politics in Israel*, p 121.
14. Yoram Peri, 'Party-Military Relations in a Pluralist System,' *Journal of Strategic Studies*, vol 3, September 1983, p 50.
15. Samuel P. Huntington, *The Common Defense: Strategic Programs in National Politics* (New York, Columbia, 1961).
16. Martin Edmonds, *Armed Services and Society* (Boulder, CO, Westview Press, 1990), p 175.
17. Samuel P. Huntington, 'Organization and Strategy', in Robert J. Art, Vincent Davis and Samuel P. Huntington, *Reorganizing America's Defense* (Washington, DC, Pergamon–Brasseys, 1985), p 235.
18. Perlmutter, *Military and Politics in Israel*, pp. 123–124.

This paper is based on a forthcoming book by the author, *Civil Military Relations: The Israeli Case*. The book, scheduled for publication in 1993, is the result of research undertaken at the Jaffee Centre for Strategic Studies (JCSS) at Tel Aviv University.

Chapter 13

1. The author would like to acknowledge assistance, during trips to Israel in May 1990 and December 1991, from the late Dan Horowitz, Moshe Lissak, Shlomo Avineri, Haim Ben-Shahar, Benyamin Rabinovitch, Asher Susser, Gad Ben-Ari, Assa Lifshitz, Yossi Olmert, Abraham Friedman, Shaul Schiff, MK Abdel-Wahab Darawshe, Mohammed Darawshe, Aziz Haldar, Azmi Sharaf, MK Yossi Beilin, Yoram Peri, Arnon Soffer, Yosseph Shilhav, Michael Romann, Ora Ahimeir, David Bligh, Rabbi N. L. Rabinovich of Ma'ale Adumin and many others, including all the other contributors to this book. Meetings outside Israel have taken place with, among others, MK Dan Meridor, MK Ehud Olmert, MK Ze'ev (Benny) Begin, Yitzhak Ritter and Natan Sharansky.
2. FO 371/111071 Evans (Tel Aviv) to Eden, 10 May 1954, Kew.
3. The Ethiopians were still being described as 'the most difficult group to absorb' by the minister for absorption, Yair Tsaban, in February 1993 when he defended the policy of letting some of them have special grants up to 99 per cent of the price of an apartment in the coveted central area, where they were most likely to get jobs. The Russian-language press had protested outspokenly against this discrimination. Tom Sawicki in *The Jerusalem Report*, 25 March 1993, p 5.
4. Interview with Gad Ben-Ari, *dovar* (spokesman) of the Jewish Agency, Jerusalem, May 1990. For a different Israeli view on this see the 'Last Word' column of Hirsh Goodman, editor-in-chief of *The Jerusalem Report*, 25 February 1993, where he accused the Jewish Agency and the Israeli government of doing all they could to scare Jews into leaving

Russia for Israel at once and not doing nearly enough to enrich life for Jews living there. Arguing that 'the best *Aliyah* is motivated *Aliyah*', Goodman contended that proper motivation could come only out of education and ideological commitment.

5. The number of Soviet immigrants from September 1989, the start of the mass immigration, to December 1992 was 400,455, when the total population was 5.192 million. Of these 52,000 were engineers, 20,000 teachers, 11,000 doctors and 8000 scientists. There were 10,000 artists (painters, musicians, dancers), 4000 athletes and more than 3500 economists. 25.7 per cent of the immigrants were aged 18 and under, as compared with 41.1 per cent of the general population; 60.4 per cent of the immigrants were between the ages of 19 and 65, contrasted with 49.9 per cent in Israel generally (Israel Central Bureau of Statistics and Natan Sharansky, 'A Demand for Hope', *The Jerusalem Report*, 8 April (1993).

6. *U.S. House of Representatives Committee on Appropriations, Hearings before Subcommittee on Foreign Operations*, 21 and 23 February 1992, p 149. Evidence of Professor Stanley Fischer. By mid-1992 108,000 new immigrants were at work and 43,000 were registered unemployed. Of these employed 19 per cent were working as academics and scientists, 37 per cent as factory and construction workers and 24 per cent in services.

7. Survey of Tazpit Research Institute, July 1991.

8. *Hearings*, p 111. Alvin Rabushka, *Scorecard on the Israeli Economy: A Review of 1991* (Jerusalem, Institute for Advanced Strategic and Political Studies, March 1992).

9. See, for example, profile of Shamir by David Makovsky in *Jerusalem Post International*, 20 June 1992.

10. *Hearings*, p 113. In 1982–8 total net investment from abroad was $185 million, an annual average of $26 million. In 1988 it grew to $88 million but in 1990 there was a net negative foreign investment of $144 million. On the other hand, foreign grants and charities rose in the nine years 1982–90, from an annual rate of $2.616 billion to one of $5.790 billion, including $3.188 billion in net intergovernmental remittances. (Rabushka, *Scorecard*).

11. State of Israel, *Absorption of Soviet Jewry Immigration. Economic and Humanitarian Aspects* (1992), submitted as evidence to US House of Representatives Appropriations Subcommittee, February 1992.

12. Figures from *The Jerusalem Report*, 16 July 1992.

13. According to an opinion survey, less than one-third of the new immigrants profess belief in God, compared with just over half of the general Jewish population of Israel. More strikingly, no fewer than 84 per cent want the religious laws in Israel abolished or whittled down, whereas that was the wish of only 55 per cent of the general public. (Leon T. Hadar, 'The 1992 Electoral Earthquake and the Fall of the "Second Israeli Republic"', *Middle East Journal*, autumn 1992.

14. Yoel Marcus, *Ha'aretz*, 25 September 1992.

15. Natan Sharansky, *The Jerusalem Report*, 3 December 1992, p 35.

16. *The Jerusalem Report*, 13 August 1992, pp 26–7. See also Yigal Kotzer and David Rudge in *Jerusalem Post*, 21 August 1992, p. 9a.

17. Surie Ackerman in *Jerusalem Post International*, 14 March 1992. See also Batsheva Tsur in *Jerusalem Post International*, 17 October 1992, and Peter Hirschberg in *The Jerusalem Report*, 22 October 1992, pp 22–3.

18. Of a total of 268 kibbutzim, 165 are affiliated to Labour through Takam (the United Kibbutz Movement) and another 86 are more left-wing, being members of Hakibbutz Ha'artzi (the National Kibbutz Movement) and affiliated to Mapam, one of the components of Meretz; the remaining 17 being to the Religious Kibbutz Movement, Hakibbutz Hadati.

19. This remains true despite the relatively good performance of the economy during 1992, which has been variously assessed according to whether one highlights the real rate of GDP growth of 6.4 per cent or the per capita growth rate, which was a modest 2 per cent in 1992 after being a negative figure in 1991. See for a bullish view, 'The Israeli Economy: On a Healthy Growth Path,' Economics Department, *Bank Hapoalim*, February 1993 and, for a much more pessimistic assessment, Alvin Rabushka, 'Why Don't Ordinary Folks Feel Richer?' in *Jerusalem Post*, 5 March 1993, p 6.

20. Members of the Health Fund pay dues to the Histadrut and not to the Kupat Holim itself. The fund is obliged to make a substantial contribution to Histadrut overheads. For a vigorous defence of the Kupat Holim Clalit, see Arie Caspi in *The Jerusalem Report*, 25 March 1993, p 55.

21. Abraham Friedman, Executive Director, The Jerusalem Institute for Israel Studies. Interview (Jerusalem), May 1990.

22. Rabin address to Labour supporters, Tel Aviv, 23 June 1992. (BBC–SWB IV June 25, ME/1416 A/1). Rabin interview, Tel Aviv IDF Radio, July 2 1992 (Federal Broadcasting Information Service, 6 July 1992, p 48).

23. In 1990 it took from 15 March to 11 June to form a new government. In 1988 the goverment was formed on 22 December after the Knesset election of 1 November. The same delays were sometimes true of earlier periods, e.g. in 1955 the election of 26 July was followed by a government on 2 November. Ministers of a resigned government are by law locked into their portfolios until a new government takes office.

24. Israel Television Network, 23 October 1992 (FBIS, 26 October 1992, pp 28–9).

25. Rabbi Deri's ability to hold the post of minister of the interior under both Shamir and Rabin was especially noteworthy in that from his first day in office in Shamir's last government it was public knowledge that he was the object of a major criminal investigation. Shas generally has a problem with the criminal law. In 1993 one of its ex-MKs was given a five-year sentence for forgery, theft and false accounting, and a second received a (much lighter) sentence for similar offences. A current Shas MK, Rafael Pinhasi, had been deputy minister for religious affairs for only a few weeks when the Knesset lifted his parliamentary immunity so that he could stand trial on charges of fraud and criminal conspiracy.

26. Azmy Bishara in *Yediot Aharonot*, 25 June 1992.

27. See 'The Forgotten Ones: The Unrecognized Arab Villages', *New Outlook*, January/February 1993, pp 40–1.

28. Yigal Schleifer, Profile of Abdel-Wahab Darawshe in *Jerusalem Post International*, 7 March 1992, p 12. Also Dan Leon in *New Outlook*, March/April 1992.

29. Ahmad Tibi, 'Citizen. Not-Citizen', *New Outlook*, June/July 1992.

30. Elie Rekhess, 'New Approach, New Power', *Jerusalem Post International Edition*, 27 February 1993, pp 14–15.

31. Interview with David Bligh (Jerusalem), May 1990. Jacob M. Landau, *The Arab Minority in Israel, 1967–1991* Oxford, Clarendon Press 1993 pp 192–3. The Rabin government has made a start on narrowing the wide gap. For example, of the 1700 executive positions in the Israeli government structure 17 are currently held by Arabs (15 Druze, 2 Muslims). The government is proposing to increase this number to 50 (the proportionate figure would be upwards of 250). In addition, under the new concept of 'development zones' enterprises in Arab areas will for the first time be eligible for some subsidies and tax exemptions.

32. Rabin's message to International Conference on Anti-Semitism at Brussels, broadcast on Qol Yisrael, 9 July 1992 (FBIS July 9, p. 33).

33. *Jerusalem Post*, 13 November 1992. p 1b; Sarah Honig, 'Likud Leadership.'

34. Until the big membership drive in preparation for the March 1993 primaries it had never been too clear exactly how many members the Likud had but it was thought to be about 70,000 (Eric Silver in *The Jerusalem Report* 30 July 1992). It now appears to be larger in absolute terms than the individual membership of the British Labour Party.

35. See article in *Hadashot* by Doron Me'iri on 30 January 1992, which discussed the existence of the extreme right-wing organizations *Hashmona'im* and *Herev Gid'on* (Gideon's Sword).

36. Gershom Gorenberg, *The Jerusalem Report* 30 July 1992, 'A stay in opposition could prove once and for all that the NRP is obsolete – that modern Orthodox Israelis don't need to have a separate party.'

37. Aviezer Ravitsky, 'Exile in the Holy Land: The Dilemma of Haredi Jewry', in Peter Y. Medding (ed), *Israel, State and Society 1948–1988* vol V (Oxford, Oxford University Press, 1989); Dina Porar, 'Amalek's Accomplices: Anti-Zionist Ultra-Orthodoxy in Israel during the 1980s', *Journal of Contemporary History*, vol. 27, no 4, October 1982.

NOTES ON CONTRIBUTORS

Mordechai Bar-On is a Fellow of the United States Institute of Peace and president of the New Israel Fund. He served 20 years in the IDF including as chief education officer (1961–8) and nine in the World Zionist Organization as head of the Youth Department (1968–77). He was a Member of the Knesset (Civil Rights Movement) in 1984–6, and a fellow of the Ben-Gurion Research Centre at Sdeh Boqer, 1989–91. His books include *Peace Now: A Profile of a Protest Movement* (Tel Aviv, 1985) and *The Gates of Gaza: Israel's Defence and Foreign Policy 1955–57* (Tel Aviv, 1991).

Yehuda Ben-Meir is a Lecturer in the Department of Psychology, Bar-Ilan University, Ramat Gan, and a senior research associate of the Jaffee Center for Strategic Studies. He was a Member of the Knesset (National Religious Party) from 1971 to 1984 and was deputy minister of foreign affairs, 1981–4. He is the author of *National Security Decision-Making: The Israeli Case* (1986) and *Civil–Military Relations: the Israeli Case* (1993).

Menachem Friedman is Professor in the Department of Sociology and Anthropology at the Bar-Ilan University, Israel. In 1991–2 he was chairman of the research group on religion and society at the Institute of Advanced Studies, Hebrew University of Jerusalem. His publications include *The Haredi (ultra-Orthodox) Society–Sources, Trends, Processes* (The Jerusalem Institute for Israel Studies, 1991), and he co-edited (with Emmanuel Sivan) *Religious Radicalism and Politics in the Middle East* (State University of New York, 1990).

Itzhak Galnoor is professor of Political Science, Hebrew University of Jerusalem, and author of *The Partition of Palestine: Decisions within the Zionist Movement* (1993). He is the editor of the International Political Science Association Book Series on Advances in Political Science and has published extensively on comparative politics and the Israeli political system.

Emanuel Gutmann is Professor of Political Science at the Hebrew University of Jerusalem and president-elect of the Israeli Political Science Association. His main research interests are relations between church and state and between religion and politics in western democracies and in Israel. He has been active in Israeli politics as a member of the Labour Party.

Majid Al-Haj is senior lecturer in the Department of Sociology and Anthropology, University of Haifa. He was visiting professor at Carleton University, Ottawa, in 1989–90. He is the author of *Social Change and Family Processes* (Westview Press, 1989) and *Arab Local Government in Israel* (Westview Press, 1990), and has just completed a monograph on 'Education, Empowerment and Control: The Case of the Arabs in Israel'.

Yitzhak Klein is a lecturer in the Department of Political Science, Bar-Ilan University, Ramat Gan. He writes on comparative reform processes in Eastern Europe, the liberal democracies and the third world, and contributes columns to the press.

Keith Kyle is a research fellow with the Middle East Programme of the Royal Institute of International Affairs, Chatham House, and Visiting Professor of History, University of Ulster. His previous career in journalism was mainly with *The Economist* (1953–60) and BBC Television (1961–82). He is the author of *Suez* (Weidenfeld & Nicolson and St Martin's Press, New York, 1991 and 1992). He was convenor of the Middle East Group at the RIIA (1974–90).

Pinchas Landau is a British-born financial journalist who migrated to Israel in 1976. He has been financial correspondent of the *Jerusalem Post* and author of two special reports on the Israeli Economy for *The Economist Intelligence Unit* (1987 and 1992). He has written and lectured extensively in Israel and abroad on the Israeli economy and financial system.

Joel Peters is Lecturer in International Relations in the Department of Politics at the University of Reading and an Associate Research Fellow in the Middle East Programme of the Royal Institute of International Affairs. He has been a visiting scholar at the Truman Institute for the Advancement of Peace and a Lady Davis fellow, both at the Hebrew University of Jerusalem. He is the author of *Israel and Africa: The Problematic Friendship* (British Academic Press, 1992).

Juliet J. Pope is Lecturer in Politics at Queen Mary and Westfield College, London University. She studied Middle East politics at St Antony's College, Oxford, and was a Lady Davis fellow at the Hebrew University of Jerusalem. The doctoral thesis on which she is currently working concerns the political discourse of Israeli women.

Sammy Smooha is Professor of Sociology at the University of Haifa. A specialist on comparative ethnic relations, he has published widely on the internal divisions in Israel. His books include *Israel: Pluralism and Conflict* (Routledge & Kegan Paul, 1978), *Social Research on Jewish Ethnicity in Israel* (Haifa University Press, 1987) and *Arabs and Jews in Israel*, vols 1 and 2 (Westview Press, 1989 and 1992).

Ehud Sprinzak is Professor of Political Science at the Hebrew University of Jerusalem, author of *The Ascendance of Israel's Radical Right* (Oxford University Press, 1992) and co-editor (with Larry Diamond) of *Israeli Democracy Under Stress* (1993). He is the associate editor of the journal *Terrorism and Political Violence*, a consultant to several Israeli government agencies, a frequent commentator on television and radio and a leading campaigner for political reform.

INDEX